Housing and social inequality

LIBRARY AND LEARNING RESOURCES CENTRE
Northern College, Barnsley. S75 3ET

Please return this book by the last date stamped below.

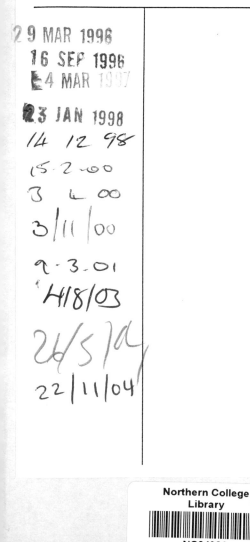

First published 1990 by
Hilary Shipman Limited
19 Framfield Road
Highbury
London N5 1UU

British Library Cataloguing in Publication Data
Morris, Jenny
  Housing and social inequality.
  1. Great Britain. Housing. Socioeconomic aspects
  I. Title   II. Winn, Martin
  307.336

ISBN 0-948096-23-3

Cover design by David Bennett Books

Typeset by Florencetype Ltd, Kewstoke, Avon
Printed and bound by Biddles Limited
Guildford & King's Lynn

Contents

List of tables and figures   iv

Introduction   vii

Chapter 1   Housing inequality and housing
             policy   1

         2   Housing and class   35

         3   Housing and race   78

         4   Housing and gender divisions   117

         5   Housing inequality and social
             problems   159

         6   Housing studies and sociology   212

             Conclusion   243

             Bibliography   245

             Index   255

Tables and figures

1.1 Homelessness in England 1980 and 1989   10

1.2 Housebuilding in Britain 1976–88   19

2.1 Socio-economic groups
     by tenure of heads of household   39

2.2 Income of households in council housing
     (Great Britain)   42

2.3 Socio-economic group of council tenant
     purchasers compared to all borrowers   47

2.4 Class composition of the electorate
     1964 and 1983   67

2.5 Housing, class and vote   69

2.6 Council house sales and vote   70

2.7 Characteristics of council house purchasers   71

3.1 Tenure patterns by ethnic origin of household   79

3.2 Dwelling type by ethnic group   82

3.3 Amenities by ethnic group   85

3.4 Numbers of adults and children
     resident in households, by ethnic group   94

4.1 Tenure by sex and marital status
     of head of household, Great Britain 1984   118

4.2 Tenure by sex – households over the age of 60   120

4.3 Age, price and type of property purchase
     and amenities, by sex of borrower   121

4.4 Selected characteristics of women who move
     out of the marital home at breakdown of
     their first marriage   124

4.5 Women with and without dependent children
– percentages working full time and part time,
by marital status 126
4.6 Household structure of families
applying as homeless 129
4.7 Individuals in one-person households,
by age and sex 140

Figures

2.1 Socio-economic group
of household heads in work:
tenants and buyers 45
2.2 Number of wage-earners in household:
tenants and buyers 46

Acknowledgements

We would like to thank Tim Brown, Jane Darke, Anthony Heath and Peter Malpass for their comments on sections of this book and Hilary Macaskill for her work in editing it. Special thanks are due to Anne Winn whose willingness to take on additional childcare responsibilities made it possible to complete the book on time.

Introduction

The initial motivation to write this book emerged from our experience as teachers and examiners for the Institute of Housing. We were convinced that housing management and housing provision needed to be set in the context of the wider social structure. We wanted to be able to introduce our students to work which directly related a sociological understanding to housing issues. The problem was that, with very limited exceptions, the material needed to do this is not easily available. There is a wealth of empirical material (i.e. research which does not attempt theoretical explanations of the data which is gathered) which can be utilised by intrepid sociologists trying to teach housing students but much of this material is not very accessible to students.

Housing studies tends to focus on housing policy and there are few publications which explore how housing fits into the wider social structure. On the other hand, sociologists, with a few exceptions, have not concerned themselves with housing. As a result, the sociology of housing is poorly developed and highly fragmented. It is very difficult for part-time students (as the majority of housing students are) to read the original housing research and the material which provides the sociological framework and then knit it all together.

Our aim in this book has not been the over-ambitious one of setting out a blueprint sociology of housing. Rather we intend to bring together the relevant research and theoretical debates which we hope will be useful to both students and to other academics in the task of bringing a sociological understanding to housing issues. In doing so, we have attempted to identify the questions which will be uppermost on the agenda of developing a sociology of housing. However, the prime determinant of how we wrote this book was the desire to make the existing research material and theoretical debates more accessible to students.

The book is divided into six chapters. The first identifies what is meant by housing inequality, briefly discussing the nature of the phenomenon in Britain today, and then moves on to an analysis of how housing policy has exacerbated the experiences of housing inequality. This first chapter is a starting point in the sense that it covers the material with which, we would argue, the housing studies literature has in fact been overly concerned. An analysis of housing policy needs to be incorporated into a sociology of housing rather than being the main focus for research as it has tended to be.

It is in the material of the subsequent chapters that we believe the basis for a sociology of housing is to be found. Chapters 2, 3 and 4 analyse the available research on the relationships between housing inequality and the major social divisions of class, race and gender, identifying some of the theoretical questions which such material raises.

Chapter 5 uses the examples of 'problem' housing estates, homelessness and racial harassment to explore the relationship between housing and wider social processes and inequalities. These phenomena are an important part of the day-to-day reality faced by housing managers. Our purpose, as in the three preceding chapters, is to focus on the way in which housing inequalities do not arise in a vacuum inhabited only by housing policy-makers and housing practitioners but must be set within their wider socio-economic context. This chapter examines the explanations which have been offered of the three phenomena and, through analysis of the shortcomings of these explanations, illustrates the importance of a sociological understanding for housing practice.

Chapter 6 is concerned with identifying the agenda for a sociology of housing. The first part of the chapter outlines the few theoretical contributions which have been offered by sociologists and others to a 'theory of housing'. Our purpose is to identify both criticisms of the different positions and what they each have to offer, and our central concern here is to make these ideas more accessible to students. The second part of the chapter, in identifying the issues which are raised by these contributions, discusses a series of questions which we believe are key concerns for future sociological research.

The issues with which this book deals are very much part of the underlying concerns of the new syllabi which are being developed as part of the Institute of Housing's restructured professional qualification. Those working in the provision and management of housing are concerned with one of the most important scarce resources in an increasingly unequal society. The professionalism of housing managers must rest, not only on the application of more technical and practical skills, but also on a body of knowledge which enables an understanding of the wider social processes and conflicts within which the housing manager operates. We hope that this book makes a useful contribution towards this.

1 | Housing inequality and housing policy

Housing is one of the scarce resources which determine the general quality of life, and its uneven distribution is an important aspect of inequality in Britain today. In the first part of this chapter we look at the nature of housing inequality, briefly discussing some of the links between housing inequality and other social factors. This first section then addresses the question of whether housing inequality is merely a residual phenomenon or whether the evidence of housing inequality is indicative of a more general housing problem – an integral part of the social structure of Britain in the last part of the twentieth century. While we argue in the following three chapters that there are clear relationships between the experience of housing inequality and the social divisions of class, race and gender, in this chapter we explore the way in which housing inequality has been influenced by the course of housing policy during the 1980s. The second section of the chapter therefore analyses the relationship between housing inequality and housing policy.

I

Housing inequality

There are three aspects to housing situation which can be seen when measuring housing inequality. Firstly, there are the issues of access to housing, security of tenure and opportunities for mobility; that is, whether someone is able to get the housing they need, and once they have it, to be

1

secure in their occupancy. Then there are the physical characteristics of the home which are an important dimension of advantage and disadvantage – space, number of rooms, heating and insulation, state of repair, environment surrounding the home and so on. Finally, some people enjoy opportunities of access to credit and capital as a result of their housing situation while others do not.

All three of these aspects of housing situation are important facets in an individual's general experience of advantage and disadvantage. While there continue to be inequalities in access to and security of housing, together with differentiation of the housing stock in physical terms and inequalities of access to credit and capital through housing, housing situation will always be an expression of inequality.

Housing is also an important factor in any consideration of inequality because of the way that housing situation has been shown to be a causal factor in other aspects of people's lives, principally health but also educational attainment and employment opportunities(1). Housing situation is therefore not only an expression of inequality but also has an effect on other inequalities.

The experience of housing advantage and disadvantage can be clearly shown to be related to the major social divisions of class, race and gender and this is explored in Chapters 2, 3 and 4. For example, semi-skilled and unskilled manual workers and those who are unemployed find it difficult to get access to housing and when they do, it is frequently (within each housing tenure) to housing in poor condition, in unpopular areas with inadequate community amenities. Such groups' occupancy of their housing is often insecure, whether because it is temporary accommodation for homeless households or because their financial precariousness brings rent or mortgage arrears.

At the other end of the social scale, Ray Forrest's and Alan Murie's sample of households living in some of the most desirable housing in Bristol illustrated how housing advantage is related to a male head of household's employment history(2). Their research showed how the experience of progressing up the career ladder in multinationals, smaller businesses and the professions brings with it increasing housing advantages, including substantial subsidies of housing costs from the employer.

The housing situation of these households is in stark contrast to that of the homeless families in Jean Conway's study of bed and breakfast accommodation(3). The absence, or inadequacy, of a male wage – either through single parenthood, unemployment or low-paid manual or service-sector work – brings a high risk of homelessness. This is particularly clear in the context of rising house prices coexisting with a population group whose low wages and/or job insecurity places them in a poor bargaining position(4).

Although we focus in later chapters on the three main social divisions of class, race and gender, it is important to recognise that there are other social characteristics which are also associated with housing inequality. Two key factors are age and disability. There is now substantial research to illustrate that both young people and older people experience particular housing disadvantage. For young people the problem can be most clearly measured as one of access to housing: homelessness amongst young people has increased significantly in recent years(5). For older people it is the experience of poor housing conditions which becomes increasingly common(6).

The housing inequalities experienced by disabled people are illustrated by the fact that homelessness has increased amongst disabled people at double the rate for other groups during the 1980s(7). The fact that two-thirds of disabled people are elderly means that they are also at risk of experiencing the poor housing conditions which are a feature of the housing situation of older households.

Housing inequality and tenure

Housing tenure – that is, the legal basis of occupancy of a dwelling – has been an important concept in housing

3

studies, not only in debates on housing policy but also in studies of housing inequality. As Barlow and Duncan state, 'Housing tenure is commonly used as a basic statistical and conceptual shorthand in housing research'(8). However, as they also identify, the meaning of tenure is historically and socially variable and this undermines the assumption that there is an integral link between housing tenure and housing inequality. Peter Kemp, from his historical studies of housing, argues that the legal status of owners and tenants varies both within the tenures and over time. Thus:

> To simply categorise occupiers as either 'owners' or 'tenants' is to ignore an important element of complexity and variations. Hence tenures should rather be viewed as bundles, or configurations, of property rights and obligations, the precise mix of which is liable to some important variations, albeit within limits. These configurations are not immutable but vary over time and space. For example, the council tenant in the 1980s has security of tenure, the 'right to buy', the 'right to exchange' and the 'right to repair', but in the 1970s did not. These configurations are also relational in the sense that changes in one tenure can affect the meaning of other tenures.(9)

Another common misuse of the concept of tenure is to make simplistic assumptions about the relationship between housing tenure and the experience of housing inequality; in particular, it is assumed that housing advantage attaches to being an owner-occupier while disadvantage is an inherent part of being a tenant. Thus it is general practice to use statistics which establish the relationship between class, gender, race and tenure as evidence of how housing disadvantage, measured as the likelihood of being a tenant, is related to being working-class, a woman or black.

Some of the inadequacies of this practice are developed further in the later chapters on class, race and gender divisions. It will be seen that owner-occupation is not an homogeneous tenure and that the terms on which a household enters the owner-occupied market are closely related to wider social and economic factors. For the moment, we want to examine the evidence on the relationship between tenure and housing advantage to challenge the assumed benefits of owner-occupation.

If there are major differences between tenures it is between the private rented sector and the other two tenures of owner-occupation and the public rented sector. In terms of housing conditions (measured by amenities and state of repair) there is little to choose between owner-occupation and council housing(10). The tenure which differs significantly on amenities is the privately rented furnished sector where 26 per cent of households do not have sole use of a bath or inside toilet. Owners outright are worse off than either council tenants or those buying on a mortgage, but only by a couple of percentage points. Thirty-nine per cent of council tenants do not have central heating, compared to 16 per cent of owners buying on a mortgage and 28 per cent of owners outright, but again the largest difference is between these tenures and the private rented sector where 68 per cent of unfurnished tenants and 56 per cent of furnished tenants lack central heating(11).

The English House Condition Survey found that 42 per cent of dwellings in the private rented sector, 13 per cent of owner-occupied dwellings and 11 per cent of local authority dwellings were in poor condition. In terms of the cost of repairs, an owner-occupier is likely to need to spend more on his/her property than needs to be spent on local authority dwellings but again the private rented sector requires the highest expenditure(12).

The owner-occupied sector has a larger percentage of houses than either of the other two tenures and this is a major reason for dwellings in this tenure being, on average, larger than in the council or private rented sectors. However, space standards in the private housebuilding industry have been declining during the last 30 years. The average floor space decreased by about 15 per cent between 1960 and 1980 with average plot sizes decreasing more than that(13). However, this figure conceals the increasing variation within the owner-occupied sector in that detached four-bedroom

5

houses increased from 4 per cent of the market in the early 1960s to over 20 per cent in 1979 while the percentage of dwellings with floor space below 750 square feet was also on an upward trend(14). The 1980s have seen a further squeeze on the size of dwellings in the first-time buyer market – in both the new build and conversions market – while the high-price, high-quality sector has also continued to expand. There is now a clear division within the owner-occupied sector in terms of the new properties coming onto the market, which further weakens the case for the dividing line – in terms of standard of housing – being drawn across tenure lines.

Another part of the debate about the significance of tenure stresses the capital gains (real and potential) which owner-occupation brings, arguing that this results in a social and economic division which cuts across class. The identification by Peter Saunders of 'consumption cleavages' uses tenure as an empirical measurement of social division, arguing that the way in which owner-occupation is a source of accumulating wealth has a profound effect on social identity and social action(15). Again, our chapter on class divisions identifies that there is great variety within the owner-occupied sector in terms of whether to be an owner means to be able to accumulate wealth. Research on these variations and on whether being an owner- occupier changes people's political affiliation generally stresses the importance of social and economic factors other than housing tenure(16).

As owner-occupation has become the mass tenure over the last 20 years, it is important to recognise that, despite political rhetoric, such a development is not necessarily a measure of an increased standard of living for the country as a whole. As Mark Boleat and Adrian Coles point out, the poorest countries in the world have a very high level of owner-occupation because the poorer people are the less able they are to pay rent(17). Bangladesh, with the lowest gross national product (GNP) per capita, thus has the highest level of owner-occupation (90 per cent). Amongst the wealthier countries there is no correlation between GNP and levels of owner-occupation; Switzerland, with the highest GNP per capita, has the lowest level (30 per cent) while New Zealand has under half Switzerland's GNP per capita but owner-occupation stands at 71 per cent of the population (1980/81 figures).

It is also important to recognise that there is no inherent relationship between owner-occupation and wealth within a country. While in Britain, there is a clear correlation between household income and tenure, this is more a result of the way in which existing subsidy structures and conditions of entry constrain people's choice of tenure rather than any inherent relationship between housing advantage/disadvantage and tenure. As Boleat and Coles point out:

> In Britain the subsidy system operates in such a way that the poorest people are better off as tenants, and middle and upper income people are better off as owner-occupiers(18).

Is there a 'housing problem'?

In the mid-1970s a complacency amongst politicians on housing inequality could be identified and this had its most clear manifestation in the 1977 Housing Policy Review. The prevailing view was that there was no longer a shortage of housing; indeed, there was a crude surplus. The slum clearance and high building levels of the 1950s and 1960s had significantly modernised the stock, and the switch to rehabilitation in the 1970s was hailed as a shift of priorities from 'the numbers game' of building as much housing as possible to the priority of preserving existing communities and improving existing dwellings. The 'area approach' (manifested by General Improvement Areas and Housing Action Areas introduced by the 1969 and 1974 Housing Acts respectively) was part of an assertion that the 'housing problem' was now about poor housing conditions concentrated in particular localities.

7

Similarly, the Housing (Homeless Persons) Act 1977 was a manifestation of the idea that certain groups were in particular housing need and that these groups should have priority access to the public rented sector; council housing was therefore for those who could not gain access to other tenures. As Malpass and Murie point out, the 1977 Act was part of a move to residualise council housing – to turn it into 'welfare housing' – and was effectively a nail in the coffin of the notion that council housing was 'general needs' housing(19).

With this denial of a general housing problem, the focus of housing policy, particularly after 1979, became the encouragement of higher levels of owner-occupation. The main policy instrument for bringing this about is the transfer of existing dwellings from the public rented sector to the owner-occupied sector (through the 1980, 1985 and 1986 Housing Acts). However, by the end of the 1980s, the reduction of the public rented sector had become an important policy aim in itself. The 1988 Housing Act sought to transfer significant numbers of council dwellings to the housing association sector, the nature of which sector was also changing through the reduction of public subsidy and the increased use of private finance. The financial restrictions placed on both capital and revenue spending of local housing authorities through the 1989 Local Government and Housing Act provide a further incentive for the transfer of properties from one form of landlord to another.

The important thing about all these developments is that the emphasis shifted completely away from the provision of dwellings, or indeed even an improvement of existing dwellings, to an attempt to change the tenure structure. At the same time, recognition of the existence of housing inequality tends to be couched in terms of these being residual problems, affecting small groups of people. Furthermore, the assumption is commonly held that, far from there being a housing problem as such, it is the behaviour and/or circumstances of particular groups of people which results in their experience of housing

8

inequality. The Conservative government's stance on home-lessness is an illustration of this approach.

Table 1.1. illustrates one of the most obvious features of housing inequality, the dramatic increase throughout the 1980s of the number of homeless households. The government view is that this increase in homelessness is caused by such factors as too high expectations amongst younger people; too high void rates amongst local authority proper-ties; young women getting pregnant deliberately in order to get a council house; 'special local circumstances' such as the housing crisis amongst the Bangladeshi community in Tower Hamlets (which is laid at the door of immigration policies)(20).

Organisations such as Shelter have argued that this is an inaccurate portrayal of the reality of housing inequalities and that, while underlying social and economic factors are crucial to explaining the nature of housing inequality for particular groups of people, there is also a general 'housing problem'. What is more, housing policy has played an important role in creating a housing crisis and this is an integral part of the existing social structure. This viewpoint has also been coherently argued by Peter Malpass in *The Housing Crisis*(21).

Malpass identifies three powerful forces which have resulted in structural conditions that must be recognised as a housing crisis and which thus challenge the official complacency on housing inequality. These factors are demographic change; the ageing of the housing stock; and changes in the tenure structure. Government reactions to the first two factors, and its role in the changing tenure structure, are crucial to the nature of housing inequality today. Before analysing housing policy's contribution, we will discuss in more detail the three factors identified by Malpass as constituting a housing crisis.

Demographic changes, in the context of declining house-building, are the first factor undermining the notion that homelessness is a residual problem. The number of house-holds in England and Wales is expected to increase by 2.2

TABLE 1.1   *Homelessness in England 1980 and 1989*

	year 1980	year 1989	Increase
Number of households accepted as homeless	62,920	126,240	101%
	at 31.12.80	*at 31.12.89*	
Number of households in temporary accommodation	4,524	39,900	762%
of which			
Bed and breakfast	1,253	11,480	
Hostels }	3,271	{ 8,020	
Short life dwellings }		{ 18,400	

Source: DoE *Homelessness Statistics: England*

million between 1983 and 2001(22). There are four key features of population change which are contributing to this overall increase.

Firstly, the late 1980s and early 1990s are a period of high household formation because of the effect of the 1960s 'baby boom'. The age cohort in which people are generally looking to set up home is therefore experiencing a large increase in numbers. This demographic trend accounted for about half of the overall net increase in households of 180,000 per year during the 1980s and although there will be a decline in the numbers in this age cohort from 1991 onwards, the sharp decline will not work its way through until 1996(23).

The effect of the above has been exacerbated by a second demographic feature; the fact that over the last 20 years or so there has been increasing household formation amongst single never-married people and this trend is continuing amongst both the under-30 and the 30–44 age cohorts(24). This is not just because of the increase in the numbers in the age cohorts but is also due to an increase in headship rates – i.e. the proportion of the age group who form separate households. For both this and the following reason, one-person households between the ages of 30 and 44 are set to double in number between 1987 and 2001(25).

Thirdly, divorce and separation currently result in a net increase of around 80,000 households per year(26). Of particular significance is the fact that marital breakdown generates a demand for rented housing. Holmans, Nandy and Brown estimated that at present divorce rates, 30,000 former owner-occupiers are demanding rented housing per year and 25,000 ex-partners in tenant households are also demanding rented accommodation. (These latter figures are gross rather than net.)

Finally, although the population over retirement age is not expected to increase over the next decade, there will be a continuing increase in the number of people over the age of 75. As Malpass points out:

> Given the long-term trend towards more elderly people living alone in separate households and the current preference [in social policy] for elderly people to remain in the community rather than move into institutional care as they become more frail, there is a growing problem for many of them in securing and maintaining appropriate accommodation(27).

There were 2 million people aged over 75 in 1961 but by the year 2000 this number will have doubled to 4 million(28). This is reflected in the projected increase of 600,000 one-person households over retirement age between 1987 and 2001. Many of these will be over-75-year-olds who have survived their spouses.

The above demographic trends combine to exert an increased demand for housing but an equally important part of the picture is the ageing of the housing stock. Almost 30 per cent of Britain's total housing stock (over 6 million properties) was built before 1919. Malpass also draws attention to the fact that house building has been subject to booms and slumps over the last hundred years which result in, for example, the large number of houses built around the turn of the century all getting old together and creating a major demand for housing renewal in the form of either demolition or rehabilitation. The next major boom period in housebuilding, during the 1930s, has created a large number of properties in both public and private sectors which are now in need of refurbishment.

Over the past 20 years a considerable amount of public money has been spent on grant-aided improvements, particularly during 1982–84 when the government increased both the total amount of money available and the percentage grant paid. However, the net result has been a slight increase in serious disrepair between 1971 and 1986, while the number of unfit dwellings has declined slightly. On this evidence, huge sums of money have been spent but only a standstill in housing conditions achieved. Using data from the 1986 English House Condition Survey, Paul Walentowicz estimated that a total of £50 billion would be needed to put right all the defects in the total housing stock(29).

However, the problems with housing conditions in Britain today are not solely associated with the ageing of the housing stock. The mass production of council housing in the 1950s and 1960s has left a legacy of housing which is often unpopular, structurally unsound and a health hazard to its occupants. The Association of Metropolitan Authorities has estimated that about one million dwellings were built using non-traditional building methods and that the cost of rectifying the mistakes which were made would be between £3,750 and £5,000 million(30). Not only, therefore, is there an increased demand for housing, but the existing housing stock is ageing, over one million dwellings are in serious disrepair and there are significant structural problems with large numbers of dwellings built during the 1950s and 1960s.

The third factor which Malpass identifies, changes in the tenure structure, has been a feature of the housing system since the early part of the century. The details of the structural changes are covered in Chapter 2. Briefly, the private rented sector, from being the mass tenure, has declined to the point where it accounts for only 7 per cent of households. About 65 per cent of households are now home-owners while the public rented sector houses about a quarter of all households. Although these developments have had the advantage of potentially weakening the link between poverty and poor housing (through the expansion of council housing) and of providing many owners with 'greater security, greater freedom, better conditions, lower costs in the long term and the accumulation of a capital asset of far larger value than could ever be secured by saving'(31), they have also brought new problems.

One way in which housing inequality has increased is that access into the two main tenures is much more difficult than it ever was into the private rented sector. Council housing presents bureaucratic barriers, and certain groups in housing need are disadvantaged in their experience of entry into the sector in that either they do not conform with the household type accorded priority (single homeless people, for example) or they are subject to decisions based on prejudice or indirect discrimination (black and ethnic minority groups, single parents, etc). Owner-occupation, now the mass tenure, also features far more barriers to entry than private rented housing did as the mass tenure. Entry costs are high and movement within the tenure faces the obstacle of the 'house buying chain'. Low-income households, for whom the private rented sector was previously so important, find it particularly difficult to enter, and remain within, the sector.

The way in which owner-occupation is now the mass tenure has had other implications for housing inequality in that the expansion of the tenure has brought more and more older, inner city properties and low-income households into owner-occupation. It has thus become a very diverse tenure in terms of both housing conditions and household socio-economic status. However, the key common feature of owner-occupation is that, as Malpass puts it, as a tenure:

It individualises costs: owners are responsible for repair and maintenance. In this sense low income and mortgaged house purchase, especially in run-down inner city areas, do not fit comfortably together(32).

Our discussion in the next chapter on class and home-ownership illustrates the increasing experience of housing disadvantage within the owner-occupied sector.

Those involved in formulating and implementing housing policy during the late 1970s and throughout the 1980s were, therefore, faced with an increasing demand for housing, an overall deterioration of the housing stock and a rigidity in the tenure structure which made the housing situation of low-income households particularly difficult. However, the housing policy response to these structural features of the housing system has, in fact, exacerbated housing inequality. The next section of this chapter analyses the contribution which housing policy has made to housing inequality.

II

The political response to the housing inequalities discussed above was not determined by these realities but by political commitments within a wider arena. These political commitments were twofold (although related). Firstly, governments of all persuasions since the 1960s have been committed to the expansion of owner-occupation *as a political end in itself*. Secondly, the Conservative government since 1979 has, in addition, had a general commitment to extending the operation of market forces. This latter aim does not mean necessarily that there is less state intervention in the housing system. In fact, in some aspects there has been greater government control, in that central control of local authorities' housing expenditure and functions has been increased in order to bring about the wider aims of decreasing public expenditure and of decreasing the number of properties in the public rented sector.

It is this general thrust of privatisation which, in combination with the demographic changes and the physical problems of the housing stock, has led to housing inequality becoming an ever-more evident part of the housing system. We offer the following detailed analysis of two aspects of housing policy as examples of the way that housing policy has contributed to the creation and maintenance of housing inequality.

Housing renewal policy and housing inequality

Housing renewal can take the form of rehabilitating/improving/modernising an existing dwelling or it can involve demolition of dwellings and their replacement with new buildings (redevelopment). These processes may take place within the private sector or the public sector, or may involve the transfer of private property into the public sector, or vice versa. In his book *State Housing in Britain* Steve Merrett has identified that during the 1960s and 1970s, both Labour and Conservative governments held the assumption that demolition and redevelopment would be carried out by the public sector while rehabilitation should be left to the private sector. Merrett coined the phrase 'partitioned renewal' to describe this division of reponsibilities(33). During the second half of the 1970s, when the rehabilitation of existing council stock became an important housing policy issue, it was, however, assumed that this type of improvement of existing dwellings would take place within the public sector, using government subsidy.

Housing policy in the 1980s has steadily worn down the division of responsibilities for housing renewal identified by Merrett. As Brindley and Stoker argue in their article for *Local Government Studies*, the government:

Has developed a strategy for the privatisation of housing renewal and . . . this strategy is being pursued across a broad front to incorporate the renewal of both privately owned and local authority housing(34).

There are two main parts to this strategy, the first being to increase the responsibility of occupiers for their own housing standards. The increase in the level of owner-occupation is an important part of this aim but owners have also been exhorted to take more responsibility for the repair and maintenance of their properties. As the 1985 Green Paper on the improvement grant system stated:

> Home-ownership offers opportunities for individuals to alter and improve their homes as they wish; they must also carry the primary responsibility for keeping their property in good repair(35).

Individual responsibility has been confirmed by the 1989 Local Government and Housing Act which amended the improvement grant system to a means-tested system. Furthermore, the government clearly expects owners to make more use of the equity tied up in their homes to carry out improvement work.

However, the government's reliance on individual owners improving their own properties is likely to be frustrated by the correlation between low income and poor housing conditions. The major problem with the old improvement grant system was the evidence that a substantial amount of money went to households who could have afforded to do the work anyway and that 'targetting' of improvement grants through Housing Action Areas and General Improvement Areas merely resulted in the replacement of low-income households with middle-income households ('gentrification'). However, the problem with replacing the old system with a means-tested grant is that take-up is likely to be low. Furthermore, low-income households will continue to find it difficult to raise sufficient money to carry out improvements, a difficulty compounded by the lower value of their properties. The links so clearly established by the most recent English House Condition Survey between low income and poor housing conditions will therefore continue to be a key feature of the housing system.

The second part of the privatisation of housing renewal is the involvement of the private sector. The government wishes building societies, property developers and housebuilders to become involved in clearance and redevelopment, the form of renewal which had previously been left to the public sector. The 1989 Act places a statutory duty on local authorities to involve the private sector in redevelopment schemes. Building societies were enabled by the 1986 Building Societies Act to extend their activities to become involved in the provision of housing.

The private corporate sector is also seen as having a role in the renewal of the public sector stock. This is envisaged through a number of different devices – from barter or 'partnership' deals between the local authority and the private sector to wholesale selling off of the local authority housing stock.

It should be stressed that these private sector initiatives involve public subsidy. For example, Urban Development Grants were introduced in 1982 to encourage private sector investment by the use of public subsidy on redevelopment projects; the DoE's special unit, originally named the Urban Housing Renewal Unit, now named Estate Action, has redistributed money which had previously been allocated through the Housing Investment Programme to provide subsidy to private developers involved in rehabilitating council estates where transfer of ownership (from public to private sector) is also involved.

Indeed, Brindley and Stoker argue that the provision of public subsidy (either direct or indirect through, for example, the provision of land at below market price) is crucial to the success of the involvement of the private sector in rehabilitation and redevelopment as otherwise the profit levels to be gained are not high enough. This is recognised by government and the private sector alike, as the following statement from a senior civil servant seconded to the Phoenix Initiative, a private consultancy involved in inner city regeneration, illustrates:

> In run-down areas, individual developers or companies will not go in by themselves because the risk is too high. It has to be a co-ordinated effort. And because of the high risks involved, there has to be some form of government subsidy(36).

17

However, even with the subsidy available the evidence is that the role of private housebuilders in the areas of greatest housing disadvantage is limited. Low-income households cannot support a high enough return for these companies. Brindley and Stoker quote the director of the House Builders Federation, who said:

> Those who would be prepared to buy in these areas cannot afford to do so, and those who could afford to do so won't buy in the existing urban environment(37).

Private housebuilders therefore continue to devote the great majority of their activity to suburban and green-field sites; not only can the households buying in these areas pay the prices necessary to sustain the profit level required, but the building industry, as Brindley and Stoker point out, has always relied heavily on the capital gains from land speculation on green-field sites. Private housebuilders appear unlikely to take over the role of local housing authorities in either rehabilitation or redevelopment. This is illustrated by Table 1.2 from which it is evident that the reduction in public sector housebuilding (the other side of the coin of the government's encouragement of private housebuilders) has not been compensated for by the increase in the private sector (nor by housing association activity). It is also of significance that the collapse of the property market during 1989 is likely to result in a reduction in private sector construction over the next few years.

The government has been more successful in persuading building societies to become involved in inner city areas with poor housing conditions. This was initially achieved under the last Labour government when local housing authorities often worked in close liaison with local branches of building societies in Housing Action Areas, persuading them to drop the policy of 'red lining' (refusing mortgages in certain areas) and to make finance available for improvement as well as for purchase. Even before the 1986 Act,

TABLE 1.2 *Housebuilding in Britain 1976–88*

| Year | Housing Completions | | |
	Public (1) 000's	Private 000's	Total 000's
1976	163	152	315
1977	163	141	303
1978	131	149	280
1979	104	140	245
1980	107	128	235
1981	85	115	200
1982	50	125	175
1983	51	146	197
1984	51	157	208
1985	40	152	192
1986	35	163	198
1987	32	171	203
1988	30	181	212

1. Housing association construction figures are included within the figures for the public sector.

Source: Housing and Construction Statistics, DoE.

some of the major building societies set up separate companies to provide new and improved houses for sale and to rent, mainly in inner city areas.

It may well be that, with owner-occupation reaching saturation point, building societies will become increasingly interested in financing housing improvement, and also in schemes which take properties out of the public sector, refurbish them and let them on assured tenancies. However, as with the private housebuilders, there is a significant limitation on their activities – the ceiling on the prices which low-income households can afford. Research on low-income households in inner city areas where house prices have not kept up with regional averages indicates that building societies are reluctant to lend for either purchase or improvement(38). The groups who are most likely to occupy such property are elderly white women and ethnic minority families (particularly Asians). As Brindley and Stoker conclude:

The underlying commercial interests of building societies are likely to exclude both the dwellings and the owners most likely to be in need of assistance with housing renewal(39).

Again, the current housing policy trend will do little to tackle housing disadvantage where it currently exists in run-down areas and amongst low-income households.

Gibson and Langstaff, in an article on the prospects for housing renewal written in 1984, concluded that 'We have to grapple with the problem of managing urban decay in a way which minimises inequality or face the consequences of deepening social divisions'(40). The policy developments in housing renewal throughout the 1980s have in fact exacerbated, not minimised, inequality. This is because housing renewal has essentially been used as a vehicle for establishing the primacy of the market place in the distribution of housing. Privatisation of housing renewal deepens the rift between those who experience economic power and those who do not. At the same time, the policy is not very effective in dealing with the deterioration of the housing stock nor with meeting the increasing demand for affordable housing.

Tenure politics and housing inequality

There are a number of ways in which housing policy has affected the tenure structure during the 1980s. The general aim has been to increase owner-occupation, diminish the public rented sector and to deregulate the private rented sector. The following discussion looks at the specific policies which have been very successful in meeting these objectives.

The 'right to buy'
The right to buy provisions of the 1980, 1984 and 1986 Housing Acts were the first stage in a policy of privatising council housing. Following the 1980 Housing Act which

introduced the right to buy for sitting tenants, together with generous discounts, 500,000 council tenants took up the opportunity by 1983. However, this was only 3 per cent of the public sector stock. The 1984 and 1986 Acts increased the incentives by increasing discounts, introducing higher discounts on flats. Notwithstanding this, the proportion of council tenants who had taken active steps towards buying their property decreased from 10 per cent to 6 per cent of council tenant households between 1981 and 1986(41). While a steady trickle of tenants will exercise their right to buy each year, it has become clear that the right to buy in itself is not going to break up the public rented sector in the way that the government is now committed to doing.

However, the way in which the right to buy operates has had a significant impact on the council housing sector and has increased the tenure dimensions of housing inequality. It has done this in respect of both the types of property that have been sold, the type of household which has bought and the local variations in levels of sales.

The detailed study of the effects of the right to buy carried out by the Department of the Environment in 1988, concluded that '. . . the "typical" sold property is a three-bedroomed semi-detached house, likely to be situated in a popular suburban area'(42). The effect has been to increase the proportion of flats in the public sector, and also the proportion of non-traditional dwellings (including those with design defects) since these are also under-represented amongst sales. The proportion of two- and three-bedroom houses within the council stock has declined while the proportion of one-bedroom dwellings and two- and three-bedroom flats has increased. A higher percentage of council dwellings is now concentrated in inner city and other less popular areas as a result of local variations in the take-up of the right to buy(43).

However, these disadvantageous effects on the character of council housing have only been sustained because they have coincided with a reduction of capital investment in new council housing together with a preponderance of flats amongst the much reduced new-build and rehabilitated properties This means, for example, that in 1985 sales of houses in England and Wales exceeded new building by seven to one, whereas sales of flats amounted to little more than a third of those built(44).

Those households seeking access to council housing have experienced not just a decline in the ratio of the number of applicants to the lettings available but a decline in the quality of the stock from which an offer of housing will be made. This residualisation of council housing in terms of its physical characteristics also has a significant effect on those existing council tenants seeking a transfer. Not only is there greater pressure on the number of lettings but it is the properties that people want to transfer into, houses with gardens, which are being sold. A Greater London Council report(45) published in 1984 pointed up the particular consequences of this for the housing opportunities of single-parent and ethnic minority council tenant households who are disproportionately housed in flats above the fourth floor, in pre-1940 property and whose level of satisfaction with their housing is lower than other groups of council tenants(46). The chances for these groups of achieving better housing conditions are depleted year by year as more and more of the popular properties are sold.

Together with other factors (which are discussed in Chapter 2), the sale of properties under the right to buy has resulted in there being an increasing proportion of low-income households amongst council tenants. This is because those who have bought have predominantly been those in full-time work, with more than one income coming into the household, and skilled manual workers and non-manual workers have been over-represented amongst them(47). Table 2.2 in Chapter 2 illustrates the increasing percentage of council tenants who are in receipt of benefits. While it is clear that this is a long-term trend related to broader social and economic processes, the right to buy has exacerbated this marginalisation of council tenants.

Although the majority of council tenants are in good-quality housing and are very satisfied with their housing conditions, the right to buy has undoubtedly increased the incidence of housing disadvantage within the public sector and in particular has contributed to the closer correlation between council housing and low income. The heightening of housing disadvantage in the public rented sector is a very important part of the structure of housing inequality, as is the increasing difficulty of gaining access to the council sector.

Large-scale sales of council housing
Government policy has encouraged the sale of estates into private or housing association ownership since the early 1980s and this received legislative backing in the 1986 Housing and Planning Act. The 1988 Housing Act introduced a compulsory element in that local authorities could be forced to sell if a majority of tenants failed to vote against proposals put forward by an aspiring alternative landlord (those who didn't vote would be counted as voting in favour).

The immediate motivation (for tenants and the local housing authority) is usually the prospect of refurbishment and repair being carried out using private finance. Since this happens in a climate where public sector investment in improving the properties is unlikely, it could be argued that such a policy reduces the experience of housing inequality. However, the policy of large-scale 'transfers' is primarily about shifting properties from one tenure to another and in the process, while the conditions of the dwellings concerned may improve, housing inequality is increased.

Whether the dwellings concerned in such schemes involve sale into owner-occupation or transfer to private sector or housing association tenancies, the housing costs for the original occupants (should they remain) will increase. This is particularly the case since the 1988 Act which deregulated the private rented sector. The evidence is that the less control there is over tenancies, the higher the rent will

23

be and the lower the standard of accommodation(48). In areas of shortage of rented accommodation the economic consequences can be significant. For example, the Select Committee on the Environment heard in 1982 that, in the same block of flats, tenancies let at free market rents were almost four times that of tenancies let on a registered fair rent(49).

Rents will increase even when the properties concerned are taken over by a housing association as the fair rent mechanisms for new lettings in this tenure were also abolished under the 1988 Act. The use of private finance by housing associations – increasingly common under the new finance system introduced by the Housing Corporation – will further fuel rent increases. The National Federation of Housing Associations has expressed concern that in the current financial climate housing associations will no longer be able to cater for the low-income households whom they have traditionally housed.

In areas of high housing demand, the transfer of stock from the public to the private sector has resulted in the squeezing out of working-class communities. The process has been particularly apparent in parts of London such as Wandsworth and Tower Hamlets. In the latter borough the combined effect of the development of land by the London Docklands Development Corporation and the sale of council estates for home ownership and private renting has resulted in working-class tenants being displaced to other parts of the borough. There are increasing difficulties of access to council housing and stark contrasts of extremes of wealth and poverty coexisting alongside each other(50).

Private developers in London have made a lot of money out of the transfer of housing from the public to the private sector. In other areas where there is not such a high demand for housing from middle- and high-income households, they have encountered difficulties. In schemes such as Cantril Farm in Knowsley, bought by a trust involving Barclays Bank and the Abbey National Building Society, with Barratts appointed as the main housebuilder, investors have come up against the ceiling on profit levels imposed by the low incomes of the original occupants. Such experiences throw into question the ability of privatisation strategies to meet the housing needs of low-income households.

The government's strategy of speeding up the decline of the public sector by encouraging wholesale transfers of local authority stock under the 'Tenants' Choice' provisions of the 1988 Act is yet in its early stages of implementation and cannot therefore be properly assessed. However, two things are clear already. Firstly, that the number of transfers is likely to be much smaller than initially expected, partly because of tenant opposition. Secondly, in order for a transfer to go ahead, the investment gains will have to be very clear for the private sector. Housing which is in poor condition and occupied by low-income households is unlikely to be an attractive proposition. The strategy will therefore – in the way that the right to buy does – further separate out the better-off sections of the public rented sector from those who experience both poor housing conditions and other forms of social and economic deprivation.

The 'Tenants Choice' provisions of the Act seem most likely to be used by local housing authorities as a way of liberating themselves from the restrictions being placed on them as both providers and managers of housing. Setting up a housing association to take over council stock gives access to capital funding (from the Housing Corporation and the private finance market). However, the net result is likely to be a rise in housing costs to the individual household and a reduction in the amount of housing allocated according to housing need. Thus the policy will exacerbate the experience of housing inequality.

The deregulation of the private rented sector
The private rented sector has been declining during the course of the century. The sector, which now only accounts for 7 per cent of all households, is a diverse one, containing both high-rent luxury lettings and low-rent, poor-condition housing.

The nature of the decline of the private rented sector has thrown up three major sources of housing disadvantage. Firstly, it is generally agreed that the reduction of housing opportunities within the sector has contributed significantly towards the increase in homelessness over the last 20 years or so. This is particularly the case in terms of the increase in homelessness amongst young single people for whom this tenure has traditionally been a source of housing and for whom owner-occupation and council housing have little to offer. Secondly, there is a higher incidence of lack of amenities and serious disrepair amongst privately rented property than amongst either owner-occupied or public rented property, the experience of housing disadvantage being particularly common in the case of houses in multiple occupation(51). Landlords have little incentive to invest large sums of money in repairing and maintaining their rented property as the rates of return are so low compared to the capital gain to be made from selling into owner-occupation with vacant possession. Moreover, within the residential landlord part of the tenure, landlords are often as poor as their tenants(52). The final source of housing disadvantage is the way in which this tenure is an important source of housing for the lowest-income households, particularly elderly households, many of them single women. The lack of economic power experienced by such households is reflected in their limited housing options and thus their unequal relationship with their landlord. Harrassment and poor housing conditions are thus an important feature of their housing experiences.

However, rather than addressing these aspects of housing disadvantage within the private rented sector, housing policy has focused on attempting to revive the sector by establishing the primacy of market forces. This has been done through the provisions of the 1980 and 1988 Housing Acts which reduced tenant security (although a concession was made on strengthening action against harrassment in the 1988 Act) and enabled landlords to charge market rents.

By the second half of the 1980s, the government had

recognised that the high level of owner-occupation and the pressures on the public rented sector were inhibiting labour mobility. In particular, the South East's economic expansion was being hampered by a shortage of rented housing. While recognising the need for a healthy and expanding rented housing sector, the government was very clear that this should not be public rented housing. Instead, market forces were to be the driving force behind the expansion of rented housing. The intention was to make this possible by both the decontrol and deregulation of the private rented sector and the encouragement of new types of landlord into the sector.

In pursuit of the latter aim, the 1988 Budget introduced the first public subsidy to the private rented sector in the form of tax relief on Business Expansion Schemes involving property letting companies. The schemes which have so far been developed using this subsidy have mostly provided high-rent lettings to high-income households who are geographically mobile (and who will also be entering owner-occupation at a later date).

Previous decontrol of the private rented sector in the 1950s merely increased its rate of decline(53). However, during the second half of the 1980s conditions within the owner-occupied sector have brought about some expansion of certain parts of the private rented sector, which probably would have happened even without the formal rent decontrol brought in by the 1988 Act as landlords had previously been able to create new tenancies which evaded the Rents Acts' controls. The ready availability of mortgages in the 1980s made it easy for landlords to acquire property. A survey carried out in 1988 concluded that the upper end of the London private rented sector was increasing because high house prices made buying an inconvenient tying-up of capital for certain high-income households(54). The landlords who were attracted into the market were those providing high-rent, high-quality lettings, often company lets, or to overseas visitors, embassy employees and professional people.

Paradoxically, when the housing market took a downturn

in 1989, this also served to increase the number of residential lettings as people found it difficult to sell their properties and were forced into letting them instead. Many estate agents in the South East have now set up residential letting sections. Again, however, the lettings concerned are at the middle and top end of the market.

There may well be an increase, therefore, in the number of properties in the private rented sector but these will be of a different type of tenancy than that traditionally found in the sector. In London (which accounts for a quarter of the private rented dwellings), market rents are generally two to four times the level of regulated rents so there will certainly be a speeding-up in the decline of the housing opportunities which the sector offers low-income households. The upward pressure on homelessness will therefore continue.

The 1988 Housing Act attracted building societies to increase their activity in the private rented sector by decontrolling rents. However, the Building Societies Association recognises that such activity will be aimed at high-income households as the rents will be considerably higher than those pertaining under the old 'fair rent' system. Housing renewal of this kind will therefore make access to rented housing for low-income households more difficult as the low-rent private rented sector speedily declines and any 'revival' takes the form of high-rented provision.

At the same time, little is being done to improve conditions in the low-rent part of the tenure. In particular, the 1989 Local Government and Housing Act's introduction of a means test for improvement grants to landlords will do little to encourage the improvement of property in a poor state of repair.

To sum up this discussion of the way that housing policy has been concerned with influencing the tenure structure, we can assert that there has been a failure to address housing inequality. This has resulted in a continuation of poor conditions within the private rented sector and continuing expansion of homelessness due to the decline in housing opportunities offered to low-income households by this tenure. Moreover, the way in which housing policy has encouraged owner-occupation, in the context of reducing the public rented sector, has resulted in an increasing experience of housing disadvantage amongst owners. More and more low-income households are entering a tenure where the entry costs are high and the repairs and maintenance costs fall on individual households who are often unable to ensure that their housing conditions are adequate. Part of this process of expansion is also the pulling into owner-occupation of older, run-down properties and the housing disadvantages associated with occupation of these types of property is becoming an important feature of the owner-occupied sector.

The way in which the public rented sector is declining is splitting off the better properties and the better-off tenants from those low-income households occupying poorer-quality dwellings. At the same time, the dramatic reduction in housebuilding in the public sector (together with the loss of relets through sales) is making a major contribution to the rise in homelessness.

Conclusion

Any discussion of the effect of housing policy on housing inequality would be incomplete without reference to the changes in housing subsidies over the last decade, for these changes have been an important part of the government's privatisation strategy. The net effect of these changes in subsidy structure, together with the effect of wider economic policy, has been to increase housing costs to the individual household.

There has been a general shift from subsidy at the point of provision of housing – through capital investment in public sector housing – to subsidy at the point of consumption, i.e. subsidies to individual households in the form of either mortgage interest tax relief (and income support payment of mortgage interest) to owners, and housing benefit to tenants. Subsidy to public sector housing (in the form of Exchequer and Rate Fund Contributions) has been halved from £2,450m in 1980/81 to £1,205m in 1988/89. At the same time, subsidy to owner-occupiers in the form of mortgage interest tax relief has increased from £2,250m in 1980/81 to £5,500m in 1988/89. The housing benefit system, introduced in 1983, has also seen a steady increase from £1,980m in 1983/84 to £2,725m in 1988/89, although the number in receipt of housing benefit has declined (from 3,735,000 in 1983/4 to 3,100,000 in 1988/89 as a result of changes in eligibility).

The withdrawal of subsidies to local authorities' housing revenue accounts during the early part of the 1980s resulted in council rents increasing by 143.6 per cent between 1979 and 1985, a period during which the general inflation rate was 66.9 per cent(55). The direct result of this has been an increase in the number of council tenants on housing benefit and an increasing incentive (together with the discounts available under the right to buy) for those households paying full rent to purchase their property. The housing association sector is also experiencing rent increases. Fair rents (on new tenancies) were abolished by the 1988 Housing Act and the subsidy structure for housing associations was changed to encourage private finance to be used, thus reducing the level of direct public subsidy.

Rented housing in the local authority and housing association sectors is therefore becoming more expensive as a result of changes in subsidy levels and structures. However, the costs of home ownership have also risen significantly during the 1980s. The government's economic policy has been largely responsible for increasing the direct costs of house purchase. Real interest rates have increased, the value of tax relief has fallen (because of cuts in the tax rate) and house prices have risen during the 1980s.

Kleinmann and Whitehead conclude that:

Overall, economic trends in the 1980s point to housing in all tenures becoming more expensive for the majority of households, both as a result of price and notably real interest rate increases and because of changes in the general subsidy and taxation system(56).

More and more public money is going into subsidising housing, yet homelessness is increasing, poor housing conditions remain a major problem, and housing is becoming more expensive.

We can sum up this discussion of housing inequality and housing policy by stating that there has been a shift, not so much in the amount, but rather in the form, of state support for housing. Whereas the first three-quarters of this century saw a growth in direct state provision of housing (in the form of subsidies on the building of council housing) the last quarter of the century has seen a shift towards public subsidy of provision by the private sector. Forrest and Murie have termed this 'subsidised individualism', for the shift in subsidy structure has gone along with an ideological insistence on individual choice and preference for home ownership(57).

These changes have occurred over a period when household formation has been increasing and the condition of the housing stock has worsened. The effect of the policy has been, on the one hand, to fail to address these underlying problems, and on the other, to strengthen the link between economic position and housing situation. Those groups experiencing economic disadvantage now have a higher risk of experiencing housing disadvantage, a fact made starkly apparent by the dramatic increase in homelessness throughout the 1980s.

Notes

1. For a summary of earlier research, see A. Murie (1983), *Housing Inequality and Deprivation*, Heinemann Educational Books. See also the comprehensive review of research on housing and health in S. Smith (1989), *Housing and Health: a review and research agenda*, Glasgow Centre for Housing Research.

31

2. R. Forrest and A. Murie (1987), 'The affluent home-owner: labour market position and the shaping of housing histories', in N. Thrift and P. Williams (eds), *Class and Space: the making of urban society*, Routledge and Kegan Paul.

3. J. Conway (ed) (1988), *Prescription for Poor Health: the crisis for homeless families*, London Food Commission, Maternity Alliance, SHAC and Shelter.

4. See, for example, G. Bramley et al (1988), *Homelessness and the London Housing Market*, School for Advanced Urban Studies, Bristol.

5. C. Holmes (1986), 'The worsening crisis of single homelessness', in P. Malpass (ed), *The Housing Crisis*, Croom Helm.

6. *English House Condition Survey, 1986*, (1988), HMSO.

7. J. Morris (1988a), *Freedom to Lose: housing policy and people with disabilities*, Shelter.

8. J. Barlow and S. Duncan (1988), 'The use and abuse of housing tenure', *Housing Studies*, Vol.3, No.4, October, p.219.

9. P. Kemp (1987), 'Some aspects of housing consumption in late nineteenth century England and Wales', *Housing Studies*, Vol.2, No.1, January, p.4.

10. *General Household Survey, 1986* (1989), HMSO; *English House Condition Survey, 1986* (1988), HMSO.

11. *General Household Survey, 1986* (1989), HMSO, Table 6.22.

12. *English House Condition Survey, 1986* (1988), HMSO, Table A4.11.

13. S.S. Duncan (1986), 'House building, profits and social efficiency in Sweden and Britain', *Housing Studies*, Vol.1, No. 1, January.

14. M. Ball (1983), *Housing Policy and Economic Power*, Methuen, p.117, 119.

15. P. Saunders (1984), 'Beyond housing classes: the sociological significance of private property rights in the means of consumption', *International Journal of Urban and Regional Research* 8(2). See our Chapter 6.

16. Barlow and Duncan (1988) have a useful summary of this research; see also our Chapter 2.

17. M. Boleat and A. Coles (1987), *The Mortgage Market: theory and practice of housing finance*, Allen and Unwin, p.5.

18. *Ibid*, pp.9–10.

19. P. Malpass and A. Murie (1982), *Housing Policy and Housing Practice*, Macmillan, p.176.

20. C. Forman (1989), *Spitalfields: a battle for land*, Hilary Shipman, pp.236–7.

21. P. Malpass(ed) (1986), *The Housing Crisis*, Croom Helm.

22. *Social Trends, 17*, (1987), HMSO, p.43.

23. Department of the Environment (1988), *1985-based Estimates of Numbers of Households in England 1985–2001*, HMSO.

24. M. P. Kleinmann and C. Whitehead (1988), 'British housing since 1979', *Housing Studies*, Vol.3, No.1, January, p.6.

25. *Social Trends, 19* (1989), HMSO, Table 2.5.

26. A. E. Holmans, S. Nandy and A.C. Brown (1987), 'Household formation and dissolution and housing tenure: a longitudinal perspective', *Social Trends, 17*, HMSO, p.23.

27. P. Malpass (1986), p.13.

28. A. H. Halsey(ed) (1988), *British Social Trends*, Macmillan, p.107.

29. P. Walentowicz (1989), 'Lies, damned lies and house condition statistics', *Roof*, March/April.

30. Association of Metropolitan Authorities (1984), *Defects in Housing Part 2: Industrialised and System Built Dwellings of the 1960s and 1970s.*

31. P. Malpass (1986), p.15

32. *Ibid*, p.16.

33. S. Merrett (1979), *State Housing in Britain*, Routledge and Kegan Paul, p.110.

34. T. Brindley and G. Stoker (1988), 'Housing renewal policy in the 1980s', *Local Government Studies*, Sept/Oct.

35. Department of the Environment (1985), *Home Improvement: a new approach*, HMSO, para 1.

36. Adam Smith Institute (1988), *Altered Estates*, p.46.

37. T. Brindley and G. Stoker (1988), p.54.

38. V. Karn, J. Kemeny and P. Williams (1985), *Home Ownership in the Inner City*, Gower.

39. T. Brindley and G. Stoker (1988).

40. M. Gibson and M. Langstaff (1984), 'Housing renewal: emerging crisis and prospects for the 1990s', *Housing Review*, Vol.33, No.5, Sept/Oct, p.179.

41. *General Household Survey, 1986* (1989), HMSO, p.50, Table 6.1.

42. M. Kerr (1988), *The Right to Buy*, HMSO, p.6.

43. R. Forrest and A. Murie (1984a), *Right to Buy? Issues of Need, Equity and Polarisation in the Sale of Council Houses*, Working Paper 39, School of Advanced Urban Studies, Bristol; R. Forrest and A. Murie (1984b), *Monitoring the Right to Buy*, Working Paper 40, School of Advanced Urban Studies, Bristol.

44. *Social Trends, 17* (1987), HMSO, p.145.

45. Greater London Council (1984), *Council House Sales*.

46. Department of the Environment (1979), *National Dwelling and Housing Survey, 1977*, HMSO.

47. R. Forrest and A. Murie (1984a and b); M. Kerr (1988).

48. J. E. Todd (1986), *Recent Private Lettings 1982–84*, HMSO.

49. House of Commons Environment Committee (1982), *The Private Rented Sector, Vol.III, Appendices*, HMSO. p.45.

50. D. Usher (1987), *Housing Privatisation: the sale of council estates*, School of Advanced Urban Studies, Bristol; J. Morris (1988b), *Housing and Disabled People in Tower Hamlets*, Action for Disability Tower Hamlets.

51. A. Thomas (1986), *The 1985 Physical and Social Survey of Houses in*

Multiple Occupation in England and Wales, HMSO.
52. North Islington Housing Rights Project (n.d), *Room for Improvement: resident landlords and Islington Council.*
53. J. Doling and M. Davies (1984), *Public Control of Privately Rented Housing*, Gower.
54. *Residential Renting in London* (August 1988), prepared by Mass-Observation UK Ltd for Safeland plc.
55. M. P. Kleinmann and C. Whitehead (1988), p.10.
56. *Ibid*, p.11.
57. R. Forrest and A. Murie (1986), 'Marginalisation and subsidised individualism' *International Journal of Urban and Regional Research*, Vol.10, No.1, January.

2 | Housing and class

As Chapter 1 has shown, housing policy is tenure-constrained. Rather than dealing with the issues of access to housing and the quality of housing, policies have primarily been directed at changing the tenure structure. The literature of housing studies has tended to focus on housing policy and this has meant that a 'tyranny of tenure' has also set the academic agenda. Our discussion in this chapter on housing and class illustrates this for there is literally no other way into a study of housing than through a tenure analysis. We begin by looking at tenure and class, outlining both the changes in the tenure structure during the course of the twentieth century and the changes in the relationship between tenure and class. A major sociological debate on housing has been around the issue of whether tenure divisions have undermined class divisions; in other words, whether social class is the predominant determinant of life chances or whether the social and economic advantages which are said to be associated with home-ownership have made tenure a key determinant of life chances(1).

This chapter explores some of the research evidence on this question, looking at both the relationship between class and housing in terms of social and economic advantage and disadvantage, and also at the issue of whether housing tenure influences class consciousness. However, discussion in this chapter is confined to empirical analysis of the relationship between housing and class. The chapter does not cover the academic debate on the nature of the housing system or the theoretical discussion of its relationship with the class system. These theoretical issues are covered in Chapter 6.

Tenure and class 1900-1990

The tenure structure of the housing stock has changed fundamentally during the course of this century. Three processes can be distinguished, all of which saw their fastest development during the period after the second world war: the decline of the privately rented sector; the growth of the owner-occupied sector; and the growth of the public rented sector until the early 1980s after which it started declining in both numerical and percentage terms.

In 1951 4 million dwellings were owner-occupied; by 1988 this had increased to 14.7 million, an expansion from 29 per cent to 65 per cent of the housing stock. Over the same period, the private rented sector declined from 7.5 million to 1.6 million dwellings and in 1988 made up 7.5 per cent of the stock. The public rented sector increased steadily between 1951 and 1980, rising from 2.5 million dwellings to 7 million. By 1988, there had been a decline to 5.6 million (25 per cent of the stock), primarily as a result of the sale of council dwellings to sitting tenants(2).

These changes in tenure structure have been accompanied by clear changes in the relationship between housing tenure and class. At the beginning of the century, when 90 per cent of dwellings were privately rented, all social classes were represented in significant proportions within the tenure although conditions varied enormously. Owner-occupation was not necessarily sought after by the economically advantaged: as Daunton states in *Coal Metropolis: Cardiff 1870–1914*:

> So far as the well-off were concerned, home ownership was not considered socially necessary, the general attitude being that house purchase for self-occupation was merely another investment and not of any pressing importance(3).

Indeed, before the expansion of mortgage finance, house purchase could merely tie up capital which would be better invested elsewhere. Thus, as Peter Kemp said in an article for *Housing Studies*:

Renting from private landlords was generally seen as the normal (and an acceptable) housing tenure, while owner-occupation was not so widely regarded as the ideal tenure; many households who could have afforded to buy chose not to do so(4).

On the other hand, the public rented sector was intended from its inception to house one particular part of the population – working-class people. All the early legislation empowering local councils to build new housing and take on the role of landlord, made it clear that this was housing for workers and in fact it wasn't until the 1949 Housing Act that local authorities were given the power to provide housing for the community generally. Merrett identifies the political concerns which fuelled the inter-war expansion of public provision of housing, namely the persistence of very poor living conditions amongst manual workers in the privately rented sector and the social and economic consequences of this, such as the spread of disease, which affected society as a whole(5).

As the owner-occupied sector expanded in the inter-war period (from 10 per cent of dwellings in 1914 to 32 per cent in 1938), evidence suggests that it was spreading in an uneven fashion amongst the occupational classes. Merrett refers to two inquiries, one of which found that 18 per cent of manual workers and lower-income non-manual workers in urban areas were owner-occupiers while the other recorded 65 per cent home-ownership amongst a sample of civil servants, local government officials and teachers(6).

With the expansion of both owner-occupation and council housing in the post-war period, a clear relationship opened up between tenure and social class. This is demonstrated by Hamnett's analysis of census statistics for 1961, 1971 and 1981(7). Over this 20-year period, the level of owner-occupation amongst total households increased by 14.6 per cent compared to 5.2 per cent for the public rented sector and a decline of 19.8 per cent for the private rented sector. Table 2.1 illustrates the uneven nature of these changes amongst the different socio-economic groups (SEGs). Hamnett argues that this analysis points to a social polarisation of what have become the two main tenures. The class dimension to this polarisation is not, however, along the conventional manual/non-manual occupational divide. The social division occurs between the semi-skilled and unskilled manual occupations together with the economically inactive, and the rest of society. The significance of Table 2.1 is summed up by Hamnett:

> It can be seen that the whole of the decrease in the proportion of privately rented households in the two highest SEGs and almost all the decrease in the skilled manual groups from 1961-1981 is accounted for by an increase in the rate of owner-occupation. In the semi-skilled group by contrast, only slightly over half of the decrease in the percentage privately renting was accounted for by an increase in owner-occupation, and in the unskilled group the proportion was only one-third, the other two-thirds being accounted for by an increase in the percentage of council tenants. When we examine the figures for the economically inactive and not stated category, the contrast is even more striking. Whilst the percentage of this group who were owner-occupiers remained static at just over 42 per cent in both 1961 and 1981, the decrease in the percentage of privately rented households of 25 percentage points was totally accounted for by a similar increase in the percentage of council tenants. Quite clearly, therefore, the small overall increase in the percentage of households who were council tenants between 1961 and 1981 was entirely concentrated in the two lowest SEGs and the economically inactive(8).

In other words, as the privately rented sector declined, skilled manual workers, intermediate and junior non-manual workers and professional, employers and managers moved into the owner-occupied sector while the other socio-economic groups (the semi- and unskilled manual workers and the economically inactive – the economically worst off) moved into the public rented sector.

TABLE 2.1 *Socio-economic groups by tenure of heads of household 1961–81*

		Owner-Occupiers		Council Tenants		Privately Rented	
		%	ppc	%	ppc	%	ppc
Professionals,	1961	67.3	+8.5	6.8	+0.9	25.9	–9.4
employers and	1971	75.8	+6.9	7.7	–1.2	16.5	–5.7
managers	1981	82.7	+15.4	6.5	–0.3	10.8	–15.1
Intermediate	1961	53.4	+5.9	15.3	+2.7	31.3	–8.6
and junior	1971	59.3	+11.2	18.0	–2.9	22.7	–8.3
non-manual	1981	70.5	+17.1	15.1	–0.2	14.4	–16.9
Skilled manual	1961	40.0	+7.8	29.3	+5.1	30.7	–12.9
and own account	1971	47.8	+10.6	34.4	–3.1	17.8	–7.5
non-professional	1981	58.4	+18.4	31.3	+2.0	10.3	–20.4
Semi-skilled	1961	28.7	+7.9	32.3	+6.9	39.0	–13.8
manual and	1971	35.6	+6.0	39.2	+2.7	25.2	–8.7
personal service	1981	41.6	+13.9	41.9	+9.6	16.5	–22.5
Unskilled manual	1961	21.9	+5.1	38.9	+10.4	39.2	–15.5
	1971	27.0	+3.9	49.3	+6.6	23.7	–10.5
	1981	30.9	+9.0	55.9	+17.0	13.2	–26.0
Students and	1961	42.3 ⎫		17.1 ⎫		40.6 ⎫	
not stated	1971	⎬	+0.1	⎬	+24.9	⎬	–25.0
Economically	1981	42.4 ⎭		42.0 ⎭		15.6 ⎭	
inactive							
All socio-economic	1961	43.1	+7.3	23.6	+4.4	33.3	–11.7
groups	1971	50.4	+7.3	28.0	+0.8	21.6	–8.1
	1981	57.7	+14.6	28.8	+5.2	13.5	–19.8

The first column of figures given for each tenure represents the percentages in each of the three census years. The second column represents the percentage point changes (ppc), and whereas the top and middle figures give the percentage point changes for 1961–71 and 1971–81, the third and bottom figure gives the overall ppc 1961–81.

Source: C. Hamnett, (1984) 'Housing the two nations: socio-tenurial polarisation in England and Wales 1961–81' *Urban Studies, 43*

While the figures in Table 2.1 illustrate the socio-economic dimensions to the decline of the private rented sector, the 1980s have seen the start of a new trend – the decline of public rented housing. The policy, introduced with the Housing Act 1980, of giving council tenants the right to buy the property they rent, has resulted in the disproportionate movement of skilled manual workers, professional and managerial groups, and junior and intermediate non-manual workers, out of the public rented sector and into owner-occupation (see below). This has deepened the tenure rift between these groups and semi-skilled and unskilled manual workers.

Council housing has not always been associated with disadvantage in the way that it now is as Britain enters the 1990s. To more fully understand how this association has come about we need to look in some detail at the changes in the relationship between council housing and class which were a particular feature of the 1980s, although the trends, as we have identified, were evident throughout the post-war period.

Class and council housing

It is now a widespread assumption that to be a council tenant is to be disadvantaged, not just in housing terms, but in more general social and economic terms. Chapter 1 has clearly shown that, in terms of physical housing conditions, council housing is comparable to owner-occupied dwellings and clearly superior to the private rented sector. To some extent, therefore, the association between poor housing conditions and council housing is a myth – although there is undoubtedly a minority of council tenants who experience such conditions. The campaigning by housing activists during the 1970s and 1980s created a picture in the public mind of high-rise blocks, despite the fact that 64 per cent of council properties are houses and only 10 per cent of purpose-built council flats are in blocks of 12 stories and above. The majority of council tenants live in good-quality housing with which they are highly satisfied.

However, there *is* a reality to the association of disadvantage with council housing. But this has its roots in a wider social and economic disadvantage, and powerlessness, which is brought about by the changing class profile of council tenants. Table 2.1 has illustrated the way in which a higher proportion of low-skilled workers and those who are outside the labour market now look to the public rented sector. Hamnett's analysis also illustrated the way in which these groups form an increasing percentage of council tenants. In spite of the overall decline in the number of semi-skilled and unskilled households, they rose as a proportion of council tenants from 37 per cent to 39 per cent in 1981 and the economically inactive increased as a proportion of council tenants at almost double their overall rate of increase (23.2 per cent compared to 12.7 per cent). If we take these two groups together, representing as they do the most economically powerless groups in society, they accounted for 40 per cent of council tenants in 1961 and 56 per cent in 1981(9). By 1986, the two groups together accounted for 72 per cent of council tenants(10).

Table 2.2. is particularly interesting as it indicates that by the early 1980s council housing had been transformed from a tenure in which the different income groups were represented more or less in proportion to their representation amongst the general population to a tenure where the lowest-income groups are disproportionately represented. Willmott and Murie draw attention to a whole range of evidence on the increasing amount of poverty amongst council tenants, including the fact that the number receiving housing benefit has increased by over a third during the 1980s – by 1987, 63 per cent of council tenants were in receipt of housing benefit(11).

This concentration of the poorest sections of the population into the public rented sector led to an identification of what has been called the residualisation of council housing. Residualisation has been defined by Malpass and Murie as:

The process whereby public housing moves towards a position in which it provides only a 'safety net' for those who for reasons of poverty, age or infirmity cannot obtain suitable accommodation in the private sector. It almost certainly involves lowering the status and increasing the stigma attached to public housing(12).

There are various factors involved in bringing about this situation, some of which are part of long-term trends in housing tenure structure, others stemming from demographic trends while the impact of government policy during the 1980s is also important.

TABLE 2.2 *Income of households in council housing (Great Britain)*

	1968 %	1978 %	1983 %	1986 %
Proportion of council tenants who were among the:				
poorest 30% of all households	31	42	52	60
middle 20% of all households	23	23	23	22
richest 50% of all households	46	35	25	18

Source: Peter Kemp (1989), 'The demunicipalisation of rented housing' in M. Benton and C. Ungerson, *Social Policy Review 1988–9*, Longman

The decline of the low-rent part of the private rented sector throughout the course of this century has meant that low-income households have looked in ever greater numbers to the council sector. At the same time, the nature of access to council housing has changed. Whereas it was common prior to the Second World War for local councils to only house those whom it was sure could pay the relatively high rents, the expansion of council housing after the war coincided with greater pressure on local authorities to house those who were poorest and in greatest housing need. This pressure had its culmination in the Housing (Homeless Persons) Act of 1977, a piece of legislation which has been identified as playing a key role in the residualisation of council housing.

At the same time, the policy of all governments since 1951 of giving favourable treatment to owner occupiers has made a major contribution to a residualisation of the council sector. As Willmott and Murie state:

> The more that access to owner-occupation is extended, the more it is bound to pull in households just at the margin of being able to afford it. Increasingly that leaves behind a relatively pauperised group, those people who cannot afford to make the move(13).

While residualisation of the council sector is associated with the changes in the tenure structure, identified above, which have been going on for most of the century, there are particular developments in the 1980s which have increased the social significance of this trend. The first is the uneven effect of the economic recession of the early 1980s. Council tenants were disproportionately affected by industrial restructuring, partly because a higher proportion of them were in the most 'at risk' occupations (semi-skilled and unskilled jobs) and partly because council housing is disproportionately found in areas particularly affected by closures and redundancies. This uneven impact of industrial restructuring contributed to increasing poverty levels amongst council tenants.

A second factor is the effect of demographic trends. The number of retired people has increased generally, but the increase has been greater amongst council tenants. As Willmott and Murie point out:

> This is partly because the people who were parents with young children in the period of greatest post-war growth in council housing are now in their 60s and 70s, and partly because that is the sector in which pensioners can most readily afford to live or, to put it the other way, can least readily leave for one of the other options(14).

Council housing also becomes the preferred option for considerable numbers of elderly owners. Kleinmann and

Whitehead refer to unpublished Labour Force Survey data which show that 42 per cent of the households moving from owner-occupation to council housing are aged over 60(15).

Just as the overall increase in the number of older people has had a disproportionate effect on the profile of council tenants, so the steady increase in the divorce rate has had a similar effect, in that one-parent families are over-represented amongst council tenants. Again, this is partly because council housing is often the only option when marital breakdown brings poverty (see Chapter 4). It is also because the divorce rate is higher amongst those who have married young and such households are more likely to gain access to council housing at this early stage of their married lives.

The third factor apparent in the 1980s has been the effect of council house sales. The greater propensity for non-manual and skilled manual workers who were council tenants to take the opportunity of buying their dwelling was already evident in the voluntary sales policies of local authorities such as Birmingham City Council in the 1970s(16). Figure 2.1 gives the picture for the much larger volume of sales which has resulted from the right to buy legislation.

Economically inactive heads of household are not included here in this breakdown of buyers and tenants. Earlier research found that economically inactive buyers form a higher percentage amongst council tenant purchasers than amongst other purchasers (i.e. on the private market) and this is illustrated by Table 2.3. Indeed, the right to buy policy has undoubtedly made it possible for pensioner households, in particular, to become home-owners – primarily through the right to a mortgage which was also granted under the 1980 Act. However, economically inactive households have been under-represented amongst council tenant purchasers compared to their representation amongst all tenants. Figure 2.2 illustrates this, and also draws attention to the importance of more than one wage coming into the household to enable council tenants to purchase their dwelling.

FIGURE 2.1 *Socio-economic group of household heads in work: tenants and buyers*

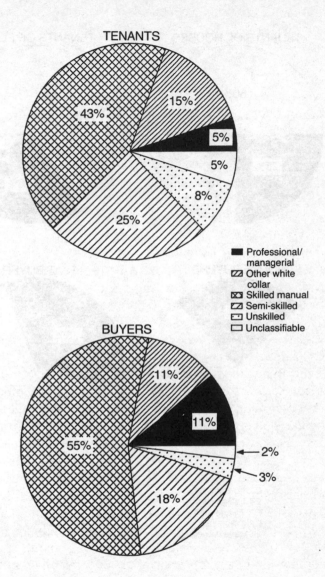

TENANTS

15%
43%
5%
5%
8%
25%

Professional/
managerial
Other white
collar
Skilled manual
Semi-skilled
Unskilled
Unclassifiable

BUYERS

11%
11%
55%
2%
3%
18%

Source: Marian Kerr (1988), *The Right to Buy: A national survey of tenants and buyers of council homes*, HMSO.

FIGURE 2.2 *Number of wage-earners in household: tenants and buyers*

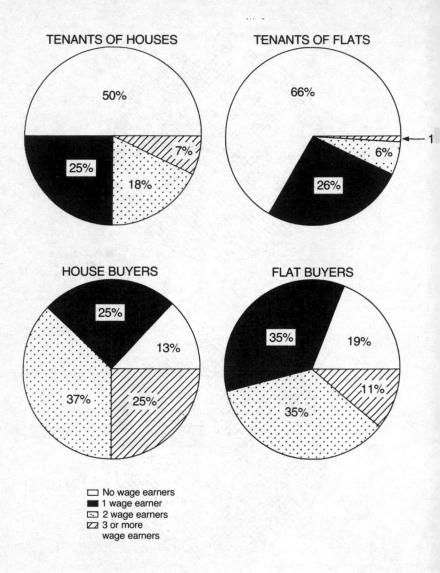

Source: Marian Kerr (1988), *The Right to Buy: A national survey of tenants and buyers of council homes*, HMSO.

TABLE 2.3 *Socio-economic group of council tenant purchasers compared to all borrowers*

Socio-economic group	Bexley %		Haringey %		Islington %	
Prof/managerial	7	(33)	6	(43)	21	(56)
Intermediate	16	(21)	10	(23)	33	(22)
Skilled manual	33	(25)	47	(21)	21	(8)
Semi-skilled manual	14	(3)	4	(8)	9	(3)
Unskilled			3		2	
Retired	18	(2)	21	(1)	3	(2)
Other	7	(17)	6	(6)	6	(9)
Not available	5		3		5	

Figures in brackets represent Nationwide Building Society borrowers in London (Nationwide, 1985).

Source: J. Morris (1986), *Council House Sales in Three London Boroughs*, London Housing Research Group.

It is undoubtedly the case that a decline of council housing, particularly when it is the most desirable property which is being sold to the better-off tenants (see Chapter 1), is contributing to a residualisation process – i.e. whereby both the housing tenure and its population are becoming marginalised. However, Forrest and Murie have pointed out that this process cannot be separated from wider social and economic changes which were having an effect even before the right to buy policy. They argue:

> In fact what is happening to council housing is the product of wider processes of economic and social change – and indeed of changes in other tenures as well as council housing(17).

In particular, they emphasise, residualisation involves issues of economic, political and social power. Three factors are identified:

a. the increasing importance of market relationships (as a result of the increase in owner-occupation) in determining access to housing and the disadvantageous effect this has on low-income groups;

b. the political powerlessness of the economically inactive, i.e. unemployed and retired people (who have increased in number and as a proportion of local authority tenants);

c. the uneven impact of industrial decline and the fact that local authority housing tends to be concentrated in the areas most affected. The selective take-up of the right to buy is aggravating this concentration.

As Balchin points out, the decline of the public rented sector has not brought about its residualisation, rather that decline happened at the same time as a section of the population in the 1980s became marginal in economic terms(18). It is conceivable that a smaller public rented sector could retain the privileged position that it had amongst rented housing up until the second world war. Instead, the increasingly rapid decline of the low-rent part of the privately rented sector coincided with the withdrawal of government support for the public rented sector and the encouragement of owner-occupation. Low-income households – in particular, those experiencing the unemployment and deskilling which was such a crucial feature of the 1980s economy – had nowhere else to go but the deteriorating council sector. The result, in terms of changes in the relationship between tenure and class structure, has been summed up by Forrest and Murie as follows:

> The public sector is catering for a progressively higher proportion of those marginalised in the labour market . . . There is a movement from a position where owner-occupation was a predominantly middle class tenure, high-quality council housing was used by the affluent working class and private landlordism catered for the poorest sections of the population towards one where council housing serves the vulnerable, low-paid and marginalised population with a highly stratified and differentiated home-ownership as the mass tenure(19).

Research has also identified that the different experiences of housing advantage and disadvantage *within* the public rented sector are related to wider social and economic inequalities. Most attention has been focused on the way in which black and ethnic minority households tend to be allocated the poorer-quality council housing (see Chapter 3) but there is evidence that class is also related to housing situation within the public rented sector. Twine and Williams, in their study of council housing in Aberdeen, state that:

> A statistically significant concentration of unskilled and semi-skilled manual households was found to exist in estates built under slum clearance and overcrowding legislation in the 1930s [the walk-up tenements which were unpopular], whereas estates built under legislation aimed at more general housing provision contained fewer households than expected [in these socio-economic groups](20)

Twine and Williams identified three possible explanations for this social segregation occurring despite the fact that the formal terms of entry to the public sector are based on housing need rather than other socio-economic factors. Firstly, there may be differential rent levels between different estates; in the past some local authorities have had deliberate policies for maximising rent income which have resulted in better-off households being allocated more expensive, and higher-quality, property. Secondly, the housing department may grade tenants and properties. This may be done formally or informally. Glasgow, for example, had a formal practice in the 1960s and 1970s which involved applicants being judged by housing visitors according to whether they were suitable for good-quality housing or not(21). The result was that the poorer households – large families, one-parent families, unemployed people, chronically sick people – were allocated the 'Group 8' estates, the low-amenity, unpopular, inter-war housing estates which had been built for slum clearance.

Informal practices most often result from the management priorities which conflict with a formal lettings policy based on housing need. Willmott and Murie, drawing on Henderson and Karn's research of Birmingham City Council's allocation practices in the late 1970s emphasise these pressures on council officers which lead to social segregation.

> Two of their main tasks are to let dwellings as quickly as possible, and to avoid management problems – those that might arise, for example, from mixing 'rough' people with 'respectable' ones. Both these objectives lead them to allocate housing in ways that make for the easiest 'fit' based on the officers' judgements about which kinds of people are likely to be most appropriate for particular estates. They seek to match the people to the dwellings and estates which they think will best 'suit' them(22).

The third factor, which makes the allocation practices referred to above possible, is that poorer households are unlikely to refuse the worst housing because their housing need is desperate. As Willmott and Murie point out:

> The ability of applicants to delay and wait for a better offer – their bargaining power within the allocation system – strongly influences which queue they are in and which property they get(23).

The temptation for housing officers, faced with pressure to keep down void rates and a knowledge that some property is difficult to let, is to offer the least popular dwellings to those who are most likely to accept them. This issue – of social segregation within council housing – is part of our discussion of both race and gender divisions and housing in Chapters 3 and 4. It is also an important aspect of the association of social problems with council housing and is thus integral to our analysis of 'problem estates' in Chapter 5.

The first part of this section on class and council housing established that there is clear evidence of an increasing proportion of council tenants being marginalised in social and economic terms – partly because of a movement out of the sector of those who are not marginalised, partly because council housing is concentrated in those areas of the country which score highly on such measurements of social deprivation as unemployment rates, and finally because council housing is the major source of low-cost housing. However, there is also evidence of marginalisation and associated social and economic disadvantages amongst increasing numbers of owner-occupiers. The following section looks in more detail at the relationship between class and home-ownership and in doing so touches on some of the theoretical debate which is dealt with in more detail in Chapter 6.

Class and home-ownership

Much has been written in recent years on the implications of expanding owner-occupation (particularly amongst skilled manual workers) for the class structure of modern British society. Interest focuses on two aspects, which are of course interrelated. The first is whether the advantages which home-ownership brings to working-class households have diminished the importance of class position as a determinant of life chances; the second is whether home-ownership has an impact on class consciousness. This section focuses on the first issue while the final section of the chapter addresses the question of class consciousness.

The previous discussion has illustrated that a tenure/class division can be identified in Britain which cuts through the working class; skilled manual workers have always been more likely to be owner-occupiers than other sections of the working class and housing policy in the 1980s has increased this likelihood. Some sociologists have argued that home-ownership brings economic advantages and increased social status and that the class composition of the owner-occupied sector therefore weakens the relationship between class and economic and social inequality(24).

The theoretical dimensions to this argument are explored in Chapter 6. In this chapter we focus on an empirical analysis of the relationship between class, tenure and social and economic inequality, using the material to examine both the question of whether home-ownership is a *determinant* of life chances rather than merely being a life chance itself and the question of whether home-ownership automatically brings social and economic advantage.

Recent analysis of data from the National Child Development Study has found a relationship between housing situation in childhood (measured by tenure and over-crowding) and 17 aspects of adult life, *irrespective* of social class. The outcomes encompass employment, unemployment and income; health; qualification; partnership, marriage and family formation; and housing. It was found that the strongest relationship in almost every area was with the tenure of the home(s) in which the cohort member grew up. The relationship of crowding with the outcome showed a similar but less strong pattern than did tenure.

The study concluded that:

> Those whose families were owner-occupiers at seven, 11 and 16, and similarly those who were not in crowded homes at those ages, were more likely, compared with those who were local authority tenants (or in crowded homes) at all three ages: to be in higher-status occupations at 23; to have higher family incomes, particularly when family situation is taken into account; to have experienced less unemployment, both currently and since completing education; to have higher qualifications; and to rate their health highly. They were less likely to have married and/or to have children; to have left home and formed an independent household; to be on a council waiting list; and to have moved home frequently(25).

This relationship between advantageous outcomes and housing tenure is irrespective of social class and could therefore be cited in support of the position that Britain 'is moving to a point where the division between households which have a property right in the home and those who do not is becoming a major determinant of life chances', as Peter Saunders and Peter Williams put it(26). The theoretical dimensions to this position are explored in Chapter 6. On an empirical level, however, it is clear that the contention that home-ownership is a *determinant* of life chances has to be set against the evidence that there is not by any means a simple relationship between owner-occupation and either housing advantage or economic advantage. The following discussion identifies the variations which exist within the tenure, identifying that being a home-owner does not in any way guarantee an experience of social and economic advantage.

The owner-occupied sector contains larger dwellings, more houses and exhibits less overcrowding than either of the other two tenures, but in terms of housing conditions there is little to choose between the owner-occupied and council sector (see Chapter 1). As the English House Condition Survey identified, the crucial factor determining poor housing conditions is the income of the household. The Survey found that poor conditions are associated, across the tenures, with particular types of household – with older households, single-person households and ethnic minority households – but the crucial factor is low income: as the report stated: 'Poor housing was related, above all, to income'(27).

We have seen that the changing relationship between tenure and class during the post-war period has resulted in a higher proportion of council tenants being low-income households. However, it is also the case that, as the owner-occupied sector has become the mass tenure, larger numbers of owners are living in poverty. This is particularly evident amongst older owners. In 1986 the average household income of the poorest 25 per cent of owners outright (the majority of whom are over 60) was £68 per week, compared to the median income for all households of £166 per week(28). Home-ownership is increasing amongst older people – because of the historical expansion of the sector – and since older people have a high risk of experiencing poverty, we can expect this to be reflected in increasing poverty levels amongst owner-occupiers in the years to come. It is also of significance that, as home-ownership increases amongst manual workers, more and more home-owners will be entering retirement without adequate occupational pensions to keep them out of poverty in old age.

As the owner-occupied sector expands, more and more low-income households are forced into owner-occupation. The economic situation of these households means that buying a property does not necessarily bring about housing advantage. They buy older property, often cannot afford to repair and maintain it and are at risk of falling into mortgage arrears and losing their home. Furthermore, some groups of low-income owners are excluded from the formal mortgage market and rely on 'informal finance' to raise loans to buy(29). This means that they do not benefit from mortgage interest tax relief, so they lose out on one of the main financial advantages of owner-occupation.

In areas of the country where there are high unemployment levels and low house price inflation, many home-owners have found that the repair bill on their property amounts to more than the value of the house(30). These people have been completely left behind in the house price booms of the 1970s and 1980s and their housing disadvantage can only increase while their housing situation depends on their own resources.

It would seem, therefore, that to be a home-owner does not automatically mean to experience either housing advantage or wider social and economic advantages. However, owner-occupation *is* a potential source of wealth accumulation in the way that being a tenant is not normally (except, that is, where 20 years as a council tenant can be converted into a 70 per cent discount on the purchase price for a sitting tenant under the right to buy legislation). A number of writers(31) have identified the way in which the increase in owner-occupation has led to a reduction in the degree of concentration of wealth in Britain. Dwellings now account for a third of total personal net wealth in Britain(32).

The expansion of home-ownership has had a part to play in the expansion of personal wealth in the form of dwellings but it is also crucially related to house price inflation which since the mid-1950s has been double general price inflation. According to a report published by the Nationwide Building Society in 1986, a property bought in 1970 on a 25-year mortgage and sold in 1985 averaged an annual return of 17 per cent net (after tax) for its owner, a higher rate of return than on any other form of investment(33). And, as Chris Hamnett has pointed out, 'As a result, home-ownership has functioned not just as a store of wealth but also as a major source of wealth'(34). The importance of this source of wealth is illustrated by the fact that the value of residential property in estates passing at death grew from £465m in 1968/9 to £3.383 billion in 1982/3 – an increase of 627 per cent and the average value of residential property being passed on increased from £3,700 to £23,000(35).

The importance of inheritance of wealth in the form of property has been emphasised by Murie and Forrest. They argue:

> At a time when free market processes are likely to become more dominant in the determination of life chances generally, the accumulation of wealth through property ownership may be a crucial element in perpetuating and creating inequalities(36).

Those households who inherit properties are unlikely to be at the early stages of their housing careers but the inheritance will enable them to 'trade up' (thus fuelling house prices) or to assist their own children in becoming first-time buyers (also fuelling house prices). Most children of owner-occupiers become owner-occupiers themselves. The wealth passed on by the previous generation of owners therefore creates an ever-widening inequality between owners and tenants in the current generation.

Supporters of a continuing increase in owner-occupation have a different perspective, stressing that capital accumulation through home-ownership spreads wealth more evenly throughout the population. The higher the rate of home-ownership the larger the number of households who will be able to accumulate capital in a way which they could never do as tenants. The increase in home-ownership is thus said to bring about a 'democratisation' of wealth – a spread of wealth amongst many more households.

However, there are variations in the potential for wealth accumulation within the owner-occupied sector. House price inflation (in real terms) is the crucial factor in making owner-occupation a source of wealth accumulation but we should not assume that this is a uniform feature of owner-occupation. On the contrary, house price trends vary and in particular they vary by area.

David Thorns has identified how the uneven impact of industrial change has meant that economic disadvantages are compounded by static or declining house prices(37). Industrial restructuring during the 1960s and 1970s – the decline of the basic industries of the North, North East and South Wales and the growth of the service sector and new industries in the South East – created regional disparities in employment opportunities. Associated regional variations in house price inflation meant that, for example, in 1979 a house in the North of England would only buy 59 per cent of a house in Greater London and only 63 per cent of a house in the South East. According to Thorns:

These figures indicate the general picture of regional dispari-ties; however they also mask the true extent of the differences between the prosperous and declining areas where in the latter cases house prices are either static or falling. The results of such marked changes upon owner-occupiers in these declining areas is to reinforce their losses sustained by the labour market change. Not only have they lost their job, but also their main private investment, their own house, is also of declining value and virtually unsellable except at a price which would represent a substantial loss to the household(38).

Most of the data available on capital gains is national and regional data and the debate has therefore focused on the North/South divide in house price inflation. There is however much more local variation and it is important to recognise that the nature of house price inflation in London and the South East has not been uniform across all classes within the region.

Research during the 1970s on the process of 'gentrification' which some working-class inner city areas experienced illustrates the way in which middle-class owners are more likely to benefit from increasing house prices. One example is Balchin's analysis of the effect of urban renewal policies in the London Borough of Hammersmith and Fulham(39). The low-cost working-class housing in his area of study had been protected from high-income demand by the low quality of the housing and the demand for housing in suburban locations.

> But in the 1960s and 1970s the units were under severe competition as a result of demand from higher-income groups – a demand increased by the availablity of improvement grants and stimulated by the cost and inconvenience of commuting(40).

Although improvement grants were directed at the areas of working-class housing in the borough, working-class people did not in fact benefit. Instead, private rented housing changed hands into owner-occupied housing or high-rent luxury accommodation. This 'forced the poor to consume less housing space, often within the same borough, and homelessness and council housing waiting lists are increasing'(41). Balchin confirmed a process identified by earlier research(42) where the rising house prices in such inner city areas benefited the new entrants who were high-income and middle-class households and actually increased the housing stress experienced by working-class households.

The class differences in wealth accumulation through owner-occupation within the South East has also been demonstrated in recent years in the London Borough of Newham. Previously one of the lowest-priced areas in London, because it was predominantly a working-class area, the activities of the London Docklands Development Corporation in the neighbouring borough of Tower Hamlets has created an economic and social desirability which the area did not have before to middle- and higher-income groups. In 1985, smaller properties in the area were affordable by people on an average wage. By 1987, they were not, prices having risen by around 50 per cent(43). Those working-class households who were already owner-occupiers had made significant capital gains but the rise in house prices has meant the area is no longer a source of affordable owner-occupation for working-class households. Instead, a high level of house sales, together with economic and social regeneration of the area are part and parcel of a changing social composition. From being a predominantly working-class area, it is now being 'gentrified' by the managerial, administrative and professional occupational classes.

Forrest and Murie have reassessed their previous work on wealth inheritance through owner-occupation, concluding that the increase in home-ownership does not in fact lead to a 'democratisation' of wealth. 'Ultimately,' they say, 'the process of intergenerational transfers of housing wealth may have more oligarchic than democratic consequences'(44) – in other words those who are economically privileged in one generation pass this privilege on to their children. This situation comes about firstly because people's experiences of home-ownership during their lifetime are determined by wider social and economic factors – class, race and gender are key influences on the terms on which someone enters and experiences owner-occupation and therefore on whether home-ownership brings significant capital accumulation to be passed on at death.

Secondly, these social divisions also influence the nature of the transfer of wealth at death. For example, working-class home-owners are more likely to come from larger families, to live in the same locality as their parents and their parents are less likely to be home-owners than the parents of middle-class home-owners. The sale of a working-class parental home will fetch a lower price than in a more prosperous middle-class area and the proceeds will be divided amongst more people. Class, race and gender may also have complicated influences on housing opportunities in old age which may freeze or erode wealth holdings (e.g. moving to a nursing home or living with relatives).

Far from spreading wealth more evenly, the operation of the housing market – with its sub-markets of high-status, high-priced dwellings and low-priced, poor-condition dwellings – is more likely to open up further divisions within the owner-occupied sector. Forrest and Murie argue that:

> A privileged minority will not only continue to hold their wealth in forms which convey real social and economic power (e.g. stocks and shares) but they are likely to pass on disproportionately large amounts of accumulated housing wealth(45).

In this way the capital gains to be made from home-ownership only serve to exacerbate inequalities which are grounded in wider social divisions.

As a final illustration of the nature of variations within the owner-occupied sector we set out below two examples which illustrate the economic context of housing disadvantage within owner-occupation and which suggest that it is not tenure which determines advantage or disadvantage but the wider socio-economic context of housing experience.

Saltley
Saltley, in East Birmingham, illustrates the interaction of class, race and housing disadvantage. As a residential area, it is surrounded on three sides with an industrial belt. Houses were built during the second half of the nineteenth century to accommodate the workers in the brick, gas, metal and railway carriage works and on the railways. These were rented houses built by a local landowner for skilled and relatively well-paid male workers and their families.

With the expansion of owner-occupation in the 1930s and 1940s and the ageing of the properties in Saltley, many of the skilled workers in regular employment moved out to the suburbs and the new, bigger, semi-detached houses. At the same time, the first wave of (Irish) immigrants moved into the area as it was now a source of relatively cheap rented housing as well as being close to employment opportunities. However, the area experienced a fundamental change in its industrial base during the post-war period. While it has remained a source of cheap housing its industry has declined as a result of productivity crises in British Leyland, in local gas-making and railway carriage manufacturing and in railway transport(46). During the 1950s and 1960s a new wave of immigrants moved in, this time from the New Commonwealth and Pakistan. They were initially pulled in through local employment opportunities but the area became even more important as a major area of settlement because of the housing opportunities offered. Council housing was closed to such immigrants initially and they looked to the private rented sector and then to owner-occupation for housing. Saltley became an important settlement area for people from Pakistan and Bangladesh and by 1981, 35 per cent of heads of households in the area were born in one of these two countries.

The class composition of the area also changed quite rapidly during the 1960s and 1970s: the proportion of professional and managerial workers in the area, which had always been low, declined still further but so did the proportion of skilled manual workers. This changing class composition was a direct result of the decline of manufacturing in the area and the expansion of distribution services. These economic shifts were reflected both in the increase in the land used for warehouse/distribution and also in derelict land. The local population was becoming marginalised: local unemployment levels were consistently higher than the national or regional average and average household income levels lower.

At the same time, levels of owner-occupation were increasing. Karn, Kemeney and Williams carried out research on owner-occupation in Birmingham and Liverpool, using 1972–74 and 1975–79 data. They found that entry into owner-occupation in Saltley meant buying a pre-1919 (98 per cent of purchasers), terraced (92 per cent), two-storey

(99 per cent) property. It meant buying with a much lower household income than the average first-time buyer(47). A significant minority of Saltley purchasers bought properties without inside toilets (14 per cent in 1979), or without a bath (16 per cent) and 89 per cent of purchasers in 1979 bought properties with no central heating. Only 8 per cent of buyers used a building society mortgage to purchase their home (the cheapest source of financing owner-occupation). The largest group (43 per cent in 1975–79) bought with short-term bank loans and 20 per cent bought with finance from a friend or relative. It is also significant that the Asian community was dramatically over-represented amongst purchasers (making up 73 per cent of purchasers).

Although the most important motivation for purchasing, according to Karn et al's research, was as an investment for the future, purchase of housing in Saltley was not a good investment. Between 1972 and 1979, prices of houses in Saltley fell by about 25 per cent relative to the average for the West Midlands. Furthermore, a house condition survey done as part of the same research found a severe state of disrepair, the majority of properties technically qualifying for compulsory purchase orders to bring them up to minimum standards.

> The estimated mean cost of improvement to a 30-year life was more than the mean price paid for the houses by buyers between 1975 and 1979. Though households spent what were for them considerable amounts of money on repairs, often at great personal sacrifice, the amounts spent were far below those required to bring the houses up to a 30-year life. In addition, levels of grant-aided work were low, even among longer-established buyers(48).

Owner-occupiers in areas like Saltley lack power – social, economic and political power. They lack power primarily because of their position within the economy. The economic disadvantage experienced by Saltley residents arose from industrial restructuring which for them meant higher levels of unemployment and a higher proportion of low-waged occupations in the area. For a significant section of the local population (i.e. the Asian community) these disadvantages were compounded by discriminatory effects of the building societies' and the local authority's role in the housing market. The way in which building societies operated resulted in Indian and Pakistani purchasers being less likely to get access to cheaper loans through mortgages and mortgage interest tax relief. Birmingham City Council operated both directly and indirectly discriminatory practices which first closed the door to council housing and then provided limited access to poorer-quality housing(49).

Racial discrimination (including its indirect effect on the local housing market) compounded the housing disadvantage experienced by Saltley residents, but the crucial factor in the history of the area was the impact of industrial decline and restructuring. Owner-occupation in this context did not constitute an experience of social and economic, or housing, advantage.

Shipcote
Shipcote is an area in Gateshead made up of pre-1914 terraced houses and flats. Originally built for private renting, the houses are now almost wholly owner-occupied. Having escaped clearance it developed into an important area for first-time buyers, many of whose parents were council tenants, living in good-quality, Wheatley and Bevan houses(50). When these new households formed, their only chance of getting into the public rented sector was into the mass housing of the 1960s. Benefiting from 1960s/1970s high employment levels, they became owner-occupiers. Grants were available from the local council for putting in amenities and these households were then able to 'trade up' as their incomes grew and as there was a plentiful supply of newly forming households wishing to move into the area. During the 1970s, the area was a key example of how, having got onto the 'housing ladder', young owner-occupiers were able to benefit from increasing house prices to ensure increasing housing advantage by moving from the bottom of the ladder to better houses further up the ladder.

However, in the 1980s, high unemployment levels hit the area. In 1984, 18.4 per cent of the working population in Gateshead were registered unemployed and the figure for Saltwell/Shipcote was 22.2 per cent(51). This economic situation reduced the supply of first-time buyers in the area and brought economic difficulties to existing owner-occupiers. These houses were now over 100 years old and, although their amenity standard was good, their state of disrepair was growing. They required large sums of money to restore their condition and in fact could be served with Section 9.1(a) notices which was where an Environmental Health Officer served a notice stating that while a dwelling was fit, it required substantial structural repairs. The owner was then entitled to a mandatory grant of either 75 or 90 per cent of the cost of works up to a ceiling of allowable cost of £4,800 – in fact the majority of houses were divided into two flats, but bought as one dwelling and counted as two dwellings for repair grant purposes. A local survey indicated that two-thirds of the dwellings could be subject of Section 9.1(a) notices(52).

However, renovation grant aid was drying up because of financial difficulties experienced by the local council. In 1984–5, the local authority spent £7m. on private sector renovation grants. This was reduced to £5.4m. in 1985–6 and to £1.5m in 1986–7.

These owner-occupiers, having been such an important part of the expansion of owner-occupation, were becoming marginalised.

Not only are they 'trapped' by the collapse of trading up but many of them belong to precisely that section of the skilled working class who are being peripheralised by deindustrial-isation expressed through redundancy and are thereby trapped in all senses . . . Owner-occupation is turning round for these people(53).

They were being marginalised in production and this led to a marginalisation of their position as owner-occupiers.

The general conclusion from our discussion must be that class position determines the terms of access into the owner-occupied sector and that while individual working-class home-owners may do very well out of owning their own home, or their parents'/grandparents' home-ownership, the expansion of home-ownership to the situation where it is now the mass tenure has meant that there is no longer a straightforward relationship between owner-occupation and social and economic advantage. To be a home-owner is not necessarily to experience either housing advantage or other social and economic advantages. This is because, rather than being a *determinant* of social and economic advantage, home-ownership may be an *expression* of such advantages. What is more, home-ownership can also be part and parcel of economic and social disadvantage and this is particularly evident in areas and amongst groups who are economically marginalised.

It is likely that the variations within owner-occupation will become ever clearer as Britain enters the 1990s. The combined effects of increasing home-ownership, an ageing population, a low-waged economy and the regional variations in economic prosperity/decline may mean that disadvantaged owners become more and more visible. For the moment, however, we can identify that class factors are crucial in determining whether the experience of home-ownership constitutes advantage or disadvantage.

Housing tenure and class consciousness

We have argued that the spread of home-ownership does not necessarily diminish the importance of class as the major social division. However, some writers, such as Saunders and Williams, have developed their argument further and insist that not only does the spread of home-ownership bring about a less clear relationship between class and social and economic advantage, but it also brings about the spread of privatism and individualism(54). This is said to challenge the

Marxist assumption that it is the experience of waged work which determines people's perceptions of their world, their place within it and their social actions. To be a member of the working class 50 years ago was supposedly to be focused on collective action and politics through the trade union movement and the Labour Party. Today, more and more working-class people are home-owners and their lives are more and more based around the home and on privatised, individual consumption.

Again, the theoretical dimensions to this argument are explored in Chapter 6. Here we wish to look at some of the empirical evidence on whether the increase in home-ownership amongst manual workers has eroded class identity. The debate on this issue commonly focuses on the decline in support for the Labour Party. It is argued that the decline of the working class – measured in occupational class terms – cannot explain the rapid decline in the Labour vote between 1979 and 1983 and 1987 or the growth in the Alliance parties. Instead, it is argued, the expansion of owner-occupation amongst skilled manual workers has predisposed them to vote in ever greater numbers for the Conservative Party as their stake in the 'status quo' increases.

A major problem with this argument is the leap which is made from the concept of class consciousness to voting for the Labour Party. We would wish to distance ourselves from the assumption that a vote for Labour is an indication of working-class consciousness. However, the argument about the relationship between the increase in home-ownership and the decline in the Labour vote is worth analysing in terms of the available evidence.

The most detailed research on the importance of home-ownership for voting patterns is that carried out by Heath, Jowell and Curtice in their study of the 1983 General Election. Their later work on the 1987 Election confirms their 1983 findings so although we refer to both works in the discussion below, we focus mainly on the more detailed analysis of the 1983 Election. Heath et al set out to examine the argument that:

Rising levels of affluence and the break-up of traditional communities are held to have eroded class solidarity. Labour in particular, it is said, can no longer rely on working-class support in the way it could a generation ago and the new breed of affluent skilled manual workers in the South of England are believed to have swung decisively to the Conservatives. The spread of home-ownership in the working class exacerbates the trend(55).

They put forward three key points to refute this analysis:

Structural changes in class composition of electorate
Heath et al emphasise the inadequacies of a methodology which uses the non-manual/manual classification to indicate the division between the 'middle class' and the working class. The internal composition of the working class has been changing in the post-war period, with self-employed manual workers increasing in number while waged manual workers have been declining in number. 'The declining propensity of the working class to vote Labour is at least partly a result of this change' as self-employed manual workers have always had a greater tendency to vote Conservative (56).

Furthermore, while manual workers have been declining as a percentage of the electorate in the post-war period, non-manual workers have been increasing. Heath et al use a measurement of class which focuses on economic interests:

> Broadly speaking, wage labourers have different interests from those of the self-employed, or from those of salaried managers and professionals. Their incomes may overlap but the conditions under which they earn that income differ quite markedly(57).

They therefore use the five classes indicated in the table below which sets out the changing class composition of the electorate between 1964 and 1983.

Heath et al calculate that if the Labour Party's share of the working-class vote remained constant, then it would have fallen by 7 per cent for no other reason than that the working class declined as a proportion of the electorate. It actually

TABLE 2.4 *Class composition of the electorate, 1964 and 1983*

	1964 %	1983 %
Salariat	18	27
Routine non-manual	18	24
Petty bourgeoisie	7	8
Foremen and technicians	10	7
Working class	47	34

Source: A. Heath, R. Jowell and J. Curtice, (1987) *How Britain Votes*, Pergamon Press.

fell by 16 per cent between 1964 and 1983, leaving 9 per cent to be accounted for by reasons other than the structural change in the class composition of the electorate.

Structural change indicates that the Conservative vote should have increased by six percentage points over the same period of time whereas in fact it declined by one percentage point (to 42 per cent). It was, of course, the rise in the Liberal/Social Democratic share of the vote which took votes away from both parties and structural change only accounted for 1.5 percentage points of its 14 point rise. Just how crucial the intervention of the third party was in 1983 is seen by the fact that the 1979 election result was close to what might have been expected given the expansion and contraction of the different classes(58). The role of the Liberal and Social Democratic Alliance in the 1983 Election undermines the validity of measuring class consciousness by party voting.

Relative class voting
Heath et al argue that commentators have 'confused a decline in *overall* support for Labour with a decline in its *relative* class support . . . Labour remained a class party in 1983; it was simply a less successful class party than before'(59). Although it is true that Labour fared worse in the working class in 1983 than it had done in other elections, it fared badly in every other class as well. Its decline was

general, across the electorate and not class-specific. In this situation, Heath et al argue, it is political factors which must explain Labour's decline rather than any class dealignment. In other words, it was not that the working class is changing its class identity as expressed by its propensity to vote Labour, rather that Labour was finding it more difficult to attract votes amongst all parts of the electorate.

Tenure and voting patterns
It is certainly true that there has always been a strong statistical relationship between tenure and voting. Table 2.5 indicates the correlation between owner-occupation and voting Conservative, council tenancies and voting Labour and also shows that this association persists even when class is controlled for.

Some commentators such as David Butler have gone further than this association between tenure and voting and contend that entry into home-ownership by council tenants is likely to lead to a shift towards voting for the Conservative party. Thus a MORI poll found that whereas council house tenants voted 49 per cent Labour to 29 per cent Conservative, the figures were almost exactly reversed among working-class voters owning or buying their homes (26 to 47 per cent)(60).

However, as Heath et al point out, it is one thing to show *association*, another to establish *cause*. And this is where we need to refer again to the unsatisfactory nature of voting patterns as an indicator of class divisions. Significant numbers of working-class voters have always failed to vote Labour. It is also important to recognise that significant numbers of working-class people have aspired to owner-occupation ever since it started to develop as a major tenure form, both because of the advantages that home-ownership sometimes brings *and* because of the lack of alternatives.

It is true that the different voting pattern of home-owners compared to council tenants does beg the question as to whether home-ownership itself affects social and political attitudes. Unfortunately, all that the statistical correlations between voting and tenure patterns in Table 2.5 show is association. They tell us nothing about cause. As Heath et al argue:

> It is quite plausible, and perfectly consistent with the data, to argue that social attitudes influence one's choice of housing rather than the other way round. This will only be true to the extent that there is some choice in the housing market for people of limited financial means. This has not always been the case, and for many people it will not be the case even now. But one of the real consequences of increasing affluence is that more working-class people have the opportunity to purchase their own home. Their values may determine whether they avail themselves of the opportunity or not. On this acount, the increasing availability of mortgages and the right of council tenants to purchase, simply allows people who already favour private property to purchase their own homes. It does not create these values; without such values, people are hardly likely to want to buy in the first place(61).

TABLE 2.5 *Housing, class and vote*

	Conservative %	Labour %	Alliance %	Others %
Salariat				
Owner-occupiers	56	12	31	1
Private tenants	54	5	34	7
Council tenants	33	36	28	3
Intermediate classes				
Owner-occupiers	59	14	26	1
Private tenants	54	23	18	5
Council tenants	25	50	23	2
Working class				
Owner-occupiers	39	37	23	1
Private tenants	28	47	22	3
Council tenants	20	62	17	1

Source: A. Heath, R. Jowell and J. Curtice (1987), *How Britain Votes*, Pergamon Press

This last sentence needs to be treated with caution in that there is clearly a wide range of factors involved in the wish to become an owner-occupier, including the lack of alternatives and, particularly for council tenant purchasers, the financial incentives offered. However, the point stands that it cannot be shown that becoming an owner-occupier will change a Labour voter into a Conservative one. Consider the following analysis of voting patterns in 1979, 1983 and 1987 of council tenants who purchased their properties compared to those who did not.

TABLE 2.6 *Council house sales and vote*

	1979 %	*1983* %	*1987* %
Local authority tenants			
Conservative	18	20	18
Labour	59	55	50
Other	9	13	17
Did not vote	14	12	15
Council house purchasers			
Conservative	32	36	31
Labour	48	39	31
Other	11	14	26
Did not vote	9	11	12

Source: A. Heath, R. Jowell, J. Curtice and G. Evans (1990), *The British Voter*, Pergamon Press.

This table indicates that those council tenants who take advantage of the right to buy already have a greater propensity to vote Conservative before they become home-owners, tending to back Heath et al's contention that social and political attitudes influence tenure choice rather than the other way round (at least in the case of exercising the right to buy). Becoming a home-owner did not lead to a greater tendency to vote Conservative; as Heath et al conclude:

There is no tendency at all for [council tenant] purchasers to become more Conservative-inclined between 1979 and 1987. The pattern of Conservative voting shows essentially the same trends over time among the purchasers as it does among the council tenants and the home-owners(62).

However, these results do show that Labour voting amongst those tenants who purchased their council property declined at a much faster rate than amongst those who did not exercise their right to buy. Almost all this vote went to the Alliance but, as a proportion of the total electorate, this shift only accounted, between 1979 and 1983 for example, for a reduction of 0.5 per cent in the Labour vote. The total Labour share of the vote fell by 6 per cent between these two General Elections, so council house sales do not, in fact, live up to their reputation of significantly eroding Labour's vote(63).

TABLE 2.7 *Characteristics of council house purchasers*

	Working class %	Incomes below £8,000 %	Not in paid work %
Local authority tenants	68	77	63
Council house purchasers	55	31	28
Other home-owners	27	30	38

Source: A. Heath, R. Jowell, J. Curtice and G. Evans (1990), *The British Voter*, Pergamon Press.

In this more recent research, Heath et al stress that tenants who exercise their right to buy have different socio-economic characteristics compared to tenants who do not. Thus they cite the evidence in Table 2.7 as explanation for why tenants were already more likely to vote Conservative before they bought – because they were more likely to have non-working-class jobs and higher incomes.

We thus come back to the importance of socio-economic position and material interests as explanatory factors. Home-owners certainly have distinct material interests and are more likely to express individualistic values rather than collectivist ones (Heath et al explore this by measuring, for example, attitudes to nationalisation, income redistribution, etc.). However, home-ownership itself does not determine these values or, therefore, account for the relationship between voting patterns and tenure.

This evidence further questions the validity of the position that ownership of domestic property creates a status group which cuts across and undermines class divisions.

The argument that tenure is the crucial determinant of political consciousness is also undermined by recent research on the importance of spatial variations in the experience of tenure. One such piece of research is Johnston's analysis of local variations in the relationship between class, tenure and voting behaviour in the 1983 General Election. Having established, as Heath does, that there were significant correlations between housing tenure and voting behaviour, holding class constant, Johnston tested the hypothesis that:

> There were spatial variations in [this correlation], such that in the relatively prosperous parts of Britain with high rates of inflation of property prices in the years prior to the 1983 election, owner-occupiers would be more likely to vote Conservative and council tenants less likely to vote Labour(64).

Johnston has two reasons for putting forward this hypothesis. Firstly:

> The greater the rate of [local house price] inflation, the greater would be the desire of owner-occupiers to protect their investments, which implies a greater likelihood to vote Conservative(65).

Secondly, in the more prosperous parts of the country, council tenants are more likely to vote Conservative, partly because such areas have fewer large council estates thus weakening collective consciousness and partly because the local Conservative administrations in these areas will be associated with making it easy for tenants to exercise their right to buy and gain from house price inflation.

Johnston's analysis of local variations in voting, using both regional and constituency-type measurements, indicate that the salariat, petty bourgeoisie and routine non-manual owner-occupiers exhibited some spatial variations in their propensity to vote Conservative, in· that the Conservative Party did better than average amongst these voters in the more prosperous areas with high house prices and the Labour Party did better in the depressed industrial areas with low property values.

Working-class owner-occupiers showed a much greater variation in their voting patterns:

> The propensity to vote Labour was significantly greater in the older industrial areas than in the 'booming' areas of small towns and agricultural South-eastern England, by a ratio of as much as 4:1.

Johnston concludes that the material advantages associated with owner-occupation in high-house-price areas, together with the diluted community consciousness in prosperous areas, are strong enough to diminish the class solidarity with the Labour Party. On the other hand:

> Where exchange values are low . . . Labour obtains significantly above-average support from this group, suggesting that the domestic property cleavage is much less important than the traditional occupational class cleavage where: a) the working class is dominant; b) the socialisation of most of the working class was probably strongly pro-Labour; c) owner-occupancy is relatively recent; and d) the potential financial benefits from owner-occupancy, and thus their desire to protect these by voting Conservative, are relatively low(66).

Johnston concludes that 'local context was apparently an important influence on how people interpreted being working-class, in both major housing tenures'(67). This confirms the significance of the heterogeneous nature of owner-occupation and the importance of its socio-economic setting.

Conclusion

As we have already mentioned, the current housing studies literature focuses on tenure, both as an expression of housing advantage and disadvantage and as a key determinant of life chances. We have, however, argued that class inequalities, rather than the tenure of a household's dwelling, are much more important in determining the experience of housing advantage and disadvantage. Empirical research also undermines the idea that tenure affects class consciousness.

Housing studies has suffered from an over-emphasis on housing policy whereas, as Forrest and Murie identify, there is a need to approach changes in the housing system 'from a more general concern with transformations in the labour market'(68). The importance of this prespective is confirmed by our discussion of the impact of labour market restructuring on areas such as Shipcote and Saltley. Forrest and Murie's own study of affluent home-owners illustrates very clearly the way in which 'position within the labour market and specific labour processes [shapes] housing histories in distinctive ways'(69).

In the future, it may be possible for housing studies to throw off the straitjacket of tenure and for progress to be made – in both research and theoretical terms – in developing a study of housing inequality which places housing, as a life chance, within the wider social structure. If this is so, then class divisions, we would argue, will be seen to be a key factor in the experience of housing inequality.

Notes

1. P. Saunders (1984), 'Beyond housing classes: the sociological significance of private property rights in means of consumption', in *International Journal of Urban and Regional Research*, 8 (2).
2. Department of the Environment (December 1988), *Housing and Construction Statistics*, HMSO.
3. M. J. Daunton (1977), *Coal Metropolis: Cardiff 1870–1914*, Leicester University Press.
4. P. Kemp (1987): 'Aspects of housing consumption in late nineteenth century England and Wales', *Housing Studies*, Vol.2, No.1, January, p.13.
5. S. Merrett (1979), *State Housing in Britain*, Routledge and Kegan Paul.
6. S. Merrett (1982), *Owner-Occupation in Britain*, Routledge and Kegan Paul, p.15.
7. C. Hamnett (1984), 'Housing the two nations: socio-tenurial polarisation in England and Wales 1961-1981', *Urban Studies*, 43.
8. *Ibid*, p.396.
9. *Ibid*, pp.394–5.
10. *General Household Survey, 1986* (1988), Table 6.10.
11. P. Willmott and A. Murie (1988), *Polarisation and Social Housing*, Policy Studies Institute, pp.32–3.
12. P. Malpass and A. Murie (1982), *Housing Policy and Practice*, Macmillan, p.174.
13. P. Willmott and A. Murie (1988), p.49.
14. *Ibid*, p.47.
15. M. Kleinmann and C. Whitehead (1988), 'British housing since 1979' *Housing Studies*, Vol.3, No.1, January, p.12.
16. P. Malpass and A. Murie (1982).
17. R. Forrest and A. Murie (1983), 'Residualisation and council housing', *Journal of Social Policy*, 4.
18. P. Balchin (1989), *Housing Policy: an introduction*, Routledge.
19. R. Forrest and A. Murie (1983).
20. F. Twine and N. J. Williams (1983), 'Social segregation in public sector housing', *Transactions of the Institute of British Geographers*, NS. 8.
21. S. Damer and R. Madigan (1974), 'The housing investigator', *New Society*, 25th July.
22. P. Willmott and A. Murie (1988), p.42.
23. *Ibid*, pp.41–2.
24. P. Saunders (1978), 'Domestic property and social class', *International Journal of Urban and Regional Research*, 2.
25. National Child Development Study (1988), 'A longitudinal study of housing and social circumstances in childhood and early adulthood', p.25.

26. P. Saunders and P. Williams (1988), 'The constitution of the home: towards a research agenda', *Housing Studies*, Vol.3, No 2.
27. *English House Condition Survey, 1986* (1989), HMSO, p.44.
28. *Family Expenditure Survey, 1987* (1989), HMSO.
29. See V. Karn, J. Kemeny and P. Williams (1985), *Home Ownership in the Inner City*, Gower.
30. *Ibid.*
31. See, for example, A. B. Atkinson and A. H. Harrison (1978), *The Distribution of Personal Wealth in Britain*, Cambridge University Press.
32. *Social Trends, 19* (1989), HMSO, Table 5.22.
33. Nationwide Building Society (1986) *Housing as an Investment*.
34. C. Hamnett (1988), *Housing Inheritance and Wealth in Britain* (unpublished paper).
35. *Ibid.*
36. R. Forrest and A. Murie (1980), 'Wealth, inheritance and housing policy', *Policy and Politics*, Vol.8, No.1, p.17.
37. D. C. Thorns (1982), 'Industrial restructuring and change in the labour and property markets in Britain', *Environment and Planning* A, Vol.14.
38. *Ibid*, p.758.
39. P. N. Balchin (1979), *Housing Improvement and Social Inequality*, Gower.
40. *Ibid*, p.227.
41. *Ibid*, p.227.
42. C. Hamnett (1973), 'Improvement grants as an indicator of gentrification in inner London', *Area* Vol.4; S. Merrett (1976), 'Gentrification' in M. Edwards, S. Gray, S. Merrett and J. Swann (eds) *Housing and Class in Britain*, Conference of Socialist Economists; C. Hamnett and P. Williams (1979), *Gentrification in London, 1961–1971*, Birmingham Centre for Urban and Regional Studies.
43. J. Gosling (1987), 'The end of the East End', *Roof*, Nov/Dec.
44. R. Forrest and A. Murie (1989), 'Differential accumulation: wealth, inheritance and housing policy reconsidered', *Policy and Politics*, Vol.17 No. 1, pp.37–8.
45. *Ibid*, p.37.
46. Birmingham Community Development Project (1977), *Workers on the Scrapheap*.
47. Karn et al (1985), p.22.
48. *Ibid*, p.108.
49. J. Henderson and V. Karn (1987), *Race, Class and State Housing*, Gower. See also our Chapter 3.
50. D. Byrne (1986), 'Housing and class in the inner city', in P. Malpass(ed), *The Housing Crisis*, Croom Helm.
51. *Ibid*, p.155.
52. *Ibid*.

53. *Ibid*, p. 166.
54. P. Saunders and P. Williams (1988).
55. A. Heath, R. Jowell and J. Curtice (1985), *How Britain Votes*, Pergamon Press.
56. *Ibid*, p.34.
57. *Ibid*, p.14.
58. *Ibid*, p.37.
59. *Ibid*.
60. D. Butler and D. Kavanagh (1984), *The British General Election of 1983*, Oxford University Press.
61. Heath et al (1985), p.49.
62. A. Heath, R. Jowell, J. Curtice and G. Evans (1989), *The Extension of Popular Capitalism*, Strathclyde Papers on Government and Politics, No. 60, Department of Politics, University of Strathclyde. See also A. Heath, R. Jowell, J. Curtice and G. Evans (1990), *The British Voter*, Pergamon Press.
63. A. Heath et al (1989).
64. R. J. Johnston (1987), 'A note on housing tenure and voting in Britain, 1983', *Housing Studies*, Vol.2, No.2, April, pp.114–5.
65. *Ibid*, p.114.
66. *Ibid*, p.119.
67. *Ibid*, p.121.
68. R. Forrest and A. Murie (1987), 'The affluent home-owner: labour market position and the shaping of housing histories', in N. Thrift and P. Williams (eds), *Class and Space: the making of urban society*, Routledge and Kegan Paul.
69. *Ibid*, p.358.

3 | Housing and race

Although research evidence dating back to the 1960s has shown housing to be a key dimension to racial inequality in Britain, it was only during the 1980s that it became a central issue in debates about housing management. Professional organisations concerned with housing, such as the National Federation of Housing Associations, the Institute of Housing and, most recently, the Association of Metropolitan Authorities have attempted to set out guidelines and codes of professional practice on race and housing(1). These publications all refer to the Commission for Racial Equality (CRE) investigation of Hackney Council(2) as being the stimulus for their initiatives but this was not the only research on race and housing carried out during the 1980s. There is now a substantial body of research evidence documenting both the nature of racial inequality in housing and the role of housing organisations in the production and reinforcement of such inequality. In this chapter we will begin by outlining the major patterns of racial inequality in housing and then proceed to an examination of the explanations that have been offered.

Racial inequalities in housing

Tenure
Colin Brown's survey of 7,306 adults throughout England and Wales clearly shows the variations in tenure patterns for different ethnic groups(3). It can be seen from Table 3.1 that Asian households are more likely to be owner-occupiers and

that Afro-Caribbeans are significantly more likely to be council tenants and housing association tenants. The table also shows that there are significant variations between different groups of Asian households. Muslim households generally have a lower rate of owner-occupation than Hindu or Sikh households and the pattern of Bangladeshi households is the reverse of that for the other Asian groups, with the lowest proportion of owner-occupiers and the highest proportion of council tenants.

TABLE 3.1 *Tenure patterns by ethnic origin of household*

	White %	West Indian %	Asian %	Indian %	Paki-stani %
Owner-occupied	59	41	72	77	80
Rented from council	30	46	19	16	13
Privately rented	9	6	6	5	5
Housing association	2	8	2	2	1

	Bangla-deshi %	African Asian %	Muslim %	Hindu %	Sikh %
Owner-occupied	30	73	67	73	91
Rented from council	53	19	24	16	6
Privately rented	11	5	6	8	3
Housing association	4	2	2	3	–

Source: C. Brown (1984), *Black and White Britain*, p. 96. Policy Studies Institute.

We have already seen that it is too simplistic to equate owner-occupation with good housing conditions. The evidence that follows suggests that in the specific case of Asian householders, owner-occupation has not improved the quality of housing and that racial inequality in housing cuts across tenures.

Area of residence

A number of studies have shown that black households tend to be disproportionately concentrated into inner city areas or areas of low demand. For example, Brown found that whereas only 6 per cent of the white households in his survey lived in inner London, inner Birmingham or inner Manchester, 43 per cent of West Indian households and 23 per cent of Asian households lived in these areas. Similarly, Jeff Henderson and Valerie Karn's study of Birmingham found that 48 per cent of white households, compared to 64 per cent of West Indian and 92 per cent of Asian households lived in what they describe as 'Industrial, Commercial and Poor Residential Areas'(4). Similar results have been found for Liverpool, Nottingham, Walsall, Leicester and Greater London(5). Within these areas there are likely to be further variations in settlement patterns with particular ethnic groups concentrated in certain areas of Britain or in certain wards within urban areas(6). There is a strong implication that black people are segregated in the less desirable residential areas. However, it has been suggested that this reflects dominant white values about preferences and that black and, particularly, Asian preferences may be different leading to a positive choice to live in inner city areas. This position will be examined later when we discuss explanations of racial inequality in housing. First we will examine the various 'objective' dimensions of the quality of housing occupied by black, Asian and white households.

Property type

Brown's survey has shown that there are major differences in the types of property occupied by black, Asian and white households. His results are summarised in Table 3.2 which illustrates that white households are far more likely to live in detached or semi-detached houses or bungalows, Asian households are more likely to live in terraced houses and that West Indian households are more likely to be flat-dwellers living in blocks of flats with more than four storeys. This table also points to some important variations within the Asian group, particularly the fact that African Asians are relatively more likely to be living in detached/semi-detached houses and that Bangladeshi households are far more likely to be living in flats. These broad patterns have also been found in studies of race and housing in specific areas(7).

Age of property

The research evidence clearly shows that black and Asian people are likely to be living in older properties than white people. Henderson and Karn say about council housing in Birmingham that:

> The most striking feature about the age of property allocated between 1971 and 1978 is the extremely old property accepted by Asians. Half of them received pre-1919 property, compared with only 8 per cent of white tenants(8).

Ward found a similar pattern in Bradford where 76.7 per cent of Indian and 87.9 per cent of Pakistani/Bangladeshi households lived in pre-1919 terraced houses compared to 28.7 per cent of white households(9). This pattern is confirmed by Brown's national survey. He found that 50 per cent of white households were living in post-1945 property compared to 40 per cent of West Indian and 26 per cent of Asian households. Pakistani households were particularly likely to be living in older property with only 14 per cent living in post-1945 property(10).

Within the public rented sector, research evidence indicates that black and Asian applicants are far less likely to be allocated new properties. For example, the CRE investigation of Hackney found that 'Whereas 25 per cent of white applicants were given new property, only 3 per cent of black applicants received such accommodation'(11).

The limited research that has been conducted on housing associations suggests that an applicant's area of preference can have a strong influence on the type of property allocated. Pat Niner's research on the Family Housing

TABLE 3.2 *Dwelling type by ethnic group*

	White %	West Indian %	Asian %	Indian %	Paki- stani %	Bangla- deshi %	African Asian %
Detached house/ bungalow	18	4	7	8	3	1	10
Semi-detached house/bungalow	36	19	19	21	10	8	27
Terraced house	31	44	59	58	79	40	48
Flat in building up to 4 floors	9	16	8	7	3	31	6
Flat in building over 4 floors	2	11	4	2	2	12	5
Other	4	5	4	3	3	8	4

Source: C. Brown (1984), *Black and White Britain*, Table 36, p 103. Policy Studies Institute.

Association in Birmingham found that black and Asian households were actually more likely to receive new properties. The explanation for this was that most of the new properties were in Handsworth – an area of high demand for such households – and that large numbers of black and Asian people were nominated by the local authority when taking up their nomination rights on new-build properties. However, she found that such households were far less likely to receive newly improved properties(12).

The age of property is a fairly crude indicator of housing quality because there is not a simple relationship between age and desirability. Some studies have therefore looked at the allocation of properties in terms of the way that they are categorised by local authority housing workers and have found that black and Asian households are also less likely to be allocated the 'best' properties. For example, the CRE study of Liverpool, using a crude distinction between 'black' and 'white', found that white households were more likely to be allocated 'excellent' properties(13). Similarly, the Hackney study found that black households were far more likely to be housed on the less desirable inter-war estates(14).

Overcrowding

In their study of race and housing in Birmingham, Henderson and Karn found that:

> In spite of the relatively low levels of multi-occupancy and the movement of West Indians into council housing, blacks generally still live in much more crowded conditions. In 1977, 21 per cent of whites in Birmingham lived at more than 0.75 persons per room compared with 51 per cent of West Indians and 68 per cent of Asians in this situation. The contrast between the three groups is brought out even more clearly when one examines the variation from the 'bedroom standard' . . . in private rented or owner-occupied housing. Again, in 1977, only 5 per cent of white households in Birmingham lived below the accepted bedroom standard, compared with 23 per cent of West Indians and 42 per cent of Asians(15).

This evidence is supported on a national level by Brown's survey which found that: white households had a mean number of 5 rooms for their own exclusive use compared with 4.3 for West Indian, and 4.6 for Asian households; the mean number of persons per room was 0.5 for white households compared to 0.8 for West Indian and 1.0 for Asian households; and only 3 per cent of white households have more than one person per room compared with 16 per cent of West Indian and 35 per cent of Asian households(16). Brown adds that:

> Among the Asians, the Bangladeshis stand out as having very small accommodation in relation to their needs, and as sharing their dwellings most frequently. Sixty per cent of Bangladeshi families have more than one person per room; this is 20 times more than for white households(17).

Amenities

Earlier studies of race and housing revealed that there were substantial inequalities in terms of access to basic amenities(18). More recent evidence suggests that the extent of racial inequality on this dimension of housing conditions has reduced with the general improvement of standards and that broadly the same proportions of black and white households now lack basic amenities. Thus, in comparing his findings with those of the earlier Political and Economic Planning survey Brown shows that, whereas in 1974 18 per cent of white households compared to 37 per cent of black and Asian households lacked exclusive use of a bath, hot water or inside toilet, in 1982 these figures had reduced to 5 per cent and 7 per cent respectively(19). It should be noted though that this hides the particularly disadvantaged position of Bangladeshi households, 18 per cent of whom lacked exclusive use of bath, hot water or inside toilet compared to 5 per cent of white and West Indian households(20).

However, it may be that simply looking at current levels of 'need' for basic amenities is insufficient because it ignores the process through which racial inequalities have been eliminated. Johnson refers to his data for Coventry, where only 3 per cent of each ethnic group lacked an inside toilet, to illustrate this point. He notes that 26 per cent of Asian households had installed one since moving in compared to 17 per cent of whites and Afro-Caribbeans:

> Thus one could state that on taking possession 29 per cent of Asians but only 20 per cent of the other two groups *had* lacked this facility. This gives a clearer picture of the differential access (and hence relative deprivation) that a minority group may have to good-quality housing(21).

Black households have also been shown to be disadvantaged in terms of other amenities. The broad patterns are revealed in Brown's survey, the results of which are summarised in Table 3.3. This shows that black households are more likely

TABLE 3.3 *Amenities by ethnic group*

	White %	West Indian %	Asian %	Indian %	Paki- stani %	Bangla- deshi %	African Asian %
Lack exclusive use of bath, hot water or inside WC	5	5	7	5	7	18	5
No garden	11	32	21	15	21	56	18
No central heating	43	38	44	37	66	56	27
No refrigerator	6	6	11	4	19	37	5
No washing machine	22	37	44	38	61	78	22
No telephone	24	24	24	18	34	44	14

Source: C. Brown (1985), *Black and White Britain*, Table 43, p 109, Policy Studies Institute.

to live in properties without a garden, a washing machine or a refrigerator. Once again, Brown's research is useful because it points to the importance of differences within the Asian group. In particular, it highlights the extent to which Bangladeshi households are disadvantaged in terms of a range of amenities.

Access to housing

For the households concerned, the most important dimension of access to housing is likely to be homelessness, and black people can be seen to be disadvantaged in this respect. There is a dearth of information about the precise extent of black homelessness largely because of the failure of both central and local government to keep adequate ethnic records. Some of the available information is summarised in a report by the Association of Metropolitan Authorities:

The over-representation of black people amongst the homeless has nevertheless been confirmed by authorities that do keep records in this area and is readily admitted by many who do not. For example, information recently obtained by the London Research Centre from 20 London boroughs (of which nine have ethnic records) suggests that black households are some three or four times as likely to become statutorily homeless as white households, and that the problem is probably just as acute for the black British-born population as it is for recent immigrants. Moreover, this experience is not confined to London or to those who are actually accepted as homeless under the legislation: an analysis of metropolitan districts and 60 non-metropolitan authorities demonstrated the predominance of households of New Commonwealth or Pakistani origin, whilst advice and referral agencies for the single homeless also report a high concentration of young black people amongst their clients. The situation is given a further twist by the fact that black people tend to be concentrated in areas of housing stress where local authorities are least able to cope with the consequences of homelessness, and are frequently forced to resort to the most unsatisfactory forms of temporary accommodation(22).

Some of the studies of race and housing provide further evidence. Thus, for example, the CRE found that: 'Relative to their proportion in Hackney's population overall, black households were highly represented in our homeless sample'(23). Similarly, Brown's survey found that: 'Many more Asian and West Indian tenants than white tenants were housed because they were homeless'(24) and the CRE's more recent study (in 1988) of homelessness in Tower Hamlets, found that Bangladeshi households in particular experienced a high risk of having to present themselves as homeless(25).

Earlier research on race and housing suggested that the exclusion of black people from public rented housing was an important dimension of access to housing(26). More recent research suggests that this is now less important than the quality of the accommodation that is allocated; both the CRE investigations into Hackney and Tower Hamlets found that black and Asian households were offered poorer-quality accommodation. However, the length of time spent waiting for a council house is still an issue. The evidence on this is not consistent. In Hackney, the CRE found that black applicants did not wait longer than white applicants for rehousing(27). Henderson and Karn, on the other hand, found that in Birmingham 'West Indian and Asian applicants on the waiting list had to accumulate more points before they received an offer of accommodation or accepted one'(28).

Housing mobility

Various studies have shown that racial inequalities also exist with respect to the ability to move within tenures. In the public sector this can be seen in the difficulties black households experience in obtaining transfers. For example, Henderson and Karn found that 'white tenants were considerably more likely than West Indians or Asians to have moved since their original council allocation: 26 per cent had moved compared with only 16 per cent of West Indians and Asians'(29). This was true even though West Indian tenants were just as likely to be seeking to move through a transfer or exchange. Asian tenants were, however, less likely to be seeking a move and 49 per cent of Asians had not even heard of transfers(30).

Black and Asian households are also more likely to experience mobility difficulties within the owner-occupied housing market because of their disproportionate settlement in inner city areas. The consequences of this have been highlighted by Valerie Karn, Jim Kemeny and Peter Williams in their research on home-ownership in inner city areas. They challenge the assumption that cheap inner city property provides the first rung on a home-ownership ladder, reaching out to the suburbs, and argue that Asian owners in particular experience a lack of mobility.

The performance of the market in these areas in terms of price movement is much less 'impressive' than elsewhere. This leads us to suggest that, far from providing a ladder up the housing market, buying a house in these areas could ultimately constitute a major trap . . . The combination of poor houses and poor people, who are unable to maintain their homes even in their current condition, suggests that a downward spiral must now be in operation . . . The downward spiral of house condition and house price is noticeable across the spectrum of property whether owned by black or white occupants. However, it is apparent that price in particular is falling fastest in Asian areas. Given the financial mechanisms adopted by many Asians and particularly their dependence on loans from the limited resources of the local community itself, the question of disinvestment and the inner city as a trap looms even larger, with enormous implications for race relations in Britain(31).

Explanations of racial inequality in housing

Choice
It has been suggested by some researchers that the settlement patterns of Asian households in Britain are a product of cultural factors which are more important than economic structure in accounting for racial segregation(32). The cultural factors are usually presented in terms of a desire to live in areas in which there are strong community ties, where people will be close to shops, places of worship and other facilities which cater specifically for the requirements of Asian groups and where they will be able to maintain their traditions and customary lifestyles. However, if we accept that Asian people prefer to live in close-knit communities, this does not explain why they have 'chosen' to live in overcrowded conditions, in houses that are generally in a poor state of repair, in the declining areas of Britain's inner cities with all of the accompanying disadvantages.

A more sophisticated explanation has been suggested by Dahya in his study of Asian settlement in Bradford(33). He argues that the continued identification of Pakistanis with their homeland led to a withdrawal from British culture which facilitated their segregation into an 'ethnic village'. More importantly, he also argues that there was a strong desire to eventually return to Pakistan and, in the meantime, to send money to relatives at home. This, he says, led to a strong concern to minimise expenditure during their 'temporary' stay in this country to enable an earlier return migration. For this reason, council housing, which consumed a large proportion of income with no resale value, was shunned in favour of cheap owner-occupied housing which had the advantage of providing a saleable asset. Vaughan Robinson's study of Blackburn provides an interesting extension of this argument. He points to the growing trend for Asians to become council tenants and explains this partly in terms of the arrival of East African Asians who do not share the desire to return either to East Africa or the Indian sub-continent. He also points to changes in the availability of council housing whereby recent new development has provided council accommodation in areas of established Asian settlement(34).

The available research on race and housing shows that Asians do express strong preferences for particular areas but it also suggests a need to look beyond expressed preferences. Rex and Moore's account of the initial Asian settlement in Birmingham has shown that they were excluded from local authority housing and from many areas of owner-occupied housing and that there was, therefore, little choice other than to settle in lodging houses in the 'twilight zones'(35). Charlie Forman's analysis of the settlement of the Bangladeshi community in Spitalfields illustrates the way in which it became the 'preferred' area for what was just the latest in a long line of migrant communities. As he writes:

> Migrants haven't chosen Spitalfields, but were forced into its bad housing and its sweated labour in the clothing trade. There was nowhere else to go. And because there was nowhere else, they have defended it, cherished it, changed it as best they could to make it meet the needs of their different cultures and civilisations(36).

Some of the more recent studies of public sector housing have shown that the stereotyped views of housing workers concerning what black applicants deserve or 'prefer' have been as important as the actual preferences of applicants in determining settlement patterns(37). Henderson and Karn have pointed to the importance of differences within ethnic groups whereby certain areas which are sought after by some members of a particular ethnic group are also considered undesirable by other members of the same group(38).

Furthermore, the explanations in terms of 'choice' have failed to consider adequately the basis on which Asian households may have chosen to live in close-knit communities. It is simply asserted that Asian people wish to save money and that they are concerned about the threat to their cultural institutions if they were to mix socially and geographically with other sections of the population. This may be important but it also ignores the more physical threat to both property and life in the form of racial harassment that faces Asians who live outside of the established areas of settlement. Philip Sarre argues that choice and constraint in relation to racial segregation are not separable(39). The choices of ethnic minority households can only be understood in the context of a system of structural constraints which limit the range of choices open to them. At the same time, these constraints are not absolute and they do provide scope for ethnic minority households to exercise some choice over the areas in which they settle. Moreover, there is a complex interplay between the various factors in operation here. For example, the choice to live in segregated communities may be reinforced by the experience of racial discrimination, racial harassment etc. which could in turn strengthen the commitment of individuals to the traditions of the particular ethnic group thus leading to more and stronger 'choices' to live segregated lives. Similarly, the same sorts of experiences may lead to lessened expectations whereby black people stop asking for accommodation on estates and areas where they believe that public sector housing organisations will not allocate them property(40).

If housing choices for black and Asian households are made within a series of constraints, it is necessary to establish the nature of these constraints. In doing this, we will examine both wider social and economic factors and the role of organisations within the different housing tenures.

background historical

Circumstances of entry into Britain

There have been black and Asian people living in Britain since the third century AD but the most significant increase in the size of Britain's black population came shortly after the Second World War. At this time people were being 'pushed' from the Caribbean (and later the Indian sub-continent and East Africa) by the problems of over-population, under- or unemployment and in some cases, hostile political regimes. They were being 'pulled' to Britain by the ties of the Commonwealth and the fact that the shortage of manual labour, particularly for the unskilled and undesirable jobs, led the government and some employers to actively encourage them to settle here. This pattern of migration has had a number of effects.

The fact that black and Asian settlers were encouraged to come to Britain specifically to do the work that the indigenous white population was not prepared to do has had a lingering effect on employment patterns. In particular, it partially explains the fact that black people are dispropor-tionately represented in the lower-status occupational categories with lower incomes. The types of industry in which black people were initially employed have been more seriously affected by Britain's economic decline and this might also provide a partial explanation of the higher rates of unemployment amongst black people. In these ways the circumstances of entry into Britain in the post-war period have contributed to the broad pattern of economic dis-advantage which pervades the position of black people in the housing market. It has also been a contributory factor in determining settlement patterns in that the initial settlers tended to be located in those parts of the country in which the demand for their labour was highest. Within particular localities of high labour demand, the settlement process may also have provided accidental factors which have influenced settlement patterns. For example, as Kettle and Hodges write, the settlers on the ship, the *Empire Windrush*, were put up in an empty air raid shelter in Clapham:

They were found jobs by the nearest labour exchange, which happened to be in Brixton, and thus put down roots in a part of London which was beginning to decay(41).

However, although the effect of the circumstances of entry into Britain is important, it should not be overestimated. Even as an explanation of the employment patterns of the initial settlers it is limited because it fails to take account of the fact that they were relatively highly skilled(42).

Current position in the labour market
The pattern of immigration into Britain was significantly changed by the Immigration Acts passed in 1962, 1968 and 1971. These Acts restricted the size of Britain's black population in absolute terms but, more importantly, the restrictions have produced a situation in which an increasing proportion of Britain's black population is constituted either of people who have been born in Britain or who are long-term residents. As Colin Brown pointed out, by the beginning of the 1980s, the black population was over 40 per cent British-born and over half of those who were immigrants had lived here for more than fifteen years(43). The life chances of British-born black people should not be affected by the factors associated with the pattern of post-war settlement, at least not directly. However, research evidence shows that when comparisons are made between cohorts of black and white workers of the same age, experience and qualifications, the white cohort will, on average, obtain higher-status and higher-paid jobs than the black cohort(44). Since the only variables that are not controlled for are skin colour, accent and surname, this research suggests that the differences must be explained in terms of racial discrimination in the labour market. This may take the form of either direct or indirect racial discrimination. Direct discrimination refers to actions which treat people in a negatively different way *because* of the colour of their skin or their membership of a particular ethnic group. Indirect racial discrimination refers to actions which treat

particular ethnic groups in a negatively different way as the result of the application of a rule which, in principle, applies to everybody equally but which, in practice, has a disproportionate effect on particular groups. It is difficult to establish the precise extent of racial discrimination in employment but there is ample evidence to suggest that both direct and indirect discrimination continue to be of importance in modern British society. For example, the CRE has used actors of different ethnic origins to carry out spot checks on individual employers which have demonstrated the fact that they have directly discriminated against black applicants. They have also provided important evidence of indirect discrimination in employment through, for example, the practice of recruitment through 'word of mouth' or evaluating job applicants on the basis of written applications for posts that did not require an ability in written English(45).

The inequalities in employment experienced by British-born black people are further reinforced by differences in the level of educational achievement. The 1981 Rampton Report and the 1985 Swann Report both showed that Afro-Caribbean children were significantly less likely to leave school with GCE or equivalent qualifications than either white or Asian children who achieve at roughly equivalent levels. The reports also pointed to a major difference within the Asian group in that Bangladeshi children were seriously underachieving. The reasons for these poor levels of educational achievement are complex but they include direct racial discrimination, indirect racial discrimination through the stereotyping of black pupils, the inherent racism of the school curriculum (particularly in subjects such as history and geography where notions of white supremacy abound, but also in subjects such as domestic science which have largely ignored cultural variations) and the effects of poor housing conditions(46).

The wider factors of employment and educational opportunities will have obvious effects on housing opportunities. Chapter 2 has illustrated how economic position influences

93

the experience of housing disadvantage within both the owner-occupied and the council sector. The current position of black and Asian groups within the labour market – whatever the causes of this position – is clearly an important constraint on housing opportunities. However there are, as we shall see, other factors which are also influential.

Household structure

There are significant differences in household composition amongst the different ethnic groups in Britain and this is illustrated by Table 3.4.

TABLE 3.4 *Numbers of adults and children resident in household, by ethnic group*

	White	West Indian	Asian
Average no. of adults in household	2.0	2.3	2.7
Proportion with only one adult	25.0%	26.0%	7.0%
Proportion with more than three adults	6.0%	17.0%	22.0%
Average no. of children in household	0.5	1.0	1.9
Proportion without children	69.0%	43.0%	31.0%
Proportion with more than two children	5.0%	12.0%	31.0%

Source: C. Brown, (1985), *Black and White Britain*, p.45, Policy Studies Institute.

Asian households are likely to be larger than white households. They are almost four times more likely to contain more than three adults and more than six times as likely to contain more than two children. Brown found that the average size of Asian households was 4.6 people compared to 3.4 for West Indian households and 2.6 for white households(47). Thus, even if Asian workers earned as much as white workers, we would expect that in the private sector, at least, they would be less likely to be able to meet their housing needs. This difference in household structure therefore provides a partial explanation for the higher incidence of overcrowding amongst Asian households in the owner-occupied sector.

Within the public sector, differences in household structure are likely to have a different effect. For example, Deborah Phillips found that in Tower Hamlets, the younger family structure of Asian households led to them receiving a higher proportion of offers below the fifth floor(48). Also, the ability of local authorities and housing associations to meet the needs of Asian households is likely to be affected by the nature of the stock available for letting which may partially explain why black households have to wait longer or accumulate more points before being rehoused. If the larger properties are located in a particular area, this could be a factor in the geographical segregation of Asians in Britain.

However, the research suggests that these differences only constitute a partial explanation. For example, Henderson and Karn have shown that, even when differences in household structure are taken into account, black and Asian households seeking access to council housing still had to accumulate more points before being made an offer and they were allocated poorer-quality housing than white applicants(49). Household structure may be a contributory factor in constraining the housing opportunities of Asian households but the research evidence tends to show that the role of housing organisations – in both public and private sectors – is a more important factor.

The role of housing organisations

The implication of Henderson and Karn's findings (and those of other studies) is that a full explanation of racial inequality in housing must incorporate an analysis of

95

the ways in which processes within housing organisations reinforce housing disadvantage for black people. In doing this we will concentrate on the two major tenures – owner-occupation and council housing. We will also include a discussion of housing associations because, although they are still relatively small in terms of their total stock, government policy clearly intends that they should have an increasingly important role to play in the provision of housing.

Owner-occupation

The major cause of the concentration of black households at the lower end of the owner-occupied market is that they have fewer resources. However, the research evidence suggests that this is reinforced by institutions within the housing market, particularly building societies and estate agents. Earlier studies of race and housing found evidence of widespread direct racial discrimination by estate agents and individual home owners in the form of a straightforward refusal to sell property to black people in certain areas(50). Subsequent research suggests that this has been largely eliminated by the Race Relations Acts(51). However, this legislation has not been as successful in eliminating indirect racial discrimination in the access to owner-occupied housing.

For most people wishing to buy a property, obtaining a mortgage is an essential precondition but this facility is not granted automatically by building societies. They operate their own informal rules in the allocation of mortgages which sometimes result in indirect racial discrimination. Of particular importance here is the policy of 'red lining' areas of towns and cities where the society will not, in normal circumstances, grant mortgages. Building society representatives have denied that this occurs but, although it has not been possible to determine the precise extent of these practices, there is considerable research evidence to suggest that it is difficult to obtain a mortgage in certain areas(52) or for certain types of property(53). The areas that are delineated in this way are precisely the poorer, deprived and inner city areas in which black people tend to settle. Karn, Kemeny and Williams have shown that such policies have a number of effects for home-ownership in the inner city and that this results in additional costs, particularly for Asian owner-occupiers. Some households are excluded from owner-occupation altogether, those who chose to borrow from other institutions are faced with higher interest rates and hence higher repayments, and others who rely upon informal lending from relatives are not eligible for mortgage tax relief which effectively increased their housing costs. The lack of conventional building society mortgages has contributed to the stagnation of housing prices. This has increased the price polarisation between areas making it more difficult for Asian home-owners to trade up because of the smaller capital gains(54). Some buyers who have taken out large percentage loans and fallen into arrears can easily find themselves owing more than the market value of the house(55). The situation is compounded by the severe state of disrepair of inner city housing. In their survey area, Karn et al estimated that the mean cost of improvement to a 30-year life was more than the mean price paid for the houses by buyers(56).

The mechanisms that operate within the owner-occupied housing market indirectly discriminate against black households. Whilst estate agents and building societies are not responsible for the fact that black people are concentrated in the lower levels of the owner-occupied market, their internal organisational processes reinforce the housing inequalities experienced particularly by Asian households.

Council housing
In principle, council housing is allocated on the basis of housing need and, therefore, the fact that black people are disadvantaged in other spheres should not affect their access to local authority tenancies. Indeed, their greater housing need should actually place them at an advantage in this tenure. However, this is not the case and there is a growing

97

body of evidence based upon research into the policies and practices of specific local authority housing departments which shows that they discriminate against black households.

The evidence suggests that this discrimination is largely unintentional but there is some evidence to suggest that it sometimes takes more direct forms. For example, Henderson and Karn found that housing visitors in Birmingham commented negatively on the decorations of West Indian households and the cooking smells of Asian households and that they were occasionally racially abusive to applicants(57). They further found that the visitors processed black and white applicants differently. Asian applicants were frequently asked to produce their passports whereas white and West Indian applicants were not(58). All black applicants had their property checked by the visitor whereas the accounts of some of the more 'respectable' white applicants were taken on trust(59).

Further evidence of racial discrimination was revealed in the way that visitors asked questions about the rent levels that applicants could afford. The net result was that Asian applicants were recorded as wanting a low rent which had a subsequent affect on the quality of housing that they were allocated(60). Henderson and Karn's explanation of this stresses the importance of the visitors' preconceived assumptions about what Asian people would want rather than an outright refusal to consider Asian applicants for higher-rented properties. This is an example of the way in which racial stereotyping by housing workers can produce housing inequalities. An examination of the research evidence suggests that this is an important factor in the allocation of council housing and that it can take various forms.

Some of the evidence suggests that housing workers may operate with clearly unfavourable stereotypes of black people which influence their practice. For example, Phillips found evidence of 'suspicion and resentment' and 'overt racism' towards Bengalis amongst the staff in the Tower Hamlets housing department which resulted in differential treatment for Bengali applicants(61). There are other instances in which the stereotyped views are based upon what housing officers believe that somebody from a particular ethnic group would prefer. If, for example, a black applicant has no recorded area preference there may be a tendency to assume that he or she would prefer to live in an area in which it is known that other black people of the same ethnic origin are already settled. Although the officer concerned may be acting with good intentions, it may nevertheless result in racial discrimination if this does not reflect the true preferences of the applicant. The importance of this has been clearly demonstrated by Henderson and Karn who asked tenants which areas they had not wanted at the time of their allocation. They found that the estates that were listed were of two types: estates that were not wanted by a particular racial group because they were regarded as unfamiliar or remote; estates that were popular with a racial group but not with the particular individual. On comparing these findings with the listings of the most popular estates based upon recorded preferences, they found that a number of estates appeared in both the top ten most popular and most unpopular for particular racial groups. In the case of two estates that were listed as popular they found that there were significantly more people who did not wish to live there. 'For whites this applied to Chelmsley Wood (30 for and 136 against) and, for West Indians, Handsworth (12 for and 95 against)'(62).

It has been suggested that the need to employ racial stereotypes is generated by the institutional operation of local authority housing departments, particularly the pressure to fill vacant properties(63). To understand this it must first be appreciated that:

> Contrary to the public's view, the day-to-day process of allocations in any local authority does not involve finding properties to 'suit' people but rather finding people to 'suit' properties(64).

99

This results from the need to manage the housing stock efficiently by keeping the void rate as low as possible:

> However, these goals have undoubtedly resulted in a number of working assumptions and practices which are discriminatory and inconsistent with the council's policy of providing equal housing opportunities for all groups. For example, there has been great pressure on lettings staff to achieve a high acceptance rate for offers and, indeed, this has become an acknowledged part of their professionalism. An unofficial target of one in two acceptance rate for first offers is taken for granted. However, in order to achieve this target, staff have had to make assumptions about the sort of vacancy applicants (both black and white) are likely to refuse or accept. In order to maintain a high acceptance rate for poor as well as good property, it has been particularly important to identify the type of applicant who will accept poorer accommodation, or to create circumstances under which they have no alternative but to accept(65).

Black applicants are likely to suffer from these institutional pressures for a variety of reasons. On the one hand, they encourage the development of 'benign' stereotypes such as those mentioned above which lead to black applicants receiving a disproportionate number of offers in areas of existing black settlement. On the other hand, the relatively powerless position of black households and their greater housing need place them in a position in which they are more likely to be compelled to accept offers of poorer-quality accommodation, particularly in the case of homeless applicants (of whom we have already seen that a disproportionate number are black) where many local authorities adopt a policy of only making one offer(66).

Policies adopted by local authority housing departments have also been shown to result in indirect racial discrimination. Of particular importance are rules regulating entry to council housing and rules concerning the allocation of properties. During the early stages of post-war settlement in Britain, black and Asian households were largely excluded from council housing because of residence qualifications operated by most local authorities(67). These circumstances have since changed mainly because black people are more likely to satisfy local authority residence requirements. Nevertheless, they continue to have a disproportionate effect upon black households and the practice has recently been condemned by a report of the Local Authority Housing and Racial Equality Working Party, published by the AMA(68).

Asian households, in particular, have had restricted access to council housing where owner-occupiers have been excluded from the council waiting list. Rules of this kind are common in local authority housing departments, although recently some authorities such as Leicester and Wolverhampton have begun to accept owner-occupiers onto their active waiting lists(69). Such exclusions were initially introduced on the assumption that owner-occupiers were economically self-reliant and that councils should prioritise those households in greatest housing need(70). However, whilst in principle this applies equally to all social groups, Asian households are more likely to be owner-occupiers and are therefore more likely to be excluded. Moreover, as we have shown in Chapter 1, the assumption that owner-occupiers are in a position of less housing need is not true for households at the lower end of the owner-occupied housing market where Asian households are concentrated. The patterns which show that Asian households are more likely to be living in overcrowded conditions in the poorer areas of the inner cities are a reflection of the sort of owner-occupied housing in which Asian families live. Asian households can be seen to have been caught in a 'Catch 22' situation. Having been initially excluded from council housing through the effects of residence qualifications and forced into poor-standard owner-occupied housing, this is now being used as the reason for their subsequent exclusion from the local authority sector.

The allocations policies adopted by many local authorities are based upon ethnocentric assumptions about what constitutes a normal family structure. This is assumed to be a nuclear family consisting of a married couple and dependent children. This model is not even an accurate reflection of white household structures; only 28 per cent of all households conform to this description(71). It is particularly inaccurate for the Asian population, many of whose households consist of an extended family network comprised of a number of 'nuclear' families. Allocations policies based upon assumptions about the normality of the nuclear family do not allow for different household structures. Consequently, the tendency has been for them to be either excluded from council housing or compelled to restructure themselves to fit with the 'normal' pattern. In Birmingham, for example, brothers or cousins have been required to register their families separately. Henderson and Karn's findings illustrate some of the ways in which various aspects of local authority housing policies combine to compound the discrimination against Asian families. The attempt to house grandparents with their children faltered because they were likely to be living in a different house as owner-occupiers. Moreover, the entry rules were justified in terms of the lack of suitable accommodation which was itself the product of development strategies which indirectly discriminate against Asian families(72). We could add to this that the development policies are, in turn, affected by national government housing finance policies which have militated against the development of larger units of accommodation(73).

Afro-Caribbean family structures are also more likely to vary from the nuclear family model in that there are a larger proportion of cohabitees and female-headed single-parent families. In this case, indirect discrimination at the point of entry to the waiting list occurs if the authority has a policy which restricts the eligibility of these types of household. Henderson and Karn found that this was the case in Birmingham(74). Although they describe Birmingham as unusual in this respect, it is not unique. Gray's research has shown that the local authority housing department in Hull, for example, operated a policy of total exclusion of cohabitees(75).

In the case of homelessness, local authorities have a legal obligation to house certain categories of people. They also have discretion over how rigidly they implement the legislation and how they interpret the definitions of priority need(76). For example, single people and childless couples may be deemed to be 'vulnerable' in special circumstances but many local authorities adopt policies which exclude young single people. Again, in principle, this applies equally to all social groups but in practice it is likely to disproportionately affect young Afro-Caribbeans who are more likely to leave home as a result of family disputes.

The route through which households gain access to council housing has been shown to affect their prospects of obtaining good-quality accommodation, with homeless cases usually being offered the least desirable property. The research also shows that white households predominate in the more favoured routes of entry whilst black households are disproportionately represented amongst homeless cases and other less favoured routes(77). The Local Authority Housing and Racial Equality Working Party Report recommends that all housing cases should be offered property throughout the quality spectrum. Thus 'if homeless applicants constitute 30 per cent of all those rehoused during the year, they should where possible receive 30 per cent of the best properties and no more than 30 per cent of the worst'(78). However, the remedy cannot be as simple as this recommendation implies. The fact that some rehousing categories are allocated better-quality housing than others is a reflection of the institutional processes that we have already discussed. The pressures to be 'efficient' compel local authorities to try to let their less desirable property quickly and the relative powerlessness of the homeless and other groups in desperate housing need compel them to accept.

Allocation policies are an important constraint on access to council housing and may lead to both direct and indirect discrimination. For example, if local authorities adopt a policy (either formally or informally) of allocating smaller properties to single-parent families, indirect racial discrimination is likely to occur. In Birmingham, Henderson and Karn found that there was an unofficial policy against allocating houses to single-parent families and that, because there are more West Indian households in this category, there was indirect discrimination. This was further compounded by more direct forms of racial discrimination whereby the rule was more likely to be applied to black single-parent famiilies than to white single-parent families(79).

Henderson and Karn have also shown that indirect discrimination operating through allocation policies was a contributory factor in creating the situation whereby Asian households in Birmingham were concentrated into older, pre-1919 properties. There were several factors involved. Firstly, there was discrimination against large households. Secondly, there was discrimination against families displaced by slum clearance – a particularly important route into council housing for Asians. Thirdly, the pre-1919 property acquired by the council contained a greater proportion of larger property than the purpose-built stock. Henderson and Karn suggest that all of these factors played a part but they stress that any effects that they might have had were compounded by more direct forms of racial discrimination. The result was that, regardless of their reason for rehousing or size of household, Asian households received poorer-quality housing(80).

The explanation preferred by Birmingham City Council representatives was that pre-1919 property was the only type of property available in the inner ring of the city which was where Asians wanted to live. However, as we have already seen, the assumptions made about the area preferences of ethnic minority groups and even the expressed preferences in the local authority records are unreliable indicators of where Asian households prefer to live. It may well have been the case that there was a self-fulfilling prophecy in operation whereby housing officials assumed that Asian households preferred certain areas and allocated them properties in these areas regardless of the fact that they were older properties. Even if this were not the case, and supposing that Asian settlement patterns reflected their true area preference, it is still possible to identify an element of indirect racial discrimination in that the correlation between older properties and areas of Asian settlement must be at least partially a reflection of the local authority's development policy. One reason why the only type of property available in areas of Asian settlement is pre-1919-acquired property must be that the authority has failed to develop new-build sites in those areas.

Housing associations

Given the importance that national housing policy attaches to housing associations, it is perhaps surprising that this sector has been neglected by the research on race and housing and, indeed, by research on allocations generally(81). A major exception is Pat Niner's study(82) which examines the policies and practices of two associations in Birmingham – the Bournville Village Trust (BVT) and the Family Housing Association (FHA). However, as the report points out, housing associations are characterised by tremendous variety – for example, in terms of their size, their historical development, the people that they aim to house, their structures, and their methods of operating. Consequently, there are limits to how far we can generalise from this one study and there is a clear need for more research, particularly on different kinds of associations.

The sheer number and variety of housing associations operating within British cities may, in itself, have racially discriminatory consequences. Knowledge of housing associations is limited amongst the white population, but the indications are that black and Asian people are still less likely to be aware of the work of housing associations or may regard them as white institutions (with the exception of the small number of specialist black and Asian housing associations)(83). Table 3.1 shows that there is a higher proportion of West Indian and Bangladeshi households within the tenure than for other racial groups but this is primarily due to the focus of housing association activity in London being within the major areas of settlement for these two population groups. Given that they are likely to be in greater housing need and to the extent that housing associations aim to house those people in greatest need, we might expect a still higher proportion of black and Asian households to be located within this tenure.

The fact that housing associations tend to operate in specific localities within cities may, in fact, serve to reinforce the geographical segregation of the black population. Niner suggests that people are likely to be attracted to those associations which either operate in the area where they live or where they want to live. As a result, FHA, which operated largely in the inner area of Birmingham, received many more applications from black people than BVT, which operated outside these areas. This pattern was reinforced by other factors. For example, FHA had close links with the Catholic Church and the Irish community which resulted in the situation where 18 per cent of their applicants were born in Ireland. At BVT, 30 per cent of applicants had existing links with the estate – current residence, relatives on the estate, employed by Cadbury Schweppes etc. Given that existing tenants were predominantly white, this tended to reinforce the current racial composition of BVT tenants.

The channels of approach used by housing associations can also affect the racial composition of their tenants. Associations have links with a variety of organisations who refer applicants for housing to them, as well as agreements on the housing of applicants nominated by the local authority. Niner points out that the different referral agencies brought applicants of a very different racial mix and she concludes that:

> It would seem possible to 'orchestrate' racial mix by judicious selection of referral agencies. The selection of organisations with special status was certainly of considerable significance:

only a quarter of European allocations came through the 'special' channel, compared with 47 per cent of Caribbean and 70 per cent of Asian allocations(84).

The way in which associations operate their nomination agreements with the local authority can also affect the housing opportunities of black people. At FHA the nomination agreement with the council meant that if someone was housed who had not actually been nominated by the council but who happened to be on the local authority's waiting list this was counted against the nomination quota. The result of this practice was that FHA could claim that they fulfilled the nomination agreement with the council even if the council did not actually make any nominations. In this way, FHA retained effective control of the selection process instead of the council being able to influence who was housed through exercising their nomination rights. Niner suggests that, in practice, this made little difference in the case of FHA but there is clearly potential here for indirect racial discrimination to occur. Niner found that:

Asians in particular seem more likely to apply to the local authority rather than to housing associations, perhaps because they are less familiar with the housing opportunities associations might offer(85).

Niner suggests that the sort of arrangements operated by FHA are likely to result in a situation whereby the allocations counted against the authority's nomination rights will disproportionately favour white applicants who may have fewer points than the black and Asian applicants who are excluded by such procedures. The implication is that if the local authority made genuine nominations then a higher proportion of properties would be allocated to black households although of course it is equally possible that the local authority would operate discriminatory practices itself in the nomination of applicants to housing associations. The CRE's investigation of nominations made to housing associations by Liverpool City Council did indeed find that black applicants were treated less favourably than whites(86).

Niner's research also points to the importance of the initial assessment of applicants' suitability for inclusion on the waiting list. The associations that she studied both attempted to prioritise cases in accordance with the level and urgency of their housing needs and she found that, in the case of these two associations, this was likely to favour non-white applicants. However, she also points out that housing need may be assessed in different ways and that black and white applicants are likely to experience different forms of housing need. Thus, black applicants are more likely to experience overcrowding and to lack secure accommodation of their own whilst white applicants are more likely to be moving from a distance to take up employment, to be leaving tied accommodation or suffering the effects of divorce, separation or bankruptcy. Housing associations have considerable discretion as to how they prioritise housing needs and to which sorts of housing need they address themselves. Such choices will inevitably have implications for racial inequality in access to housing.

More direct forms of racial discrimination resulting from the exercise of individual discretion by housing staff are likely to operate in similar ways to those that have been identified in local authorities. However, they are potentially more important in housing associations who have greater discretionary power. Unlike local authorities, housing associations are not constrained by statutory obligations in relation to slum clearance or homelessness. They are constrained by non-housing legislation, for example on race and gender; by guidelines from the Housing Corporation and the National Federation of Housing Associations; and by nomination agreements with local authorities on properties funded by Housing Association Grants (HAG) but these constraints are less restrictive than those faced by local authorities. Moreover, housing associations are not publicly accountable in the way that local authorities are. Thus, although their policies and practices must have the tacit approval of the housing association's management committee, this is unlikely to be as restrictive as the control exercised by the elected representatives who compose local authority housing committees.

For these reasons, housing associations enjoy far more discretion as to whom they house than do local authority housing departments. This has the advantage of enabling housing associations to be more flexible in the way that they allocate their properties but it also creates the potential for housing association staff to use their discretionary powers in racially discriminatory ways and, if it is found that discrimination occurs, it is more difficult to identify the precise causes. Niner found that, in practice, in the two associations that she studied greater discretionary powers held by housing officers did not always result in racial discrimination. More research is clearly required to find out if this is typical and to identify the processes that generate good practice in housing associations.

Niner's research has highlighted some of the major areas of the allocation process within housing associations upon which such research might usefully focus. Firstly, discrimination may occur at the point of preliminary advice and guidance. However, because this is often given over the telephone, there are difficulties in keeping ethnic records on enquiries. Secondly, discrimination may occur in decisions as to whether to include an applicant on the waiting list. Niner found that the process at FHA was almost neutral in its effects on ethnic minorities whilst at BVT it actually favoured black applicants because their housing characteristics were more likely to fit with the priorities of the association's staff(87). However, she does point to the fact that the actual processes involved in selection and the ways in which priorities were fixed did vary between the two associations and that the net result was to produce differential housing opportunities for various applicant groups. She concludes this section by suggesting that other associations are likely to be equally variable in their practices.

Thirdly, discrimination may occur in the actual allocation of properties. Niner found that at FHA there was a broad relationship between the size of property allocated and household size, but that within each household type black households were more likely to be allocated smaller properties. For example:

Twenty-three per cent of European single-parent small families received a house, only 7 per cent of Caribbean and Asian single-parent small families did. Similarly, 53 per cent of two-parent European families got a house; no comparable black families did(88).

She adds that whilst these differences may be partially explained in terms of area preferences it is also clear that housing staff were using their discretionary power in ways which discriminated against black households. Because Niner's research was restricted to analysing records she was not able to fully explore the precise way in which this discrimination occurred but she was able to make one interesting observation. She found that the majority of West Indian single-parent households were headed by an unmarried young woman whereas white single-parent families were more likely to be a product of divorce or separation with the result that they were more mature families. She offers the thought that housing staff may have assumed that the older households have a greater need for additional space(89).

Niner also examined the quality of allocations as measured by the age of the property. She found that black households were actually more likely to be allocated new properties. She explains this by pointing to the fact that, firstly, black households were more likely to be nominated by the local authority for HAG-funded new-build schemes and, secondly, the majority of new properties were in Handsworth which was an area in which black people were more likely to be allocated properties. The pattern for newly improved property was very different. Although the numbers were

110

small – 12 European and two black households – black people were clearly less likely to be allocated these properties. They were located either in Edgbaston or Erdington which were areas in which black applicants were unlikely to be housed. However, Edgbaston was an area for which black applicants expressed a strong demand which suggests that direct forms of discrimination were in operation, possibly involving stereotyped views about where black people either deserved or preferred to live(90).

This also leads into a final point about race and housing associations. As with local authorities, the area in which new-build and newly improved properties are located is not entirely neutral and housing associations do have some control over their own development programmes. They are constrained by the Housing Corporation through, for example, zoning arrangements for rehabilitated properties and their own priorities for the types of new-build properties that they are prepared to fund but, nevertheless, where associations operate across a number of areas, they will retain some discretion over where they concentrate their activities and what types of property they develop there. Such decisions will clearly have implications for racial inequality in housing. Present inequalities will be at least partially a product of previous development decisions and any attempts to remove racial disadvantage in housing in the future will have to encompass housing development policies.

Conclusion

What constitutes good- or poor-quality housing must inevitably involve a subjective element which makes it difficult to make broad generalisations about any specific measure of housing quality. However, there is ample research evidence to show that, across a wide range of possible measures, black households fare significantly worse than their white counterparts.

This cannot be adequately explained in terms of differences in the composition of the black and white population. The circumstances of settlement in Britain in the immediate post-war period and the differences in household structures both contribute to the housing disadvantage experienced by black people but they provide no more than a partial explanation either directly, in terms of the operation of the housing market, or indirectly, through their effects on the position of black people in employment. The view that the variations in settlement patterns and quality of housing are a product of conscious choices, particularly by Asian households, to live in cheaper inner city areas is also at best a partial explanation since it ignores the framework of constraints within which such choices are made.

The inescapable conclusion from a review of the literature on race and housing is that housing workers and housing organisations play a key role in the production of racial inequalities in housing. This occurs not so much through direct discrimination against black people (although this is a factor) but rather through a battery of rules, procedures, and stereotypical views which indirectly discriminate against black people in a variety of subtle (and not so subtle) ways.

However, before leaving this discussion, it should be pointed out that the strength of this conclusion results partly from the fact that we have chosen to focus on 'housing' issues. Although the role of the housing profession is important, it operates in circumstances which are not entirely of its own choosing. Racial inequalities in housing cannot be divorced from the broader social context. Black households are disadvantaged not just because they are discriminated against by housing workers but also because of their wider experiences in employment, education, and other social institutions which leave them with fewer resources to compete in the private sector and which make them more vulnerable to the possibility of becoming homeless. Racist stereotypes are not manufactured in isolation by housing organisations but rather they are produced in the wider social context and refined in their application to housing. A complete analysis of racial inequality in housing ought to incorporate an examination of the interrelationship between housing and other spheres of social life and an understanding of the structural causes of racism in British society.

Notes

1. National Federation of Housing Associations (1982), *Race and Housing: a guide for housing associations*. Institute of Housing, Professional Practice Series, *No 2. Race and Housing: Monitoring* (1985); *No. 3. Race and Housing: Consultation* (1985); *No. 6. Race and Housing: Allocations* (1986); *No. 7. Race and Housing: Recruitment* (1986). Association of Metropolitan Authorities, *A Strategy for Racial Equality in Housing: 1. Racial Harassment* (1987); *2. Homelessness* (1988); *3. Allocations* (1988); *4. Local Housing Strategies* (1988).
2. Commission for Racial Equality (CRE) (1984a), *Race and Council Housing in Hackney*.
3. C. Brown (1984), *Black and White Britain*, Policy Studies Institute.
4. C. Brown (1984), p.62; J. Henderson and V. Karn (1987), *Race, Class and State Housing*, Gower, p.31.
5. Commission for Racial Equality (1984b), *Race and Housing in Liverpool*; A.Simpson (1981), *Stacking the Decks*, Nottingham Community Relations Council; CRE (1985), *Walsall Metropolitan Borough Council: practices and policies of housing allocation*; D. Phillips (1981), 'The social and spatial segregation of Asians in Leicester', in P. Jackson and S. Smith (eds), *Social Interaction and Ethnic Segregation*, Academic Press; J. Parker and K. Dugmore (1976), *Colour and the Allocation of GLC Housing*, Greater London Council.
6. Henderson and Karn (1987); D. Phillips (1981); CRE (1985), *Ethnic Minorities in Britain*.
7. See, for example, Henderson and Karn (1987); CRE (1984b); A. Simpson (1981): CRE (1984a).
8. Henderson and Karn (1987), p.71
9. R. Ward (1987), 'Race and access to housing', in S. Smith and J. Mercer, *New Perspectives in Race and Housing*, Glasgow Centre for Housing Research, p.213
10. C. Brown (1984), p.105.
11. CRE (1984a), p.22
12. P. Niner (1985), *Housing Association Allocations*, Runnymede Trust, p.108.
13. CRE (1984b), p.18.
14. CRE (1984a), p.22.
15. Henderson and Karn (1987), p.30.

16. C. Brown (1984), p.107.
17. *Ibid*, p.74
18. See, for example, Henderson and Karn (1987), p.30; Runnymede Trust (1980), *Britain's Black Population*; D. Smith (1977), *Racial Disadvantage in Britain*, Penguin.
19. C. Brown (1984), p.127.
20. *Ibid*, p.109.
21. M. Johnson (1987), 'Housing as a process of racial discrimination', in S. Smith and J. Mercer, *New Perspectives in Race and Housing*, Glasgow Centre for Housing Research, pp.166–7.
22. AMA 1988, *Homelessness*, p.2.
23. CRE (1984a), p.23.
24. C. Brown (1984), p.81.
25. Commission for Racial Equality (1988): *Homelessness and Discrimination: report of a formal investigation into the London Borough of Tower Hamlets*.
26. See, for example, J. Rex and R. Moore (1967), *Race, Community and Conflict*, Oxford University Press; W. Daniel (1968), *Racial Discrimination in England*, Penguin.
27. CRE (1984a), p.19.
28. Henderson and Karn (1987), p.69.
29. *Ibid*, p.88.
30. Other research has produced broadly similar findings. See, for example, CRE (1984a) p.28; P. Niner (1985).
31. V. Karn, J. Kemeny and P. Williams (1985), *Home Ownership in the Inner City*, Gower, pp.6–7
32. For an assessment of such arguments see P. Sarre (1986), 'Choice and constraint in ethnic minority housing' *Housing Studies*, Vol.1, No.2, April.
33. B. Dahya (1974), 'The nature of Pakistani ethnicity in industrial cities in Britain' in A. Cohen (ed) *Urban Ethnicity*, Tavistock.
34. V. Robinson (1980), 'Asians and council housing', *Urban Studies*, Vol.17, p.326.
35. Rex and Moore (1967).
36. C. Forman (1989), *Spitalfields: a battle for land*, Hilary Shipman, pp.4–5.
37. See, for example, Henderson and Karn (1987); H. Flett (1984), 'Bureaucracy and ethnicity' in R. Ward (ed), *Race and Residence in Britain*, Economic and Social Research Council; D. Phillips (1986), *What Price Equality?*, GLC Housing Research and Policy Report No 9.
38. Henderson and Karn (1987), p.162.
39. P. Sarre (1986).
40. See, for example, D. Phillips (1981).
41. M. Kettle and L. Hodges (1982), *Uprising*, Pan, p.40.
42. P. Fryer (1984), *Staying Power*, Humanities Press, p.374.

43. C. Brown (1984), p.2.
44. See, for example, C. Brown (1984), p.158; A. Bhat et al (1988), *Britain's Black Population*, p.67.
45. Commission for Racial Equality (1982), *Massey Ferguson Perkins Ltd: report of a formal investigation*; CRE (1985), *Beaumont Shopping Centre: report of a formal investigation*.
46. See, for example, B. Coard (1971), *How the West Indian Child is Made Educationally Subnormal in the British School System*, New Beacon Books; A. James and R. Jeffcoate (eds) (1981): *The School in the Multicultural Society*, Harper and Row; M. Sarap (1986), *The Politics of Multiracial Education*, Routledge and Kegan Paul.
47. C. Brown (1984), p.44.
48. D. Phillips (1986), p.26.
49. Henderson and Karn (1987) p.69.
50. See, for example, W. Daniel (1968).
51. See, for example, D. Smith (1977); Runnymede Trust (1980).
52. P. Williams (1978), 'Building societies and the inner city', in *Transactions of the Institute of British Geographers*, Vol.3, No.4, p.26. This article also contains a useful discussion of some of the other research in this area.
53. Commission for Racial Equality (1985), *Race and Mortgage Lending: report of a formal investigation*.
54. Karn, Kemeny and Williams (1985), p.40.
55. *Ibid*, p.49.
56. *Ibid*, p.108.
57. Henderson and Karn (1987), p.206.
58. *Ibid*, p.201.
59. *Ibid*, p.203
60. *Ibid*, pp.205–6.
61. D. Phillips (1986), pp.36–7.
62. Henderson and Karn (1987), p.162.
63. D. Phillips (1987), 'The institutionalisation of racism in housing', in S. Smith and J. Mercer, *New Perspectives in Race and Housing*, Glasgow Centre for Housing Research, p.146; Henderson and Karn (1987), p.45.
64. Henderson and Karn (1987), p.216.
65. D. Phillips (1986), p.40.
66. AMA (1988), *Homelessness*, p.18.
67. See, for example, J. Rex and R. Moore (1967), Chapter 1.
68. AMA (1988), *Allocations*, p.3.
69. *Ibid*, p.5.
70. *Ibid*, p.4.
71. *General Household Survey, 1986*, (1989), HMSO, Figure 3B, p.10.
72. Henderson and Karn (1987), p.58.
73. AMA (1988), *Allocations* p.7.
74. Henderson and Karn (1987), pp.57–8.

75. F. Gray (1976a), 'Selection and allocation in council housing' in *Transactions of the Institute of British Geographers*, Vol.1; F.Gray (1976b), 'The management of local authority housing', in Political Economy of Housing Workshop, *Housing and Class in Britain*.

76. See, for example, P. Niner (1989), *Homelessness in Nine Local Authorities*, HMSO; A. Evans and S. Duncan (1988), *Responding to Homelessness*, HMSO.

77. See, for example, D. Phillips (1986), p.11; CRE (1984b) p.24; CRE (1984a).

78. AMA (1988), *Allocations* p.14.

79. Henderson and Karn (1987), pp.78–82.

80. *Ibid*, pp.73–5.

81. J. Stearn (1988), 'How do they house?', *Housing*, June/July.

82. P. Niner (1985).

83. National Federation of Housing Associations (1985), *Race and Housing: ethnic record keeping and monitoring*, pp.11–12.

84. P. Niner (1985), p.75.

85. *Ibid*, p.122.

86. CRE (1984b).

87. P. Niner (1985), p.83–5

88. *Ibid*, p.89.

89. *Ibid*, p.101.

90. *Ibid*, pp.106–7.

4 | Housing and gender divisions

Discussions of housing policy and housing inequalities are commonly carried on with no reference to the way in which women experience the housing system differently from men. This chapter analyses the housing situation of women and seeks to show that, while Chapters 2 and 3 have established that both class and race are crucial determinants of housing advantage or disadvantage, gender divisions are also important sources of housing inequality.

In doing this, we will focus on particular groups of women. This does not mean, however, that these groups constitute some form of 'special need'. Rather, what is under discussion are the circumstances in which it becomes obvious that underlying gender divisions have a significant influence on housing inequalities. The final section of the chapter will look at explanations of the relationship between housing inequality and gender.

Women's access to housing

Table 4.1 illustrates the different tenure patterns for male- and female-headed households. However, before looking at the significance of these different tenure patterns we need to address the fact that 77 per cent of the population in Britain live in households 'headed' by a married or cohabiting couple(1) so most women live in households where there is a man present (usually husband or father) and which, by statistical convention, are described as 'male-headed households'. It could be argued therefore that access to housing independent of a man is an issue which only affects a small minority of women.

117

TABLE 4.1 *Tenure by sex and marital status of head of household, Great Britain 1984*

| | Heads of Household | | | | |
| | Men | | | | |
Tenure	Married %	Single %	Widowed %	Divorced/ separated %	All men %
Owner-occupied, owned outright	22	17	43	12	23
Owner-occupied, with mortgage	50	33	8	41	46
Rented with job or business	3	4	1	3	3
Rented from local authority/New Town	20	20	37	28	21
Rented from housing association or co-operative	1	2	3	3	1
Rented privately, unfurnished	3	10	8	10	4
Rented privately, furnished	1	13	1	4	2

Continued

On the other hand, it should be recognised that one in four households is headed by a woman and the housing opportunities for such households are also of crucial importance to women living in male-headed households. Most women will go through stages in their lives when they either wish to, or are forced to, be part of a household where there is not a man present – such as younger single women, women experiencing relationship breakdown, and older women. The opportunities and constraints for all women are therefore indicated by the housing experiences of the 25 per cent of households which, at any one point in time, are headed by a woman.

At first sight it seems that households headed by a woman are more likely to own outright. However, this is a statistical distortion owing to the longer life expectancy of women.

TABLE 4.1
Continued

	Single %	Widowed %	Divorced/ separated %	All women %
		Heads of Household Women		
Owner-occupied, owned outright	25	42	11	31
Owner-occupied, with mortgage	19	3	27	12
Rented with job or business	1	–	1	1
Rented from local authority/New Town	33	43	48	42
Rented from housing association or co-operative	4	3	4	4
Rented privately, unfurnished	10	8	6	8
Rented privately, furnished	9	1	2	3

Source: General Household Survey, 1986 (1989), Table 6.13, p 57, HMSO.

Just over half of all female-headed households are over pensionable age and many of these have inherited the matrimonial home after the death of their spouses. Table 4.2 indicates that, if we compare like with like – i.e. by taking just those households over the age of 60 – households headed by older women are in fact less likely than households headed by an older man to be owners outright.

Only 12 per cent of female-headed households are buying on a mortgage compared to 46 per cent of male-headed households. The greater difficulty that women have in gaining access to the major tenure is particularly apparent in high-house-price areas such as London where, in 1986, only 12 per cent of such households received income sufficient to take on an average London mortgage compared to 54 per cent of male-headed households(2). According to one of the major building

TABLE 4.2 *Tenure by sex – households over the age of 60*

| | Household heads over the age of 60 | |
	Male %	Female %
Outright owners	51	43
Owners with mortgages	7	2
Local authority/New Town tenants	31	39
Housing association tenants	2	4
Private rented tenants	9	12

Source: Labour Force Survey 1984, Housing Trailer (1986), Department of Employment.

societies, women are finding it increasingly difficult to get access into owner-occupation, illustrated by the way in which the position of women borrowers in terms of the prices they are paying for houses relative to their incomes has worsened more sharply compared to that of men during the 1980s(3). Between 1978 and 1988, the house price/incomes ratio for women increased by 45.9 per cent compared with only 31.3 per cent for men so that by 1988 women were borrowing on average almost four times their income compared to men who were borrowing on average three and a half times their income.

What is more, when women do gain access to owner-occupation in their own right, they enter the sector on worse terms than men in that they buy cheaper, older property. Table 4.3 shows, for example, that in 1986, 36 per cent of women mortgagors bought pre-1919 property compared to 23 per cent of male borrowers.

It is also significant that the women who are most likely to be owners are women over the age of 60, most of whom will have inherited their property from a spouse or parent. These women are also most likely to be occupying pre-1919 properties in some state of disrepair. We will return to this point later in the chapter.

It could be argued that the difference in the tenure of male- and female-headed households is the result of male-

TABLE 4.3 *Age, price and type of property purchased and amenities, by sex of borrower*

| | Borrower | |
	Male %	Female %
Age of property:		
Pre-1919	24	34
1919–1944	18	16
1945–1970	23	20
Post 1970, not new	26	23
New	9	7
Properties with full or part central heating	77	71
House type:		
Detached houses	15	7
Semi-detached houses	27	21
Terraced houses	33	38
Bungalows	8	5
Purpose-built flats	12	21
Converted flats	5	8
Average price	£59,002	£53,152

Sources: Lending to Women: July 1988 and *Lending to Women, 1978–1988,* Nationwide Building Society.

headed households being more likely to be double-income households. Undoubtedly, the presence of a second wage, even if – as in most households – the woman's wage is from a part-time and/or lower-paid job than the man's, is an important contribution to mortgage repayments. However, it is also clear that it is the lack of a *male* wage-earner which puts home-ownership out of reach of many households headed by a woman rather than the lack of a *second* wage-earner. Fifty-one per cent of single-parent households, the majority of them headed by a woman, have household incomes below £80 p.w. whereas only 8 per cent of married couple households with dependent children and where the woman is not working (i.e. a single-wage male-headed household) are in the same position(4). Of course, the higher rate of unemployment/economic inactivity amongst single parents is an important factor in this economic differential. The importance of women's economic position generally is discussed in more detail later on in the chapter.

The importance of a man's wage coming into the household is evident from recent analysis of 23-year-olds in the National Child Development Study. Of those who had set up independent households by the time they were 23, cohabiting or married 23-year-old women were over 100 times more likely to be owners than single women, holding other factors constant. For men, however, being married or cohabiting had no direct effect on tenure. The same study also highlighted the importance of a man's wage for entry into owner-occupation when single men and women's tenure was analysed: of those who had left the parental home, 29 per cent of single women compared to 76 per cent of single men had become owners by the age of 23(5). Although two-thirds of the owner-occupying couples in this study were in households where both man and woman were in waged work, further analysis of income and job security confirmed that 'women must typically rely on their partners' income and employment to attain owner occupation'(6).

Table 4.1 illustrates the importance to women of housing to which access is gained through housing need. Council housing is far more important for female-headed households than it is for households headed by men. 42 per cent of female-headed households are council tenants. Council housing is particularly important for women experiencing relationship breakdown: 48 per cent of households headed by a divorced or separated woman are in the public rented sector.

We will now look in some detail at the housing situation of women who are not in a male-headed household in order to highlight the relationship between gender and housing disadvantage. We will begin by looking at the experience of relationship breakdown, focusing within this discussion on the particular issues of lone parents and of domestic violence. We then move on to look at the housing experiences of single women and of older women.

Relationship breakdown

Relationship breakdown is a common experience; 17 per cent of women under 30 who married between 1975 and 1979 had separated within six years of their marriage(7). On current trends, one in three marriages will end in divorce. Alternative sources of housing are crucial to enabling men and women to leave an unhappy relationship. It is often assumed that women remain in the marital home when a marriage ends. In fact, as Oriel Sullivan shows in her analysis of Family Formation Survey data, nearly half of women experiencing marital breakdown leave (or both man and woman leave) the marital home and, as Table 4.4 indicates, even where there are children there are still four out of ten women who have to move when their relationship breaks down.

It appears that class differences in whether women have to leave the marital home at relationship breakdown are very slight. Other factors have more impact; women are more likely to stay put if they are older, local authority tenants or if they have children.

It is particularly significant that women are less likely to have to find alternative accommodation when their relationship breaks down if they are already local authority tenants. As Sullivan argues:

> This may reflect the fact that they are more likely to have been able to afford to retain their home than is the case for either privately renting tenants or owner-occupiers (who may have high rents or mortgages which they are unable to afford on their own)(8).

Table 4.1 illustrates the importance of public sector housing for divorced and separated women. These figures are partly a reflection of higher divorce and separation rates amongst those in the public rented sector, this situation partly coming about because marital breakdown is correlated with age of marriage and so is becoming a council tenant. In other

TABLE 4.4 *Selected characteristics of women who move out of the marital home at the breakdown of their first marriage*

	Percentage moving
Total	46
Age at breakdown	
16–29	53
30–39	37
40–49	27
Tenure at breakdown	
Owner-occupied	45
Local authority	35
Private rented	59
Husband's social class	
Non-manual	46
Manual	44
Births in first marriage	
No	56
Yes	41

Source: Family Formation Survey, 1976, taken from O. Sullivan, 'Housing movements of the divorced and separated', in *Housing Studies, Vol. 1, No. 1, 1986, p.38.*

words, the younger the age at marriage the greater the likelihood of becoming a council tenant, but early marriage also brings higher risks of later divorce or separation(9).

However, this correlation is only part of the picture and it must be recognised that the prime importance of council housing for women experiencing relationship breakdown is the fact that the public rented sector provides access to housing according to housing need rather than ability to pay. Sullivan's research indicates that amongst divorced and separated women who have to move at relationship breakdown, and who do not remarry, there is a substantial fall in the proportion who remain owner-occupiers and a rise in those who become local authority tenants. The importance of local authority housing to women experiencing relationship breakdown is also illustrated by Holmans, Nandy and Brown's analysis of OPCS longitudinal data; amongst men and women married in 1971 but divorced in 1981, the proportion of men who were local authority tenants fell (from 32 to 22 per cent) but the proportion of women housed within the public sector rose (from 30 to 37 per cent)(10).

Owner-occupation offers restricted housing opportunities for women in the event of relationship breakdown. As Pascall points out, although women's legal rights to the marital home at relationship breakdown have improved over the last 20 years, these rights are meaningless if a woman wishes to leave her marriage and yet has not the economic resources to find alternative independent housing(11). If a woman wishes to end her marriage – and 73 per cent of divorce decrees in 1987 were granted to the wife(12) – but her husband refuses to leave the marital home, alternative sources of housing take on a crucial importance.

Even where the sale of the marital home brings a capital gain, many women will find it difficult to take on a new mortgage because their income is unlikely to be high enough to sustain the repayments. Only 29 per cent of all married women are working full time(13). Table 4.5 indicates that married women are less likely to be working full time than unmarried women and that having dependent children makes it particularly unlikely that women will be working full time, whatever their marital status. Even when women are working full time they are likely to be on a low wage: in 1988 women's average full-time wage was 67 per cent that of the average male full-time wage(14).

In the event of relationship breakdown, therefore, many women will have insufficient income to sustain owner-occupation, unless the mortgage repayments on the existing marital home are low or she receives financial support from her ex-husband. It is not surprising there-fore that the public rented sector is such an important source of housing for women in the event of relationship breakdown.

TABLE 4.5 *Women with and without dependent children – percentages working full time and part time, by marital status*

	Full time %	Part time %	All working %
Women with dependent children			
Lone mothers			
single	13	12	25
widowed	14	42	56
divorced	23	26	49
separated	16	23	39
All lone mothers	18	24	42
Married Women	15	35	50
Women without dependent children			
Married	42	28	70
Non-married	56	15	70

Source: General Household Survey, 1986, (1989), pp. 102–4, HMSO.

Powerlessness is a crucial element in women's relationship with local housing authorities when seeking alternative sources of housing in order to leave an unhappy relationship. Having somewhere to go is probably the single most important factor in enabling a woman to leave her husband and in this sense housing policy and practice can make it either possible or impossible for women to leave their husbands.

There has been very little research on this aspect of women's experiences. One exception is Mary Brailey's study of women's access to public housing in Scotland(15). In two of the four areas studied by Brailey in Central Scotland, people applying for alternative accommodation because of relationship breakdown would not receive any help unless they were literally roofless or would be within the month. What is more, in one area, following a woman's application as homeless owing to relationship breakdown, the standard practice was to interview her husband to ask him if he was willing to 'keep' his wife or 'take her back'. If he was, she was not deemed homeless regardless of the strength of her wish to separate or the reasons for it. A typical letter sent by the housing department read:

> Your husband has indicated that he is quite willing for you to return home, and due to there not being any question of violence, you cannot be considered as homeless(16).

Another Scottish study found that such policies were not uncommon(17).

As the pressure on public sector housing has increased during the 1980s, so women seeking council housing because of relationship breakdown have found it more and more difficult to attain such housing through the waiting list or transfer list. Women with dependent children have turned more and more to their statutory rights under the homeless persons legislation to enable them to achieve access to independent housing. Of course, women without dependent children do not usually qualify as a priority category and the rapid decline of the private rented sector – and in particular, the low-rent part of the sector – has made it even more difficult for women to find alternative sources of housing.

Even for women with dependent children who qualify as priority homeless, the housing opportunities have narrowed. As the number of homeless households rose during the 1980s, so did the use of temporary accommodation by local authorities. In particular, it became more and more common for homeless households to be placed in bed and breakfast accommodation which is usually some distance away from their local community. Such an experience means living in overcrowded conditions with poor cooking facilities; isolation from family, friends and services such as GPs and health visitors; a disruption in children's education; a risk to mental and physical health(18).

All this acts as a pressure on women to go back to their husbands or cohabitees. Mary Brailey writes:

All the women who had spent time in bed and breakfast spoke of others who had been there at the same time and had returned to their husbands, 'not because they wanted to, but because they couldn't stand it any more'(19).

Lone parents

Women experience particular difficulties at relationship breakdown when they have dependent children. Lone parents are an increasingly important section of the population, primarily because of their increase in numbers due to divorce and separation. Eight per cent of households comprise a lone parent, but they make up 14 per cent of families (13 per cent are female lone parents). The majority of one-parent families have resulted from a marital breakdown – 9 per cent of all family households(20).

One-parent families are over-represented amongst households accepted as homeless by local authorities. Unfortunately, the DoE no longer collects statistics on household composition of homeless households but during the early 1980s (when they did collect such statistics) one-parent families accounted for 31 per cent of all homeless households in London and 40 per cent in Metropolitan Districts (figures for first half of 1981).

A more recent, postal, survey carried out for the DoE by Angela Evans and Sue Duncan asked local authorities to estimate the proportion of one-parent families amongst those accepted as homeless in 1985/86. On average it was reported that one-parent families 'represented two-fifths of acceptances and the differences between types of authority were not great'(21). That one-parent families headed by a woman are grossly over-represented amongst those experiencing homelessness is also clear from Pat Niner's case studies of policies and practices on homelessness(22). In five out of seven authorities, as Table 4.6 shows, lone mothers made up the majority of *family* households who applied as homeless.

As Evans and Duncan point out, this high representation of one-parent families amongst those applying/accepted as homeless is not surprising as DoE statistics on homelessness

128

TABLE 4.6 *Household structure of families applying as homeless*

	Woman with children or pregnant woman %	Man with children %	Man and woman with children or woman pregnant %
Cardiff	65	5	31
Gloucester	72	–	26
Hillingdon	37	5	58
Newcastle	67	2	31
New Forest	54	2	44
Nottingham	78	2	20
Westminster	45	6	48

Source: Pat Niner, *Homelessness in Nine Local Authorities – Case Studies of Policy and Practice* (1989), Table 5.4, p.84, HMSO.

Figures were only given for seven authorities owing to difficulties in collecting comparable data on household composition for the other two.

indicate that relationship breakdown accounts for about a fifth of those accepted as homeless. Many women experiencing relationship breakdown will also be represented amongst the biggest category of those accepted as homeless, namely those whose friends or relatives are no longer willing/able to accommodate them.

There is evidence that one-parent families, when they gain access to the public rented sector, do so on disadvantaged terms compared to two-parent families. For example, the London Docklands Housing Needs Survey found that 14 per cent of one-parent families lived in blocks of flats on the fourth floor or above, compared to 7 per cent of two-parent families. Furthermore, one-parent families expressed a greater degree of dissatisfaction with their housing condition: 44 per cent were dissatisfied compared to 32 per cent of other family households(23).

Homeless households are generally disadvantaged in the allocation process and, whatever the local authority's intentions of fairness, are likely to be allocated the most unpopular property. This is because, as we have discussed in previous chapters, allocators tend to find applicants for properties rather than properties for applicants, principally because of the management imperative of keeping down void rates. If a local authority has within its stock certain areas, estates, types of dwellings which are less popular than others (and this is almost always the case) then those who have the least bargaining power will be offered the most unpopular dwellings because they are the least likely to turn such an offer down. The desperation of homeless applicants is compounded by the practice of 'one offer only' policies which are often applied to homeless applicants. Evans and Duncan's survey found that three-quarters of local authorities made only one offer of permanent accommodation to homeless households(24).

One-parent families enter the public rented sector, therefore, on particularly disadvantaged terms as they are grossly over-represented amongst homeless applicants. Women's independent access to council housing is often associated with the stigma which is associated with homelessness generally quite apart from the stigma attached to being a single parent.

However, there is also evidence that single-parent families are discriminated against in direct terms (rather than indirectly through being housed as homeless) when allocated council housing. The DoE's own Housing Services Advisory Group admitted that 'all fatherless families tend to be to some extent stigmatised and hence given the most stigmatised lettings'(25). Mary Brailey's study found that lone mothers rehoused because of marital breakdown tended to be housed in unpopular tenements. 42 per cent of them in one area were allocated tenement flats, compared to 25 per cent of all homeless aplicants and only 13 per cent of all allocations(26).

The reliance of lone parents on the public rented sector partly accounts for other aspects of housing disadvantage. For example, across tenures they are less likely to be living in detached or semi-detached houses than two-parent families (35 per cent compared to 56 per cent)(27). Fewer of them have access to central heating (52 per cent compared to 67 per cent for two-parent families). However, a more significant difference in housing conditions between one- and two-parent families is the higher incidence of overcrowding. Twenty per cent live in overcrowded conditions compared to 9 per cent of two-parent families and, as Oriel Sullivan points out, this is mainly a reflection of the fact that divorced and separated people in general are more likely to be sharing housing with relatives or friends than married couples(28). One-parent families tend to move more often than two-parent families(29). This is mainly due to using a succession of friends and relatives in order to leave an unhappy marriage, a situation that women are forced into because a lack of alternative housing.

Domestic violence
It is worth considering separately the situation of women experiencing violence at the hands of their partners for, if such women have difficulty in fleeing violence, this high-lights the powerlessness which women experience generally. The incidence and prevalence of domestic violence is notoriously difficult to assess. Not only do most incidents go unreported but there is also evidence that even when reported such assaults are more often than not unrecorded by the police. Susan Edwards' research on two police stations in London found that only 12 per cent of incidents which were reported to the police appeared in the official records. Extrapolating from the local figures, she estimated that over the whole London area there were just under 60,000 reported incidents per year (of which only 7,000 would be recorded by the police as assaults)(30).

Assaults by a husband or partner tend to be under-recorded in self-reporting crime surveys which are otherwise quite successful at arriving at an accurate assessment of the incidence of crime. Stanko(31) argues that this is because women are reluctant to admit to being the victims of domestic violence because the dominant idea that 'only 'bad' girls get hurt means that rather than being exposed as 'bad', women stay quiet'(32) Hough and Mayhew, in their analysis of the British Crime Survey emphasise that the under-reporting of domestic violence in the survey probably resulted from the 'assailant being in the same room at the time of the interview'(33).

The Islington Crime Survey, using more sensitive interviewing techniques, registered a higher incidence than the British Crime Survey and estimated that a quarter of all assaults in the borough involved an attack on a woman by her partner. Extrapolating from these figures, the London Strategic Policy Unit estimated that this meant a London-wide incidence of 750,000 attacks per year.

The last major survey of the experience of women fleeing domestic violence was carried out in the late 1970s and indicates both the seriousness of such violence and the difficulties that women have in leaving a violent partner. Binney, Harkell and Nixon interviewed 656 women living in 128 Women's Aid refuges in 1978 and concluded:

> Our findings challenge the idea that battered women are not serious about leaving violent men. They also show that finding any sort of accommodation, let alone accommodation which meets their needs, makes leaving home a gruelling experience for most women. That so many women finally made a separate home for themselves attests more to their strength and determination than to the co-operation of the statutory agencies involved(34).

The average length of time women had suffered violence was seven years and ranged from a few months to 40 years; the average age of women in the refuges was 31 but ranged from 17 to 70:

> Most women had wanted to leave their violent partner from within the first year of marriage but their main obstacle had been that they had nowhere to go(35).

Most of the women in the refuges had attempted to leave home before – three times on average – but because the source of alternative accommodation was staying with friends or relatives, they had not been able to make a permanent break:

> There was seldom enough room [with the relative or friend] for a woman to stay with her children for long and she was easily found by her husband or boyfriend. The importance of keeping her whereabouts secret was clear from the pressures that came into play once a woman was found. Although some women had genuinely sought a reconciliation, all too often women described being simply worn down by their husband's persuasions to return. A proportion had been literally forced back – physically or because of threats – while others did not want to impose their husband's behaviour on friends or relatives: 'I went to my parents and of course, he came – I left him because of his hitting and kicking me – and I went home to them, but he came there and I had to go. I went back really to keep the peace because my parents weren't able to cope with it'(36).

This study found that housing departments were generally unhelpful when women approached them for emergency accommodation. Only 8 per cent of the women had been referred to refuges by housing departments, who tended instead to either refuse to take the situation seriously, or at best to place the woman in bed and breakfast accommodation, or a hostel or reception centre where their violent partner had little difficulty in tracing them.

Brailey's study covered four authorities in Central Scotland, one of which turned away 42 per cent of all those women applying as homeless because of violence. In these cases, it was common for the file to record comments such as 'occasional minor assault' and 'violence not serious'(37). The Binney, Harkell and Nixon study found that most housing departments in England and Wales did not take the experience of violence seriously, the emphasis being on reconciliation and the assumption that women would usually go back to their husbands anyway. If women are not provided with alternative, safe housing this of course becomes a self-fulfilling prophecy. Their study found that only 16 per cent of women had returned to their partners one year after the original interviews; it is undoubtedly of significance that women who manage to get to refuges are more likely to find alternative safe housing.

A more recent study of homelessness procedures in nine local authorities confirms one of the findings from this earlier study – that women fleeing domestic violence found it more difficult to leave their partner than anyone else. Thus Pat Niner concluded:

> In general, it seemed that the likelihood of applicants fleeing domestic violence reaching a 'solution' through homelessness procedures was less than applicants experiencing other causes of homlessness, and the 'failure' was disproportionately likely to be due to applicant not pursuing the application(38).

Evans and Duncan's study highlighted the additional difficulties confronting women without dependent children. They found that 15 per cent of local authorities did not treat such women as homeless at all and that another 58 per cent of authorities, while accepting that they were homeless, nevertheless did not automatically define them as being in priority need(39).

The experience of the women in Binney, Harkell and Nixon's survey who managed to find permanent alternative accommodation when the follow-up interviews were done 18 months after the initial survey, demonstrates both the importance of the public rented sector for all women experiencing relationship breakdown, and the way in which housing inequalities are perpetuated. Eighty-three per cent of the women who had found permanent accommodation were in council housing but nearly half of them described their housing conditions as poor, with 70 per cent needing repairs doing when the woman moved in(40).

Generally, therefore, women experiencing relationship breakdown rely to a large extent on the public rented sector to enable them to find alternative accommodation. They are therefore particularly disadvantaged by the decline of council housing during the 1980s. The difficulties that women experience in trying to find accommodation separate from a male partner can be summed up by one woman in Mary Brailey's study who said in despair:

> It's terrible when there's nowhere for a woman to turn to and that's really what's happening now. There's no way a woman can walk out of a marriage and get a house and start on her own and make a life of her own(41).

Single women

Single women are less likely to gain access to the major tenure, owner-occupation, than single men. Table 4.1 indicates that 19 per cent of single women are buying on a mortgage compared to 33 per cent of single men. As we have already seen, Munro and Smith's analysis of the National Child Development Study illustrates that the tenure differences between young men and women are in fact greater than this; of those who had set up independent households by the age of 23, only 29 per cent of single women, compared to 76 per cent of single men were owner-occupiers(42). The much higher figure of owner-occupation for single men in this age cohort than for single men of all ages, is a reflection of the increase in owner-occupation in the last 15 years, but this greater importance of the owner-occupied sector has evidently not had such a big impact on young single women.

However, it is not possible to conclude from these figures that single women have fewer housing opportunities than single men as there is no research on whether single men and women within each age cohort have similar aspirations for setting up home independently. What is known is that the rate of household formation amongst single people generally increased for most of the 1980s and that there is a considerable unmet demand for household formation amongst this group. The London Housing Survey 1986–7, for example, estimated that there were 242,000 potential

single-person households in the capital (potential households being those of the 873,000 single-person concealed
households who expressed a desire to live separately)(43).

It can also be argued that, as economic status becomes
ever more important in achieving access to housing (because
of the expansion of owner-occupation and the decline of the
public rented sector) single women, along with other types
of female households, are at a disadvantage compared to
male-headed households. Thirty per cent of 'not married'
women below retirement age are economically inactive
compared to 11 per cent of men below retirement age(44).
Furthermore, 15 per cent of single women in work are
working part time whereas the number of men working part
time is negligible.

Given these economic disadvantages exhibited by single
women, it is not surprising that households headed by a
single woman are under-represented amongst those households buying on a mortgage. However, this is the only type
of woman-headed household which is not over-represented
amongst council tenants and this is an indication of the
difficulty that women have in gaining access to the council
sector unless they have dependent children. All the same, a
third of households headed by single women are council
tenants (compared to 20 per cent of single men). Some of
these households will be single women with children (it is
not possible to separate these households out from single
women without children in the public rented sector) who will
often have gained access to council housing through the
homeless persons legislation. Single women without children
find it increasingly difficult to qualify for council housing as
the pressure grows on allocations. Unless they can qualify as
'vulnerable' (owing to physical or mental illness, age or
other special reason) there is little chance of achieving
independent housing.

Sophie Watson and Helen Austerberry's research on single
women's homelessness drew attention to the invisibility
of single women's housing needs. As they point out:
'Because fewer women are to be seen sleeping rough, there

is an assumption that fewer women then men become homeless'(45). Austerberry and Watson adopted a wider definition of homelessness in order to make visible the housing needs of single women. In the context of a more general discussion about the meaning of the words 'home' and 'homelessness', they state that there is a continuum against which housing situation can be measured, with sleeping rough at one end and absolute security of tenure in the form of outright ownership at the other. They go on:

> There would be little disagreement with the notion of the former state as literally homeless and the latter as not. In between, however, lies an extensive grey area, ranging across hostels, hotels, temporary accommodation, sleeping on friends' floors, licences, to insecure private rented accommodation, mortgaged accommodation and so on(46).

The accommodation available to single homeless people is mainly for men. A national survey carried out of hostels and lodging houses in the early 1970s, for example, concluded that women accounted for less than one-tenth of the hostel and lodging house population(47). However, as Austerberry and Watson point out this is because most of the provision is for men and specifically excludes women. For example, the Birmingham Standing Conference on Single Homelessness reported in 1981 that bedspaces for women in Birmingham made up only 6 per cent of all bedspaces for the single homeless(48). Nationally it is estimated that emergency provision for men exceeds that for women by 9:1(49).

However, if we take other expressions of housing demand amongst single women it becomes clear that those women who are in accommodation for single homeless people are only the tip of an iceberg. Collection of statistics from local housing advice agencies has indicated that women make up between 40–50 per cent of those single people who contact them with housing problems(50). 'Up-market' hostels are a much more important source of housing for single women than are the types of hostels which men use: for example in London in 1981 there were 760 bedspaces for women in direct access hostels and 8,000 in the 'up-market' hostels(51). Unless under threat of eviction, women in these types of hostel would be unlikely to be officially defined as homeless, although it is clear that such accommodation does not usually constitute a 'home'.

Other measurements of housing need include local authority waiting lists. Austerberry and Watson collected information on single people registered on the waiting lists of 17 London authorities and found that between 50 and 79 per cent of them were single women(52). Single people have been the most rapidly increasing group registering on council waiting lists during the 1980s.

The economic circumstances of single women pose a barrier to owner-occupation and if they do not have children this poses a barrier to council housing. However, the tenure to which single women have traditionally looked to meet their housing need – the private rented sector – has, over the years, provided fewer and fewer housing opportunities. There is a clear difference in the position within the sector of women over the age of 60 and younger women. It is the controlled, unfurnished private rented sector which is a significant source of housing for women over 60. A GLC survey on the private rented sector in London, for example, found that 83 per cent of single women private tenants over the age of 60 held protected tenancies, whereas only 48 per cent of single women tenants under the age of 60 did so(53).

This situation is a result of both the overall decline of the private rented sector and legislative changes which made it possible to create unprotected or less protected tenancies. The decline of the controlled and unfurnished part of the sector has meant no new such tenancies being created. On the other hand, older households entered the tenure when it was possible to gain such tenancies and they have remained there as there are limited alternatives for low-cost housing. We discuss the situation of older women in more detail in the next section.

The GLC survey found that single women below the age of 60 were more likely to lack exclusive use of amenities than any other household type in the private rented sector – only 41 per cent of them had exclusive use of amenities compared to an average 64 per cent for all household types. Again 51 per cent of single women private tenants lived in either poor or very poor condition housing, compared with an overall figure of 40 per cent for the whole sector. It was also younger single women who were most likely to experience harrassment, 12 per cent of them reporting such experiences.

Lesbian women, like gay men, often find that the general assumption that heterosexuality is the norm leads to housing problems. London Lesbian and Gay Switchboard has found that 25 per cent of its callers were in housing difficulties and often needed emergency assistance. In 1983, the London Gay Teenage group carried out a survey of young lesbians and gay men and found out that 11 per cent had been thrown out because of their sexuality; the percentage for lesbians was higher (14.5 per cent) than that for gay men (9 per cent).

Women who do not live in a household where there is a male wage-earner are generally economically disadvantaged. The housing implications of this disadvantage for women without children are then compounded by the failure of policy-makers to place the housing needs of single women on the political agenda.

Older women

Ten per cent of the population live alone. However, if we break down the population according to age and gender we can see that living alone is a much more common experience for older women, predominantly because of women's longer life expectancy. Table 4.7 illustrates that women over the age of 75 are almost three times as likely to be living alone as men in the same age group.

Fifty-three per cent of woman-headed households consist of women over the age of 60 living on their own (another 7 per cent are in two-person pensioner households). This is a much greater concentration than amongst male-headed

TABLE 4.7 *Individuals in one-person households, by age and sex*

| | Proportion who lived alone | | |
| | Men | Women | Total |
	%	%	%
16–24	4	3	4
25–44	7	4	5
45–64	8	13	10
65–74	17	38	29
75 and over	24	61	48

Source: General Household Survey 1986, (1989), Table 3.3, p.11, HMSO.

households, of whom 20 per cent are two-person pensioner households and only 5 per cent elderly men living on their own. The housing experiences of older women are therefore an important part of any consideration of gender divisions and housing. A particularly important dimension is the fact that the number of people over the age of 85 (the majority of them women) is forecast to increase by 60 per cent between 1981 and 2001, although the growth in the 60–75 age group is slowing down owing to the decline in the birth rate during the 1920s and 1930s.

While increasing numbers of retired people have experienced better standards of living in old age during the last 20 years, this is based on the spread of occupational pensions and is therefore determined by labour market experience during their working life. As Bull and Poole point out:

The total income of all pensioners as a whole has been growing but not all pensioners have shared equally in it. To ignore this fact is to ignore the great diversity of economic circumstances within a population which spans over 30 years of age as well as to neglect the extent to which inequalities of wealth between groups of the working population are perpetuated into old age(54).

As women are disadvantaged within the labour market during their working lives, this economic disadvantage is carried over into old age, although it may be mitigated to some extent by a husband's occupational pension. Older female-headed households have a high risk of being in poverty. This arises both because of women's general economic disadvantages and also because their savings in retirement have on average to last longer than for male-headed households. Many women experience an old age characterised by poverty which lasts for 30 years.

However, this group is more likely than other households headed by women to be owner-occupiers, predominantly because they will have inherited their home from a spouse or parents. Their high risk of being in poverty means they are also at risk of not being able to repair and maintain their property. This is reflected in the analysis of the English House Condition Survey which found that people aged over 75 (the majority of whom are women) were more likely than other groups to have homes which were unfit or lacked amenities and that elderly persons living alone (again the majority of them women) were more likely to be living in poor conditions compared to elderly couples(55).

As mentioned above, elderly women have been dispro-portionately represented amongst tenants in the protected part of the private rented sector. In London, which accounts for the largest share of the private rented sector nationally, elderly women tenants are more likely than any other group to be lacking amenities(56). However, although the private rented sector is an important source of housing inequality amongst older women, it is declining in significance because of the long-term decline of the private rented sector. The local authority and housing association sectors have become a much more important source of housing for older people, and particularly for older women.

Table 4.2 indicates that 43 per cent of households headed by women over the age of 60 are in local authority and housing association accommodation compared to 33 per cent of male-headed households over 60. Again, this is undoubtedly linked to women's economic disadvantages. It may also be linked to the provision of sheltered accommodation in the public rented and housing association sectors (although the significance of sheltered housing should not be overestimated as it only accounts for 5 per cent of all pensioner households). There is little information about the household characteristics of owners and tenants of private sector sheltered housing but the research on the subsidised sector indicates that the majority of tenants are women – 80 per cent in one study of the tenants of a sheltered scheme run by Anchor Housing Association(57). Since access into private sector sheltered housing depends on ability to pay, we would expect that female-headed households would be under-represented. It could be argued therefore that households headed by older women have been disadvantaged by the shift from public sector provision of sheltered housing to private sector provision which took place during the 1980s.

Five per cent of the population over the age of 60 is in some form of residential – that is, institutional – care. The majority of people in residential care are women, partly because of women's longevity. The overriding reason for entering residential care is the lack of suitable housing with personal care support. Public expenditure cuts in housing and social services during the 1980s made it less likely that such requirements would be met within the older person's home – and women of course are less likely to have the economic resources to meet their own requirements. At the same time, the availability of funding residential care through DSS board and lodging payments brought about the expansion of private sector residential homes(58).

There is concern about the standards and quality of service provided in these establishments(59) but very little research or political action on this aspect of what could be called 'hidden homelessness'. The Centre for Policy on Ageing questions the way in which residential care is often the only option for those confronted with what are essentially housing problems and argues that that many people could stay in their homes given support(60).

Fennell et al argue:

> Suffering from the double burden of ageism and sexism, older women have for too long been marginalised by society at large and by the literature stemming from sociology, gerontology and feminism(61).

Such invisibility is also apparent in housing studies and is reflected in the way that older women's interests are not addressed in housing policy debates.

Gender divisions and housing

The above analysis of women's housing experiences enables us to identify that, over their life cycle, housing advantage and disadvantage is crucially linked to whether women live in a household where there is a man present, and, when they do, their housing situation is primarily determined by the man's social and economic status. When women are dependent on their own social and economic status – for example, young single women, women who choose not to live with a man, women experiencing relationship breakdown and older women who have outlived their spouses – it is that status which makes them vulnerable to housing disadvantage.

The academic debate on gender divisions and housing is emerging out of a purely descriptive approach, where the focus tends to be on particular groups of women and where it is difficult to avoid presenting women's issues as some kind of 'special need'. Feminist sociology is concerned with identifying not just the evidence of women's experience of housing inequality but also the sources of this experience and how it relates to women's general socio-economic position. There is also a growing recognition that a gender dimension to the analysis of housing systems and policies is necessary to understand their socio-economic and political context. The final part of this chapter seeks to establish the current stage in the debate and to highlight some unanswered questions.

The theoretical debate about women's experience of housing inequality stresses the significance of women's economic inequality in structuring the pattern of inequality. It is important, therefore, to summarise this evidence. On the face of it, women's economic situation has improved during the past 20 years. Women now constitute 43 per cent of the workforce(62) and legislation has established the principle of equal pay and outlawed discrimination on the grounds of gender or marital status.

However, key differences can be identified in the nature of men's and women's participation in the labour force. Table 4.5 has already established the fluctuating economic activity rate over women's life cycle and the importance of part-time work at particular stages in that life cycle. Men do not experience the same fluctuations, and the percentage of men who are part-time workers is negligible.

Furthermore, the rise in women's employment conceals the continuing sexual divisions within the labour force. Women are concentrated into certain industries, and into certain types of jobs. As Linda McDowell points out, there are two types of sexual division evident within the labour force. The first is 'horizontal segregation', a term used to describe the fact that half of all employed men work in jobs where at least 90 per cent of the workforce is male and half of all women where at least three-quarters of their co-workers are women(63). The second is 'vertical segregation' which occurs:

> Within those occupations where both women and men are employed, [where] despite almost two decades of equal opportunity legislation that makes discrimination on the basis of sex illegal, women remain concentrated at the bottom of the hierarchies of pay and promotion opportunities(64).

These two forms of segregation result in women's average pay rates, for full-time work, being significantly lower than men's – 67 per cent in 1988(65).

In terms of housing opportunities, it is not just the economic disadvantages that women experience when they are in full-time work, but the fact that, over their life-cycle, women are very likely to go through periods of not being in paid employment and of working part time. These economic disadvantages of course become more and more important as owner-occupation increases, for secure, full-time employment is necessary in order to become and remain an owner-occupier.

An important link with women's employment experiences is the continuing sexual division of labour within the home. A number of studies carried out during the 1980s indicate that women continue to take the major responsibility for both housework and child care(66). These studies are confirmed by the fact that, while having young children has no effect on men's economic activity rates, it is the most important factor influencing whether or not women work, or whether they work full time or part time(67). Women's caring role is not, however, confined to caring for young children. The ageing of the elderly population – i.e. the increasing number of frail elderly – has resulted in an increase in 'informal caring'. Such caring for an elderly relative is usually carried out by women and the demands on their time are likely to come during their forties and fifties when otherwise they would be looking to returning to full-time work as their children grow older.

Women's caring role, both in terms of the care of young children and of adults, takes place in the context of inadequate community support. They receive very little help with caring which means that their participation in the labour force is curtailed and they become dependent on either their partners' wages or on state benefits. While not denying the importance of the woman's wage to most household finances, it is clear that the man's wage will be the most important contribution to the household. Whether the man's wage is low, non-existent through unemployment, or whether there is a man in the household at all, will to a large extent determine whether woman's caring role is carried out in poverty or not – including whether it is carried out in adequate housing conditions or not.

Gender divisions in the labour market, therefore, can be identified as being an important factor in determining the nature of women's housing opportunities. However, this is not a one-way causal relationship but, in fact, a complex interrelationship between the housing system and housing policies and the labour market. One example of this is illustrated by Linda McDowell. Her analysis of cities linked the position of women in the labour market with the spatial divisions of urbanisation by identifying the importance of the physical separation of work from home in the organisation of the urban environment:

> During this century, the operation of the land market, both unregulated and regulated by state control, has resulted in the separation of what British planners have euphemistically termed 'non-conforming' uses – domestic and productive activities(68).

She identifies how the growing separation of home and work was associated with the economic segregation of women, particularly at times of suburban expansion (for example, in the period immediately following the Second World War):

> The structure of urban housing markets legitimates the ideological significance of privatised family life and domesticity and institutions in both the public and private sectors operate on these assumptions in the production, allocation, and location of housing. Thus the division of space reflects and influences the social relations between men and women in cities(69).

In other words, we can identify the importance of women's exclusion from the labour force at particular historical periods, and their generally 'flexible' attachment to the labour force, for the way in which cities are structured. The separation of the public and the private which results also then serves to legitimise women's role within the home: as McDowell identifies, the 'anti-urban ideal' is very much associated with women's domestic role. It is also, of course, significant that women have very little say in the design of cities or dwellings. The whole process is an important part of women's powerlessness(70).

However, the complexities of the relationship between capitalism, the patriarchal household and the housing system are also illustrated by the tensions which are created by the separation of home from work, particularly in the current situation. Industrial restructuring during the 1980s has increased the importance of women's (part-time) work within the economy(71). Other demographic changes, namely the decline in the number of young workers, have made married women even more important as a source of cheap labour. At the same time, the increase in the number of over-75-year-olds has increased the caring role which women carry on within the home. Furthermore, all these developments have occurred at a time of decreasing community support for women's unpaid labour.

Thus, while in the past the ideology of the separation of home and work may have served capital well – in the encouragement of women's unpaid labour in the home – there are some circumstances where this ideal may be put on the back burner because women are needed in ever greater numbers in the labour force. It may also be that this demand for women's labour will change the state's approach to the desirability of women caring for children and adult dependants in isolation and with no help from outside agencies.

All this is part of the socio-economic background to the theoretical debate on women's housing inequality. Watson identifies the focus for feminist sociologists when she argues that:

> Housing policy and provision . . . assumes and is structured around the patriarchal family form. This structuring acts to create and reinforce women's dependent economic status and domestic role. Intricately related to this dominance of the family model is the marginalisation in the housing system of households which do not fit this traditional model. Many of these households . . . are headed by women(72).

Watson summarises a more general recognition by feminists that housing policy is part and parcel of an ideological support, and encouragement, of the 'nuclear family' (i.e. husband, wife and children). This can certainly be identified from the language in which policy is put forward – and by all governments in the last 40 years. Housing policy statements, from the 1945 White Paper of the Labour Government to the Conservative Party's 1979 Manifesto, are dominated by the assumption that the 'normal' household, whose housing needs must be addressed, is comprised of a married couple and their children. As Mary Brailey argues:

> According to these assumptions, the family – two parents and children – is the focal point of the life-cycle of individuals. Home and family are almost synonymous. Other sorts of household – single people, childless couples, one-parent families – are seen as formative, transitional or residual stages of the family. It is argued that the housing needs of people in these other stages may only be legitimately met if it can be done without prejudice to the position of families. People who live outside the framework of the family – older, unmarried people; people living together in groups; those who choose to have children as single parents; gay couples – are regarded as deviants, to be viewed with either pity or suspicion(73).

Focusing on the local authority sector, Brailey argues that both the provision of housing and its allocation assumes that the family is the 'normal' household type and other household types are either not considered at all within definitions of housing need, or are considered to have a 'special' housing need. This is particularly evident in the case of the statutory rights to a public sector dwelling given to certain groups through the 1977 Housing (Homeless Persons) Act (now consolidated within the 1985 Housing Act). These statutory rights have been very important in enabling women to get access to affordable housing but not because women as such are given any priority. Rather, a woman's rights under the legislation, with very limited exceptions under the 'vulnerable' categories, are entirely based on her having dependent children or being pregnant. As Frances Logan points out:

> It is a continuation of the philosophy already observed in matrimonial law generally of creating a seeming priority for women which is in fact a priority for the bearers and carers of children, and not for women themselves(74).

We can extend Brailey's analysis to the owner-occupied sector and point out that a housing policy with the aim of encouraging owner-occupation assumes that households will have a full-time wage-earner with an unbroken working career. We have shown that women's economic life-cycle does not generally conform to this pattern. Housing policy, by asserting that owner-occupation is the tenure suited to most people's housing needs, assumes therefore that women will be part of a male-headed household and that their housing needs will be synonymous with this household type.

Brailey highlights the implications of all this for women:

> The effect of this bias towards the nuclear family hits hard on all other groups of people. But this is especially significant for women, since to be reluctantly forced into or trapped within marriage means, for many women, being expected to provide domestic help, childcare and emotional support for no pay and the status of a dependent adjunct both in her own eyes and in the eyes of the world(75).

Women's role within the family is an undoubtedly important part of the state's rhetoric on housing policy and Conservative politicians' statements do highlight the nature of women's oppression. A commitment to 'family values' has been a particularly strong motivation of the Thatcher government. However, it will not do to explain women's disadvantage within the housing system in terms of a straightforward support of the nuclear family. Ideas do not exist within a vacuum but in a historically specific material context and the state is quite capable of changing its stance on women's role within the home: the most obvious instance being during the Second World War when women's labour was needed outside the home and the ideological stance was that it was women's duty to leave their children in state-run nurseries. Current demographic trends which have resulted in a shortage of young workers – a traditional source of cheap labour – are now creating a similar atmosphere of encouragment for women to work outside the home.

Could it be argued that housing policy is an ideological expression of economic interests? The two major traditions in sociology, functionalism and Marxism, would answer this question in remarkably similar ways. Both focus on the importance of the roles performed by the 'family' in modern capitalist society. Thus, functionalism insists that the modern nuclear family with its division of labour between husband and wife is the most efficient way of carrying out two vital functions of socialising children into society's norms and values and of 'stabilising the adult personalities' (i.e. providing a stable emotional environment, particularly for the male worker, which will give him both the incentive to work and emotional protection from the alienation of the harsh economic world). Using socio-psychological models of roles within small groups but fundamentally resting on a biological deterministic view of gender roles, Talcott Parsons argues that the division of tasks into the 'expressive' role of the woman and the 'instrumental' role of the man is an inevitable result of the demands of a modern industrial economy. The sexual division of labour within the home – i.e. where the woman performs a 'caring' role and the man goes out to work – is thus a function of the economy's, and society's, demands(76).

The Marxist tradition within sociology also focuses on the importance of the family's role, and women's role within it, for capitalist production. The two major emphases within modern Marxist sociology have been around the importance to capitalism of the reproduction of labour power, and the notion of women as a reserve army of labour.

It has been argued that capitalism needs women's unpaid labour in the home because this is the best way of reproducing the conditions of production. There is difficulty in determining exactly what is meant by 'reproduction' but Edholm, Harris and Young state that three, analytically separate, parts to the concept can be distinguished – social reproduction, reproduction of the labour force and biological reproduction(77). The concept has been used in various ways but one of the most important has been the 'domestic labour debate', which revolved around the argument that:

> Women's unpaid work in the home serves to reproduce both the forces and the relations of production: at an economic level the housewife's labour reproduces on a daily and generational basis the labour power of the worker, and at an ideological level it reproduces the relations of dominance and subordination required by capitalist production(78).

Other Marxist sociologists have argued that capitalism requires a reserve army of labour – reserve in the sense that such labour can be pulled into the workforce in times of expansion and expelled in times of economic contraction without the potential of social disruption. A woman's primary role as carer within the home, supported by a male wage, is said to make it possible for her to fulfil this role, and also makes her a source of cheap labour as her wages do not have to support a family(79). This type of explanation for women's economic position has been questioned by the fact that during the 1980s recession, it was predominantly men's jobs which were disappearing and that industrial restructuring in fact resulted in an increase in part-time jobs for women. However, it could still be argued that women are an important source of cheap, and flexible, labour and that it is their role within the home which makes them so.

If we follow either the functionalist or the Marxist perspective in explaining women's social and economic experiences, we could argue that the housing system – where both the operation of the public housing sector, and the private market make it difficult for women to get adequate housing for themselves and their children unless they are part of a male-headed household – is an important part of the state's support for this system of unpaid labour, this support being necessary to the capitalist economy.

Michele Barrett, however, argues that 'it is inadequate to attempt to grasp the character of women's oppression in contemporary capitalism in terms of the supposed needs of capitalism itself' (80). To do this is to fall into the functionalist trap of teleology; that is, the assumption that by establishing a function of a social process we can explain its existence. Furthermore, it leaves us with the problem of explaining women's oppression under different modes of production. Finally, as Barrett points out, the nuclear family form of household 'is not the only possible form for an efficient reproduction of labour-power in capitalist relations of production. It is the product of historical struggles between men and women, both within the working class and the bourgeoisie'(81).

Munro and Smith's research illustrates Barrett's argument in the housing context in that they identify the difficulty with relying on capitalism's need for women's unpaid labour in explaining gender divisions in housing experiences. If the housing system and housing policy operate in the way that they do because capitalism needs the patriarchal family, why is it that some 'non-family' households (e.g. some single men, dual-income couples with no children) are not marginalised in the housing market? Munro and Smith argue that:

> While housing systems undoubtedly do operate to reproduce gender relations, they also . . . reproduce other sets of social relations. In view of this, the effect of family status cannot be considered apart from the effect of a second explanatory framework, relating to labour market conditions(82).

In other words, ability to pay for housing is the crucial determinant of housing opportunities and this economic power is not solely determined by whether a household conforms to a nuclear family structure.

Another interesting point which comes out of Munro and Smith's research is the extent to which the expansion of home-ownership amongst skilled manual workers is dependent on women's earnings. This constitutes a pressure on women to do paid work outside the home, even when they have small children, and shows up a contradiction between one government policy ('the right to buy') and another ('women should stay at home to look after their children').

Conclusion

So what can be concluded from the debate on gender divisions and housing so far? We have seen quite clearly that there is a sexual division of labour within the workforce and that women's resulting economic disadvantages both limit their autonomous housing opportunities and link the housing experiences of women in male-headed households to men's socio-economic status. But this causal relationship is not merely a one-way relationship. The 'family' is the setting for women's caring role, which in itself has a limiting effect on women's economic activity. While women's autonomous housing opportunities are also limited, this has the effect of making it more difficult for women to live outside the household structure in which they are inevitably economically dependent. However, we must also recognise that women's caring role does not only take place within male-headed households but also within female-headed households; single parents are still caring for their children and many carers of elderly people are single women – and these women also have their economic activity limited by their tasks within the home.

It is also important to recognise that there are divisions other than those of gender within the labour market, principally, of course, class and race inequalities, and these in turn are reflected in differing housing opportunities. An unanswered question is whether gender is a more important determinant of women's social and economic status than class or race, and indeed how the three social divisions interrelate. The very little research that there is on the housing experiences of black women indicates that they experience greater difficulties in getting access to adequate housing than white women do. For example, a survey carried out by the Black Women and Housing Group of women presenting as homeless in the London Boroughs of Wandsworth and Southwark, indicated that black women were likely to experience homelessness for longer periods of time than white women, were more likely to be offered poorer-quality housing and expressed greater levels of dissatisfaction with their housing than white women(83). Our previous chapter illustrated quite clearly the way in which the housing experiences of black people generally are influenced by both direct and indirect discrimination. However, much more research is required in order to be able to answer the question of how gender, class and race interact to influence women's housing experiences.

In the current context, the housing system – and housing policy itself – generates gender inequalities. However, we cannot satisfactorily explain this by reference to capitalism's support for the patriarchal family form. The most important features of the current housing scene – the spread of home-ownership, and the residualisation of council housing – are the expressions of historically specific financial, industrial and political interests (see Chapter 6). The importance of women's unpaid labour within the family may be one expression of these interests but it cannot be the whole story.

What is clear, however, is that the links between economic and housing advantage and disadvantage which are an inevitable part of these recent developments in the housing system means that women's lack of power in relation to men is compounded. While labour market position remains the primary determinant of housing experiences, women will experience difficulty in gaining independent access to housing. Any analysis of housing inequalities must remain incomplete unless the gender dimension of both housing policy and the housing market is an integral part of such an analysis.

Notes

1. *General Household Survey, 1986* (1989), HMSO, Fig 3B, p.10.
2. Greater London Council (1986), *Women and Housing*, p.54.
3. Nationwide Anglia Building Society (1989), *Lending to Women 1978–1988*.
4. *Family Expenditure Survey, 1987*, (1989), HMSO, Table 26, pp.70–1.
5. M. Munro and S.J. Smith (1989), 'Gender and housing: broadening the debate', *Housing Studies*, Vol.4, No.1, January, p.9.
6. *Ibid*, p.11.
7. *General Household Survey, 1986* (1989), p.29, Table 4.9.
8. O. Sullivan (1986), 'Housing movements of the divorced and separated', *Housing Studies*, Vol.1, No.1, January, p.38.
9. M. Murphy and O. Sullivan (1986), 'Unemployment, housing and household structure among young adults', *Journal of Social Policy*, 15, 2.
10. A. E. Holmans, S. Nandy and A. C. Brown (1987), 'Household formation and dissolution and housing tenure: a longitudinal perspective', *Social Trends, 17*, HMSO.
11. G. Pascall (1986), *Social Policy: a feminist analysis*, Tavistock, pp.140–3.
12. *Social Trends*, (1989), HMSO, p.44.
13. *General Household Survey 1986* (1989), Table 8.22, p.105.
14. Low Pay Unit (1989), *Ten Years On: the poor decade*, p.15.
15. M. Brailey (1985), *Women's Access to Council Housing*, Planning Exchange Occasional Paper No.25, The Planning Exchange.
16. *Ibid*, p.37.
17. Institute of Housing and Scottish Homeless Group (1985), *Housing and Marital Breakdown: the local authority response*, University of Strathclyde.
18. J. Conway (ed) (1988), *Prescription for Poor Health: the crisis for homeless families*, SHAC.
19. Brailey (1985), p.57.
20. *General Household Survey, 1986* (1989), p.11.
21. A. Evans and S. Duncan (1988), *Responding to Homelessness: local authority policy and practice*, HMSO, p.43.
22. P. Niner (1989), *Homelessness in Nine Local Authorities: case studies of policy and practice*, HMSO.
23. London Research Centre (1986), *Docklands Housing Needs Survey 1985*.
24. Evans and Duncan (1988), p.33.

25. Housing Services Advisory Group (1978), *The Housing of One-Parent Families*, HMSO, p.8.
26. M. Brailey (1985), p.67.
27. *General Household Survey, 1981* (1983), HMSO, Tables 2.15–2.19.
28. O. Sullivan (1986), p.36
29. Department of Health and Social Security (1974), *Report of the Committee on One-Parent Families*, HMSO, p.364; J. Nixon (1979), *Fatherless Families on FIS*, DHSS Research Report No. 4.
30. S. Edwards (1986), *The Police Reponse to Domestic Violence*, London Strategic Policy Unit.
31. E. Stanko (1985), *Intimate Intrusion: women's experience of male violence*, Routledge and Kegan Paul.
32. Quoted in *Domestic Violence: an overview of the literature* (1989), Home Office Research Study 107, HMSO.
33. Hough and Mayhew (1983), *The British Crime Survey: First Report*, Home Office Research Study 76, HMSO.
34. V. Binney, G. Harkell and J. Nixon (1985),'Refuges and Housing for Battered Women', in J. Pahl(ed), *Private Violence and Public Policy*, Routledge and Kegan Paul, pp.l66–7.
35. *Ibid*, p.l67
36. *Ibid*, pp.167–8.
37. M. Brailey (1985), p.34.
38. P. Niner (1989), p.88.
39. Evans and Duncan (1989), p.17.
40. Binney, Harkell and Nixon (1985), p.177.
41. M. Brailey (1985), p.60.
42. Munro and Smith (1989), p.9.
43. London Research Centre (1988), *Access to Housing in London*, p.17.
44. *General Household Survey, 1986* (1989), Table 8.5 and Table 8.18.
45. H. Austerberry and S. Watson (1983), *Women on the Margins*, City University, p.1.
46. S. Watson and H. Austerberry (1986), *Housing and Homelessness: a feminist perspective*, Routledge and Kegan Paul, p.9.
47. Office of Population Censuses and Surveys (1976), *Hostels and Lodgings for Single People*, HMSO.
48. Birmingham Standing Conference on Single Homelessness (1981), *Current Provision for the Single Homeless*.
49. J. Gilbert (1986), *Not Just a Roof*, Birmingham Standing Conference on Single Homelessness, p.5.
50. See Austerberry and Watson (1983); Gilbert (1986).
51. Austerberry and Watson (1983), p.61.
52. *Ibid*, p.53.
53. Greater London Council (1986), *Private Tenants in London*.
54. J. Bull and L. Poole (1989), *Not Rich, Not Poor*, SHAC and Anchor Housing Trust, p.13.

55. *English House Condition Survey, 1986* (1989), HMSO, p.41.

56. Greater London Council (1986), Table 9.16.

57. G. Fennell (1986), *Anchor's Older People: what do they think?*, Anchor Housing Association.

58. Bull and Poole (1989), p.61–2.

59. B. Holmes and A. Johnson (1988), *Cold Comfort: the scandal of private rest homes*, Souvenir Press.

60. H. Taylor (1987), *Growing Old Together*, Centre for Policy on Ageing.

61. G. Fennell, C. Phillipson and H. Evers (1986), *The Sociology of Old Age*, Open University Press, p.97.

62. *General Household Survey, 1986* (1989), Table 8.26.

63. C. Hamnett, L. McDowell and P. Sarre (eds) (1989), *The Changing Social Structure*, Sage Publications, pp.167–8.

64. *Ibid*, p.168.

65. Low Pay Unit, (1989), p.15.

66. See, for example, D. Piachaud (1984), *Round About Fifty Hours a Week*, Child Poverty Action Group; A. Hunt (1986), *A Survey of Women's Employment*, HMSO; R. Jowell et al (1988), *British Social Attitudes: Fifth Report*, Gower.

67. Family Policy Studies Centre (1987), *Inside the Family*.

68. L. McDowell (1983), 'City and home: urban housing and the sexual division of space' in M. Evans and C. Ungerson (eds), *Sexual Divisions, Patterns and Processes*, Tavistock, p.143.

69. *Ibid*.

70. See A. Ravetz (1989), 'A view from the interior', in J. Attfield and P. Kirkham, *A View from the Interior*, Women's Press; Matrix (1984), *Making Space: women and the man-made environment*, Pluto Press.

71. J. Allen and D. Massey (1988), *The Economy in Question*, Sage Publications.

72. S. Watson (1986), 'Women and housing or feminist housing analysis?' *Housing Studies*, Vol.1, No.1, p.1.

73. M. Brailey (1985), p.6.

74. F. Logan (1988), *Homelessness and Relationship Breakdown: one-parent families*, National Council for One-Parent Families, p.57.

75. M. Brailey (1985), p.7.

76. See Talcott Parsons (1964), *Essays in Sociological Theory*, Free Press, New York.

77. F. Edholm, O. Harris and K. Young (1977), 'Conceptualising women', *Critique of Anthropology*, No.9/10.

78. M. Barrett (1980), *Women's Oppression Today: problems in Marxist feminist analysis*, Verso, p.21.

79. M. Power, 'From home production to wage labour: women as a reserve army of labour', *Review of Radical Political Economics*, Vol.XV, No.1.

80. M. Barrett (1980), p.249.
81. *Ibid*, p.249.
82. Munro and Smith (1989), p.5.
83. Black Women and Housing Group (1988), *Homelessness and Black Women*. Paper presented to Conference on The Future of Race Equality in Housing, November 1988, London Race and Housing Research Unit.

5 | Housing inequality and social problems

The previous three chapters have identified the ways in which housing inequalities are manifestations of wider social and economic inequalities. The general context of housing policy and practice is thus clearly established. However, the day-to-day experience of housing managers is focused more narrowly on specific phenomena. This chapter takes three issues – 'problem' estates, homelessness, racial harassment – which are generally experienced as problems for housing management, examining both the empirical reality of such issues and the relevance of a sociological perspective.

The difficulties for housing managers presented by the three phenomena we have taken are quite clear. In the case of 'problem' estates, we are talking about housing estates/areas where property is difficult to let and where various management problems are common – vandalism, rubbish, misuse of communal space, and so on. In the case of homelessness, where the number of people presenting themselves to the local authority as homeless has increased at a faster rate than the supply of lettings to accommodate them, pressure on front-line staff is significant. There is also the financial pressure on the local authority when homeless households are placed in expensive temporary accommodation. Racial harassment is a problem for housing managers when it presents itself in the form of neighbour disputes; when fear of racial harassment means that applicants are unwilling to accept offers of property in certain areas; where actual racial harassment creates a demand for transfers. Moreover, political pressure may insist that housing managers take this on generally as a housing management issue.

From the housing manager's point of view all these phenomena are characterised by conflicting pressures – demands by tenants for a better management and maintenance service, by applicants for a home, by central government for greater efficiency, by some local politicians and organisations such as the Commission for Racial Equality for action on racial harassment, and so on. It is also important to recognise that housing managers bring their own ideas, preconceptions and prejudices to their practice. If housing management is to establish professional standards, practice must be informed by a perspective which enables a standing back from the chaotic murkiness of these conflicts, pressures and prejudices. Sociology as a discipline has a key role to play in this.

'PROBLEM' HOUSING ESTATES

It has been a characteristic feature of cities in industrial capitalist Britain that they contain 'bad' areas. Jack London's journey into the 'abyss' of the East End of London at the turn of century illustrates the horror and fear which the concentration of poverty has always evoked in the minds of those who are better off:

> Not a hansom did I meet with in all my drive, while mine was like an apparition from another and better world, the way the children ran after it and alongside. And as far as I could see were the solid walls of brick, the slimy pavements, and the screaming streets; and for the first time in my life the fear of the crowd smote me. It was like the fear of the sea; and the miserable multitudes, street upon street, seemed so many waves of a vast and malodorous sea, lapping about me and threatening to well up and over me(1).

During the nineteenth century and for the early part of the twentieth century these areas consisted of privately rented accommodation. However, with the growth of council housing and the decline of the private rented sector, particularly since the Second World War, such areas have increasingly been dominated by council housing and have given rise to the identification of so-called problem estates. The concentration of the poorest sections of the population in council housing, which we identified in Chapter 2, is an important part of this issue, as we shall see. We start, however, with an analysis of what is meant by the term problem estates, before moving on to looking at three different approaches to the phenomenon.

The commonest housing management term applied to the estates in question is 'difficult to let'. From a tenant's point of view, however, it is the kind of housing which they don't want to be offered and which if they accept, they find 'difficult to live in' and 'difficult to get out of', as Taylor puts it in one of the few attempts at looking at problem estates from the point of view of tenants(2). Such estates are predominantly characterised by poor housing conditions and inadequate repairs and maintenance.

One tenant offered a flat on London's Broadwater Farm Estate describes her experience:

> The first thing that actually hit me was the condition of the estate and the flat that I was offered itself. The estate was dirty, there was lots of vandalism, lots of grass, the flat I was allocated was in a really bad state of repair. There was no kitchen sink, there was no kitchen cupboard, there was a hole in the floor. It was just horrendous. It looked to me like squatters had lived there. All the passages had graffiti and stains all over it. It was absolutely disgusting and I was told, 'sorry, no money for decorations'(3).

The social stigma which attaches to living on these sorts of estates is also an important part of the residents' experiences of living there. They may experience problems with getting hire purchase, or with obtaining employment, solely because of the views which are held by those outside the estate of the kind of people who live there(4). Residents on a problem estate studied by Frances Reynolds reported the way in which their estate's bad reputation affected their lives:

> 'All the people at work say, oh I wouldn't like to live *there*. I really hate to have to say where I live'; 'I couldn't ask anyone here, I'd feel ashamed'; 'I do sometimes feel beyond the pale. I usually tell people that I live near Netherton village'(5).

This type of experience highlights the definition of the problem estate from the tenants' perspective. From the viewpoint of housing management, under pressure to reduce the period that a dwelling is vacant to a minimum, an estate to which applicants are reluctant to move and where existing tenants are trying to move out is a problem primarily because it presents difficulties for lettings officers and because the higher level of vacant properties is likely to lead to increased vandalism and other management problems. As Anne Power described, when writing of 20 estates which were surveyed by the Department of the Environment's Priority Estates Project (PEP):

> Empty dwellings created a chain reaction. More people refused to come and live there because of the atmosphere of dereliction. Vandalism and theft to empty dwellings increased with the volume of empty dwellings. The cost of all this damage was substantial and, coupled with the loss of rent income, generated serious financial losses. Often squatting developed(6).

Other problems for housing management which are commonly associated with 'difficult-to-let' estates are high rent arrears, and the misuse of communal facilities.

While housing managers may be in agreement about the management consequences of problem estates, there is disagreement about what should be done about them. These disagreements stem from different assumptions about the causes of the problem. The Priority Estates Project, established just before the 1979 General Election, epitomises the type of approach to problem estates which focuses on the way in which inadequacies in housing management can lead to the characteristics described above. However, the popularity of the approach has waned as the very existence of council housing has been undermined. Whereas the PEP philosophy held the basic assumption that the management of housing was a legitimate activity for local authorities (although it also encouraged tenant co-operatives), the ascendant philosophy of the late 1980s is based on the assumption that problem estates occur when state intervention distorts the operation of the free market, resulting in such things as architectural features which have a profound influence on people's behaviour, and a 'dependency culture' which prevents people taking responsibility for their own lives(7).

In order to compare these two different approaches, we will first analyse the approach of the Priority Estates Project, assessing the adequacy of its recommendations for making an impact on problem estates, and we will then discuss the perspective put forward by Alice Coleman, author of *Utopia on Trial: vision and reality in planned housing*, which is based on the assumption that state planning in itself is the problem. After this we will discuss a number of sociological studies of problem estates which have found labelling theory useful, concluding the section with an assessment as to what all these different approaches have to offer housing management.

Priority Estates Project

Anne Power, the consultant to the DoE's Priority Estates Project and the prime motivator behind the initiative, argues that a shift from women housing managers who combined the roles of rent collector, repairs clerk and welfare advisor to a male-dominated profession which split up the different parts of the housing management function and removed them to distant town halls, had a fundamental effect on the experience of being a council tenant. The consequences were particularly serious once council housing started to house the poorest sections of the working class in the context of slum clearance programmes from 1930 onwards:

> Social problems quickly emerged in the uprooted new communities, and while the women housing managers were increasingly influential on the welfare aspects of slum demolition and rehousing, they were largely ignored on matters of overall housing management by the rapidly expanding local authorities. The public landlords carried out their duties to tenants through assorted departments: Finance, Engineers, Surveyors, Sanitary Departments and Town Clerk. They threw up their own municipally oriented housing body, founded in 1932 as the Institute of Housing, which openly opposed the integrated and localised emphasis of the rival, and better qualified, Society of Women Housing Managers, founded in 1916 to carry on Octavia Hill's work and tradition(8).

A housing management service which was remote from tenants, which failed to interest itself in the social mix on its estates and was not concerned with whether an estate provided adequate social and community amenities resulted in all the characteristic features of problem estates. Power draws particular attention to the allocation of housing which, she says, was 'probably the single most dominant question' on the PEP Survey estates:

> There were above-average concentrations of many disadvantaged groups on the 20 estates. Thus homeless families, one-parent families, large families, racial minorities and unemployed adults were all over-represented(9).

This situation had come about because the presence of unpopular estates in local councils' housing stock (unpopular because of design, condition, location and/or reputation) meant that housing officers made distinctions between tenants who 'deserved' the more popular property and those who did not and/or found themselves pushed into offering the least-popular property to the most desperate as they were the only applicants who would accept it.

The concentration on the least-popular estates of the poorest and most vulnerable households was then compounded by an inefficient and inadequate housing management and maintenance service. The PEP's solution was to re-introduce the local management techniques which women like Octavia Hill and Irene Barclay had pioneered. This would mean, for example, introducing a local lettings policy aimed at creating a greater diversity of household type on an estate and fewer empty properties, local repairs teams, a local rent collection service through an estate-based management office, a resident caretaking service. These management initiatives were to be combined with investment in the external environment on the estates, improvements to cleansing services, better community facilities and, most important of all, a concerted attempt to involve tenants in the running of their estates.

These were the PEP's recommendations but not all were adopted on the estates which their survey covered. The most important measure, that of opening up local offices, had the greatest effect:

> Their impact on the local community was immediate, opening up extensive and frequent contact between landlord and tenants and providing an on-the-spot service, cutting through red tape and acting as a pressure point and arbiter with the council(10).

The challenge of the PEP approach is that it shifts the focus of what is defined as the problem from tenants to housing management. Thus problem estates become a problem *of*, rather than a problem *for*, housing management. This, together with the emphasis on measures to create a sense of community on such estates, is an important counter to the stigmatisation from which such council tenants often suffer. It is possible, within this approach, for tenants to be given more influence over their housing opportunities and housing conditions.

However, one criticism of the PEP approach is that it does not go far enough in its recommendations for local authority action. If the most unpopular estates are not to be offered to the most desperate applicants, detailed allocations policies and procedures have to be developed which encourage a social mix throughout the local authority's housing stock and which put this aim over and above the organisational priority of minimising the void rate. It is also important that housing managers do not engage in the practice identified by Henderson and Karn in their research on Birmingham City Council – that of keeping the 'good' estates good by avoiding offering such properties to certain types of household. This research, which we have discussed in Chapter 3, provides a coherent explanation of how the organisational priorities of minimising the void rate and of protecting the 'good' estates lead to a concentration of the most powerless and vulnerable households on the poorer-quality estates.

Taylor broadens the issue of allocations to problem estates by emphasising that:

> Difficult-to-let estates are just one end of the spectrum of demand. They are low-demand council housing, which contrast with high-demand council housing which may be termed 'easy to let' estates. Although the latter are not identified as a 'problem' they are part of the same housing system as their difficult-to-let counterparts . . . It is misleading to identify just one part of the council housing sector – difficult-to-let estates – as a problem without seeing them within this overall perspective. The problem is one of council house variety and its resulting differential demand(11).

Taylor then goes on to argue that a tenant's need to move to a 'better' estate is just as important, if not more important, than the need for a particular size of dwelling, yet council allocation policies are focused almost exclusively on the straightforward physical aspects of housing need, such as how many rooms a household qualifies for.

Another criticism of the PEP approach is that it does not give sufficient emphasis to this physical aspect of problem estates, tending to lay more stress on the importance of encouraging tenants to take responsibility for their housing environment. Yet most problem estates are characterised by the juxtaposition of housing which needs resources put into it to make it tolerable to live in, and households which do not have sufficient resources to do this. A local authority can make a major impact on the experience of housing inequality on its most unpopular estates by targeting investment to such estates.

At the same time, the PEP approach seems to avoid the wider socio-economic context of the estates in question. The key point is that the phenomenon of problem estates is integrally linked to the socio-economic marginalisation of certain groups of people and/or certain areas. The 'Outer Estates In Britain' research project, carried out by the Centre for Environmental Studies, illustrated the way in which certain areas of the country dominated by council housing are also experiencing the general socio-economic marginalisation of their populations in the sense that their labour is no longer required by the local economy. The areas covered by this project experienced poor employment opportunities, brought about by the decline in local manufacturing industry which was then compounded by a lack of investment in service industries. All the estates exhibited higher than national incidences of unemployment (26 per cent in 1981 compared to a national average of 9 per cent), lower rates of car-ownership (29 per cent compared to 61 per cent nationally), the proportion of professional groups was only a fifth of the national average and the number of self-employed was only a third. The report stressed:

Unemployment has increased rapidly, and the income per head and spending power within the outer estates have gone down – making it even more difficult for existing and new activities serving the local market to survive or be created(12).

167

Some of the projects in the PEP survey had recognised the underlying problem of unemployment and several of them co-operated with other agencies on employment initiatives, usually involving young people in the area. However, 'while these had value in generating short-term jobs . . . they rarely had a lasting effect on the now chronic problem of unemployment'(13). The significance of economic disadvantage is also highlighted by the issue of rent arrears. Three-quarters of the estates in the PEP survey had higher rent arrears than the council average but the projects made little impact on this.

These wider socio-economic factors, over which local authorities in general have little control and housing departments in particular even less control, do not however enable housing managers to abdicate responsibility for the deprivation on such estates and in such areas. The recognition of the underlying causes counters the tendency to write off the inhabitants of problem estates as 'problem' people and provides the justification for targeting resources – in both physical and managerial terms – on such estates. Merely the recognition that categorising applicants as either 'deserving' or 'undeserving' is an inappropriate professional practice would be an important achievement, particularly when all these categories do is provide an intellectual justification for differential treatment of the desperate and not-so-desperate.

Utopia on Trial

Alice Coleman's research project, carried out by the Land Use Research Unit of King's College, focused on the physical design of the buildings rather than the nature of local authority housing management. Her book, *Utopia on Trial*, studies the relationship between the design of dwellings and estates, and 'social malaise'. 'Social malaise' is measured by: litter-dropping; graffiti-scrawling; pollution by excrement; pollution by urine; vandalism; family breakdown leading to children being placed in care. On each of these measures Coleman found that the incidence was higher in blocks of flats than it was in houses. She then set out to identify the particular features of blocks of flats responsible for this anti-social behaviour, concluding that the five 'ringleaders of the anti-social design gang' were: the number of dwellings in the block, the number of dwellings served by each entrance, the number of storeys in the block, the number of overhead walkways, and spatial organisation (which is measured along a continuum from private to public space).

The large-scale study – 4,099 blocks containing 106,520 dwellings, and 4,172 houses in the London boroughs of Southwark and Tower Hamlets – discusses the relationship between social malaise and particular design features, using a series of statistical correlations. Coleman points out that on the basis of pure chance, it would be expected that only four or five of the 90 correlations between the six measures of social malaise and the 15 design features would turn out to be statistically significant. She goes on to say:

> In reality no fewer than 83 are positively significant and 73 of these are very highly significant. Thus, correlation analysis strongly supports the evidence of the trend lines in showing that the association of poor design with social malaise is a genuine effect, far more consistent than could be expected by chance(14).

The difficulty with this statement is that it moves from correlation to causation; correlation analysis can show that there is a relationship between sets of variables but it cannot explain the relationship. This is an important criticism of Coleman's methodology although a number of other criticisms have also been documented in articles by Peter Dickens, Bill Hillier and Peter Williams(15). However, an underlying problem can also be identified in terms of the research's theoretical framework and it is this which we will focus on.

Coleman commences by distancing herself from environmental determinism, making a distinction between determinism, possibilism and probabilism. She defines environmental determinism as 'the belief that if the environment is changed, human behaviour will also change'(16). She then defines possibilism as the view that it is perfectly possible for everyone to be good and happy regardless of the nature of the environment and, if not, it is because they are 'problem people'(17). Coleman goes on to argue that:

> In reality, both the original determinist ideology and the possibilist rebound are over-simplifications. Human beings are all individuals and react in different ways. At one end of the spectrum there are a few who will always rise above adversity, no matter how appalling their environment, while at the other end there are a few who will always be sluts and criminals, even in ideal conditions. This could mean that design acts as a sliding scale. The worse it becomes, the more people it affects adversely, and the more intense becomes the atmosphere of social malaise.
>
> The sliding scale is probabilism which is not so much an ideology, as a willingness to see what degrees of environmental influence are revealed by factual evidence(18).

Having eschewed environmental determinism, however, Coleman adopts a theoretical framework which holds certain assumptions about the biological determinants of human behaviour. She starts from Carl Sagan's argument that there are four stages of development of the brain, each having particular implications for the activity of home-making. Sagan, in *The Dragons of Eden*, argues that the fourth stage of evolution, the primate-human neocortex, is 'associated with an upright stance, permitting a greater inflow of sensory information with better manual dexterity, reasoning, foresight, concern and ethical understanding. In home-making terms these powers are reflected in innovativeness, individuality and adaptability'(19). Coleman describes the implications of this for the issue of design and behaviour as follows:

Throughout most of human history our inbuilt guidance system has led us to produce a shelter with an adjoining piece of territory and to impress it with distinctive marks of identity. The decoration, the garden layout, the boundary fence, the name plate or other signals proclaim the residence of a unique family rather than a faceless unit among the masses. Even when division of labour passed the initiative to builders and architects, there was no conflict with the territorial imperative as long as people remained free to accept or reject what was on offer. Designs that incorporated defensible territory and scope for occupants to make their mark proved popular and were repeated, while those that denied these needs proved hard to sell and were discontinued. Natural selection was still in command.

However, when the power to make one's mark was taken from the individual and vested in authority, it began to be exercised on a different scale. Individual planners and architects cannot be blamed for this, as they too were following the human instinct to make one's mark as impressively as possible. They created designs that unified whole estates, and because the mark of the individual household was seen to interrupt the unit it came to be regarded as wrong. Blocks of flats can minimise such 'intrusions' and this may be part of the reason why they have commended themselves during the Utopian epoch(20).

It is this biologically deterministic theory of human behaviour to which some sociologists will take exception. To a government committed to market solutions to Britain's housing problems, however, the assumption that market forces ('natural selection') will produce benevolent outcomes if left to operate freely is welcome. Furthermore, certain sections of the housing profession, desperate to find solutions to their problem estates which are feasible within the restrictions imposed by central government, have welcomed the prescriptions of pulling down walkways, providing gardens and other design changes which are recommended by the research.

The housing manager may justifiably take the view that it does not matter so much what theory lies behind Coleman's recommendations; the essential question is whether the recommendations will work in alleviating the management difficulties caused by problem estates. A sociologist, however, in resisting a biological determinist theory, will point to a number of criticisms of Coleman's argument which throw into question the validity of the recommendations.

Firstly, the connection between one of Coleman's design features, high-rise blocks, and problem estates is not straightforward. On the one hand, there are many high-rise estates which do not fall into this category and on the other, there are many traditional low-rise estates which do. Coleman argues that her probabilistic position means that not everybody would react to certain design features and that therefore the existence of small numbers of problem-free high-rise blocks does not invalidate her thesis. However, it is not clear that problem-free high-rise blocks make up a minority of tower blocks. When the Housing Studies Group at the Polytechnic of the South Bank carried out the first-ever national survey of tower blocks in 1984, they found that the 170 local authorities in the country who have high-rise blocks within their areas did not regard such housing as generally more problematic than other forms of housing. Indeed, they concluded that 'there is no discernible physical type of property which displays consistent problems'(21).

It could be argued that Coleman's study is based on two London boroughs which are not necessarily representative and attention could be drawn to the way that authorities such as Liverpool stated in the South Bank study that between 80–90 per cent of their high-rise blocks were not considered to be 'problem housing' by the council. That study concluded that 'the reputation of high-rise as a form of housing which is socially unacceptable is not entirely deserved'(22).

It is also important to remember that, in the previously mentioned survey of problem estates carried out by PEP, one-third of such estates were traditional low-rise estates which did not generally exhibit the kind of design features that Coleman identifies as crucial factors in causing social malaise, yet the problems of vandalism, graffiti, petty crime, etc were all present.

There are alternative explanations for the social malaise features which, it has been argued, have more credence. Spicker, in his critique of *Utopia on Trial* argues 'the root cause of the problems of depressed council estates is poverty, or the lack of material resources'(23). His central argument is that many of the problems experienced by tenants living in some high-rise blocks would fade if the residents had more material resources and concludes that:

> Design has to be considered within its social context, and the adequacy of a building's design may be directly dependent on the resources available to its occupants. In areas occupied by wealthier people, many of the problems suffered in the depressed estates could be simply overcome . . . Buildings could be regularly cleaned and maintained; the tenants can afford to go out more. One of the obvious rejoinders to *Utopia on Trial* is to ask why high-rise flats in Bayswater or the Barbican are not slums. Many of the problems in council estates would not occur if the occupants were not poor people with children. Rich people without young children could afford the heating, pay for caretaking and maintainance, furnish to avoid noise, go out more. In central London, of course, they do(24).

This raises the issue again of why it is that problem estates contain above-average concentrations of disadvantaged households, such as homeless families, one-parent families, large families and generally of people on benefits. Our discussions in Chapters 2 and 3, and the section on the Priority Estates Project, referred to the ways in which allocation systems operate to place the most desperate (and those perceived as the least 'deserving') on the most unpopular estates. Twine and Williams' research, referred to in Chapter 2, also identifies the way in which allocation systems operate formal and informal mechanisms which result in a clear relationship between desirability of council dwellings and the social class of their occupants.

Although Coleman recognises that housing management does have a role to play, her central focus is on design features and their effects. Both the PEP research and subsequent experience of those local authorities who have attempted both design modifications and management initiatives indicate that it is attention to allocation policies, local management initiatives and an efficient repairs and maintenance service which have the most signficant effects on problem estates(25). These are the conclusions reached by the Safe Neighbourhoods Unit in its assessment of the design modifications made to the London Borough of Westminster's Mozart Estate on Coleman's recommendations. On this estate it was features such as walkways and lack of private ('defensible') space which were said to cause the social malaise. The Unit concluded that:

> To look at design on its own is misleading. According to Alice Coleman, certain estates are uniquely problematic because of design but in fact many of the ones she looks at are no worse than others in the same area. And these problems are largely due to economic and social factors(26).

Alice Coleman is currently leading a government-funded initiative (with £10m per year for five years) to apply the findings of her research to particular estates and to monitor the changes in the incidence of social malaise. It will then be possible to fully assess the validity of her thesis but for the moment her critics are convinced that while design modifications may have some effect on security issues they will have little impact on the way in which tenants are able to use their dwellings and their estates. Instead, it is argued, social and economic factors are the key issues and if housing management wishes to minimise both the problems for managers and for tenants, attention must be paid to the amount of resources put into estates – in terms both of investment in the physical structure and in management and maintenance services – and to allocation policies.

Labelling theory research

There are a number of studies of problem estates which emphasise the way in which the definition of such an estate is socially constructed and depends in key ways on the perception of the estate by both outsiders and its residents, rather than on a reality of poor design, high crime levels, vandalism and so on. Sean Damer's study of Moorepark estate in Glasgow, locally known as first 'Wine Alley' and now 'the Acid Scheme', is one example of such studies(27).

The estate was first built in 1934 and consists of 516 houses with gardens. Damer first came across it when he was working for Glasgow Corporation Planning Department in 1969. The Corporation had decided to build three multi-story blocks across the road from Wine Alley but when a public exhibition on these and other proposals was held, local Govanites explained that the plan, which included proposals for two pubs, lock-ups, and landscaping, 'was daft in that the 'anymuls' from Wine Alley would sally forth from their ghetto, lay waste the landscaping, wreck the lock-ups, steal the cars, burn the multis to the ground, and mug, plunder and murder the inhabitants'(28). Damer goes on:

> So I went down to have a look at this dreadful place. Wine Alley was a bleak and depressing estate: the back and front gardens were semi-derelict, the streets were covered with broken glass, small children and large dogs. Some of the houses were empty and had boarded-up windows, which added to the depressing appearance. Large housewives with larger voices bawled raucous messages to each other, while their pre-school children grubbed happily in the mud which pretended to be the front-garden. In other words, Wine Alley was a fairly typical looking, pre-war, Scottish slum-clearance housing estate(29).

Damer's subsequent research on the estate, like that of Armstrong and Wilson on Easterhouse in Glasgow, revealed that the reputation of the estate was something of a myth. The tales that he was told of 'gangsters, money-lenders, desperadoes, murders, and mayhem of such a calibre as to make the events of the novel *No Mean City* look like a church outing'(30) were very difficult to track down. The poverty and poor housing conditions experienced by the residents were real enough but the reputation of the estate hinged more on the apocryphal stories about the activities of the 'pure scruff', 'pure bone-idle wasters' and 'anymuls' who supposedly lived there. Yet when Damer tried to pin these stories down, they either dissipated into generalised antipathy or when he did track down the few named individual characters and stories, he found 'that the events with which they were associated had happened elsehere in the city in earlier years, or had never happened, or had in fact happened alright but had happened in Govan itself and not in the estate'. He concludes:

> So I came to realise rather quickly that I was dealing with somewhat of a myth, a mythical reputation which was powerful enough to have a stigmatising effect(31).

This gap between reality and reputation has been found in respect of other estates such as Easterhouse and Broadwater Farm, although in the case of Owen Gill's research on Luke Street, a Liverpool estate, Gill is slightly more cautious(32). He stresses that the rates of vandalism and delinquency were high on Luke Street (primarily because of the high numbers of teenagers on the estate who had few other activities open to them) but he also recognises, as Damer does, the differences between the reality and the reputation. He states that 'this form of behaviour [juvenile delinquency] was exaggerated in the external perceptions of the area to produce a stereotypical picture of a consistently delinquent group of people'(33).

Damer and Gill's research, together with other research which uses a labelling theory perspective, attempts to explain the discrepancies between the reputations of the estates and the observed reality in terms of the social construction of these reputations. The details of the processes involved vary from estate to estate but a number of core features emerge.

Firstly, an important factor in the initial development of the poor reputation appears to have been the fact that the estate was built as part of a slum clearance programme. Wine Alley, for example, was built in the 1930s. Initially:

> These houses were probably the most sought-after possessions in the world of Govan. Govanites rushed to their local councillors to see if they could 'swing it' so that their families could obtain a house in the scheme(34).

However, when the scheme was allocated not only to outsiders, but outsiders from the Gorbals, the reaction of the local population turned to a venomous hostility. The inhabitants of the estate were socially isolated from the rest of Govan which created the conditions in which stereotypical views of them as social pariahs could flourish. A similar observation was made by the Gifford report on Broadwater Farm which was built in the late 1960s and early 1970s primarily to rehouse people from slum clearance schemes:

> The residents in the nearby terraced streets had opposed the plans and disliked the reality. A nearby resident of 20 years' standing described to us his views of the estate as 'like a wart on one's hand, a monstrosity, out of character for the area'. From the beginning, there began to emerge a dangerous polarisation between the estate and its neighbours(35).

Secondly, the major factor identified in the crystallisation of the poor reputation is the role of the media in exaggerating the nature of life on the estates. In Luke Street, Wine Alley and Broadwater Farm this role was performed by the local press and in the case of Easterhouse it was performed by the *Scottish Daily News*. Once the media has run a story which portrays the estate or its inhabitants in a bad light, this then creates a framework for the reporting of subsequent incidents within the same broad framework. Incidents of gang violence, vandalism, etc are presented as typical of the estate whilst similar incidents on other estates may be reported as more unusual regardless of the objective patterns of such incidents.

The third common theme in these studies is that the media stereotypes can have the effect of a self-fulfilling prophecy. The bad reputation makes the estate less desirable; only those households in the most desperate need accept offers on the estate; the void rate increases, making the estate more prone to vandalism; residents on the estate are increasingly the most disadvantaged tenants who lack material resources which makes it still more difficult for them to challenge the stereotyped view of the estate. The negative images of the estate are likely to percolate through to other institutions and professional agencies. This may result in residents on the estate finding it difficult to obtain hire purchase agreements or having to pay higher insurance premiums for house contents, etc. Moreover, once the problem label has begun to stick, it is likely that the estate will become the focus of attempts to tackle the problem. This may entail inter-agency initiatives involving social services and the housing department, for example, or single-agency initiatives, particularly in the form of an increased police presence on the estate. However well-intentioned such initiatives may be, they are likely to have adverse consequences for the reputation of the estate. Gill has shown that the increased police presence in Luke Street led to more arrests which, in turn, were reported by the local media in a manner which further reinforced the reputation of the area. On Broadwater Farm, policing methods on the estate resulted in far more serious consequences with the death of Mrs Jarrett, the ensuing disorder on the estate and the death of PC Keith Blakelock. In both cases, the effect was to create a downward spiral in the form of more policing, more arrests, more media stories, reinforcement of the negative image of the estate, making it less desirable, harder to let, and so on.

Damer also found that the residents of Wine Alley, having originally resisted the label attached to their estate, came to accept the reputation of their estate – although the reputation was never thought to apply justifiably to themselves or their immediate neighbours but to other parts of the estate where they would not venture because they were too dangerous.

The labelling theory approach to problem estates highlights the importance of broader social processes and offers some important insights into the way in which this particular 'social problem' is socially constructed. It is particularly useful in helping to explain some of the concrete manifestations of the poor reputations of these estates, such as higher levels of policing, difficult-to-let properties and the discrimination that residents experience in obtaining hire purchase, employment, etc. However, there is a strong tendency within this body of research to focus upon social reaction to the exclusion of all else. Thus, the impression is sometimes given that the application of the deviant label is largely the result of an arbitrary process in which the objective conditions of the physical fabric of the estate and the level of social malaise is largely irrelevant. This glosses over the fact that there may be real problems with the estates themselves which exist independently of their reputation. It may be that: they are geographically and socially isolated on the edge of cities; they do not contain an adequate infrastructure in the form of shops and other services; they suffer from structural defects leading to damp, condensation or other problems; they may have been designed with heating systems that are too expensive to run; the local authority may have adopted inappropriate allocations policies by, for example, allocating families with young children to high-rise blocks; the general environment may be austere; the repairs service on the estate is poor; and so on.

An analysis of problem estates needs to encompass the complex interrelationship of a variety of factors, including both the physical characteristics of the estate, such as any structural defects but also including its location; the wider social, economic and political processes that affect the reputation of the estate and its position in what Gill describes as 'the hierarchy of desirability'; the allocations policies of local authority housing departments; the material resources of the tenants; and the effects of government housing policy. Having looked at three types of explanations of problem estates, we can now turn our attention to the lessons to be learnt for housing management.

Problem estates – an assessment

The major point to be made about problem estates is that they are expressions of social inequality. Residents on such estates are not only experiencing housing inequality but other aspects of their lives are dominated by disadvantage – employment prospects, educational opportunities, health profiles and so on.

The underlying characteristic of the socio-economic position of the residents on problem estates is their powerlessness. This powerlessness manifests itself in the form of a desperate need for housing within the public rented sector because of a lack of material resources necessary to get access to housing in the private sector. We have seen in the previous chapters that the organisational imperatives within housing organisations to be efficient (by speeding up allocations procedure, reducing void rates, etc) acts as a powerful incentive to offer the least-desirable housing to these groups, especially if they present themselves to a local authority as homeless. Housing need is likely to be a product of deeper social inequalities and it will be the most disadvantaged social groups who are in the most desperate housing need.

In this way powerlessness will be a central factor in determining the pattern of access to the least desirable estates. It is also important in various other ways. Spicker's arguments about the way in which design characteristics are modified by poverty offers examples of how a lack of resources leads to an inability to counteract poor housing conditions or to cope with housing which is difficult to live in. The labelling theory research shows how the powerlessness of tenants makes it more difficult for them to challenge the stereotypical views of their estate. Taylor's article offers a further perspective in that he, at least implicitly, points to the way in which tenants' perceptions are given very little credence. The very novelty of his terms 'difficult-to-live-in' and 'difficult-to-get-out-of' ought to raise questions about the partisan way in which the problem has conventionally been defined as 'difficult-to-let'.

This leads us on to identify the important role that housing management plays in the creation and perpetuation of problem estates. The most obvious way in which this occurs is through allocations policies. It is clear that, in the past, many local authorities have had an explicit policy to operate 'sink' estates. Few would admit this now but many operate single-offer policies for homeless applicants which is likely to amount to the same thing. Even where such policies do not exist, the organisational pressures referred to earlier will be important. In addition, there is evidence to suggest that the dominant ideology within housing management, with its distinction between 'deserving' and 'undeserving' clients, is likely to reinforce these institutional mechanisms(36). We would also stress that housing management should not be seen in isolation. It is clear from the labelling theory research that the attitude of housing officers to a particular problem estate is likely to be moulded by the reactions of other agencies, particularly the media but also the police and social services.

Perhaps still more importantly, just as housing need is an expression of wider social inequality so housing management is constrained by wider processes. Public rented housing is part of the state system and it is constrained by government policies. The pressures to keep voids below a certain level and the inadequate investment in poor-condition public sector housing, are not natural or inevitable features of council housing. They emanate from the policies pursued by central government which are designed to impose a closer control on local authority spending.

These are some of the elements of the broad framework in which housing operates. The essential point to grasp is that housing management mediates between the manifestations of powerlessness on the one hand, and economic and political constraints on the other.

HOMELESSNESS

There is a general consensus that homelessness is a serious social problem but there is also disagreement about the nature of the problem, its causes and, therefore, appropriate policies. We want to look at how the problem of homelessness is generally perceived, exploring the way in which certain assumptions about the causes of homelessness underlie this perception and the extent to which housing policy and practice have been influenced by these assumptions.

Definitions and measurements of homelessness

Much of the current debate on homelessness has been based on an implicit acceptance of the official definition of homelessness. This has been framed by the Housing (Homeless Persons) Act 1977 which has subsequently been replaced by Part III of the Housing Act 1985. Homelessness is defined as lacking secure accommodation free from violence or the threat of violence. In such a situation people may present themselves as homeless to a local housing authority who will be obliged to offer them accommodation if they fall into one of the priority need groups listed in the legislation, if they have a local connection with the district, and if they are not classed as intentionally homeless within the meaning of the Act. If a homeless household fails to fulfil one of these requirements then the local authority's obligations are limited to giving advice on alternative sources of housing.

As Lorraine Thompson points out in her analysis of the

legislation, the Housing (Homeless Persons) Act of 1977 was not actually intended as the solution to the problem of homelessness(37). Rather, it was a compromise between those who questioned the legitimacy of the demand that local authorities house the homeless and/or expressed a concern about their ability to do so, and those, such as the Joint Charities Group, whose ultimate aim was that all homeless households should have statutory rights to accommodation. The Act was heavily influenced by the view held by many local housing authorities that a duty to house homeless people would interfere with the provision and management of housing for 'ordinary' people. As one local authority officer put it, 'I have to pay attention to the ordinary standards of decent people. We don't want these dead-legs. They muck up the books and make life a misery for ordinary folk'(38). It was this kind of attitude, together with the fear that local authorities would not have enough resources to deal with all homeless households, which resulted in a very limited definition of homelessness being enshrined in the legislation.

There are two underlying problems with the way in which the homelessness legislation dominates the perception of homelessness. The first is a failure to consider what is meant by the term 'home'; instead homelessness is taken to mean lack of 'accommodation'. In consequence, the housing needs of a number of different groups of people will remain concealed. Single people forced to share accommodation, or remain in their parents' household; women wishing to leave an unhappy marriage; disabled people in residential establishments: these are examples of groups which have a need for accommodation which they regard as their own home, rather than merely a roof over their heads. However, this need is neither recognised within the general definition of homelessness nor measurable by the statistical sources available.

The second underlying problem is the way in which the legislation distinguishes between those who are 'deserving' of local authority help and those who are not, through the qualifications laid down in the Act of priority need, local connection and intentional homelessness. The result is not just an undermining of the legitimacy of the housing need of those groups who do not qualify under these terms, but also an under-recording of such people within the statistics on homelessness.

Glen Bramley, in *Homelessness and the London Housing Market*, has recognised these problems in his attempt to distinguish between common sense and official definitions of homelessness, asserting that: 'The definitions provided by the legislation are not alone sufficient to comprehend the nature of homelessness'(39). He goes on to identify seven categories of housing situation, ranging from people who literally do not have a roof over their heads, to situations in which households are sharing involuntarily or where certain members of the household may prefer to live separately. These are all forms of homelessness, he suggests. What they have in common is 'the lack of a right or access to their own secure and minimally adequate housing space'.

The failure to develop a more comprehensive concept of homelessness has meant that housing policy generally does not address the needs of those whose homelessness is concealed. Moreover, research into the extent and nature of homelessness has been almost totally reliant upon official statistics. The narrow perception of homelessness therefore results in problems of measuring it. There is a series of difficulties involved here. Firstly, the official statistics can only measure the number of people who are accepted as homeless by local authorities and/or those people who present themselves as homeless to local authorities. Both sets of figures will be heavily influenced by the legal definition of homelessness.

Households which do not come under the terms of the homelessness legislation, or whose rights are limited to receiving advice, are unlikely to register a demand for housing. Austerberry and Watson's study of single homeless women living in hostels found that:

Only 15 out of 102 women interviewed had even heard of the Housing (Homeless Persons) Act and only one of these knew that she had rights under it, despite half of the sample being in emergency accommodation and therefore homeless according to the Act(40).

Similarly, Randall's research on the young people at Centrepoint Soho (an emergency centre for young homeless people) found that as many as 90 per cent of those interviewed had not been in contact with any local authority since becoming homeless(41).

However, the official figures on homelessness are not only inadequate because they do not represent those whose homelessness is concealed or who do not qualify under the meaning of the legislation, but also because they do not even provide an accurate count of applications to local authorities. Glen Bramley has explored these difficulties in his analysis of the measurement of homelessness. Of the three major sources of official data, only the Housing Investment Programme returns are obligatory. These contain very limited data and there is no official analysis of the data, the returns for each authority being deposited in the House of Commons Library, which operates a very restrictive access policy. Statistics on homelessness for the Department of the Environment and the Chartered Institute of Public Finance and Accountancy are completed on a voluntary basis and, consequently, some authorities, particularly London boroughs and Metropolitan Districts, do not complete them. For example, almost a fifth of local housing authorities failed to complete the DoE homelessness returns for the second quarter of 1989.

The official statistics are therefore incomplete. There are also difficulties in comparing the data over time as there have been changes in the way the statistics are collected. Furthermore, within any one year, there are variations in the way that local authorities record both those who apply as homeless and those who are accepted as homeless. For example, amongst those who apply as homeless, some will fail to be accepted because they are found to be neither homeless within the meaning of the Act nor threatened with homelessness within 28 days. Others will be found to be homeless but not to fall within a priority need group. Bramley argues that local authorities are not consistent in the way that cases are classified between these two categories and this therefore makes comparison on levels of homelessness between areas very difficult(42).

The statistics on homelessness will also be affected by the particular ways in which an authority exercises its discretionary powers or, indeed, interprets its statutory duties. Thus there may be variations in the incidence of homelessness between different local authority areas which have nothing to do with the actual level of homelessness. Two recent studies have shown convincingly that local authorities have developed policies and practice on homelessness which vary considerably within the contraints imposed by the legal framework. Pat Niner's case studies of homelessness procedures in nine local authorities concluded that:

> At the level of the authority there is scope within the legislation and precedent set by the case law for discretionary interpretations which affect both the overall slant of policy and more detailed aspects of procedure. At the most basic level, it appears that authorities can use the legislative framework either as a minimum requirement for action within which applicants will be helped as far as possible and given the benefit of any doubt; or as a maximum forced on the authority, in which case the applicant will only be helped if the responsibility is absolutely unavoidable. There are, of course, intermediate points on the continuum from one extreme to another(43).

Angela Evans and Sue Duncan's questionnaire-based research was able to illustrate this with data gathered from a large number of local authorities(44). Their findings suggest that there are wide variations in reported policy and practice at all stages of the process from the accommodation types from which applicants are usually accepted to the interpretation of priority need and of intentional homelessness. Generally, they found that London boroughs and metropolitan authorities tended to be more generous in their interpretations. Niner's closer examination of a smaller number of authorities suggests that there are further differences within each of these categories. Thus, whilst neither the metropolitan authorities of Newcastle nor Nottingham had found anybody to be intentionally homeless since 1980, the London Borough of Westminster followed a particularly tough line with homeless applicants(45).

Housing policy and practice can never satisfactorily address homelessness as a social problem unless both a wider concept of homelessness and more satisfactory methods of measuring the phenomenon are adopted. As Alan Booth says in his exposure of the myths surrounding homelessness:

> Homeless people do not declare their existence; they make do with temporary solutions; stay trapped in disastrous, often violent, relationships; bed down in empty buildings; sleep outside; and live a life of poverty and loneliness(46).

Explanations of homelessness

Having identified criticisms of the commonly used definition and measurement of homelessness, we now want to look at the assumptions which are made about the causes of homelessness.

Some authors have approached a consideration of the 'causes of homelessness' through an empirical examination of the characteristics of homeless households. For example, Niner produces data on applicants accepted as homeless to show the proportions that had experienced a family dispute, relationship breakdown, mortgage default, etc. These characteristics are then described as the various 'causes' of homelessness(47). Factors such as these may well be the immediate causes of homelessness for any individual household but this does not explain why these factors result in homelessness (as officially defined). Is it the case, for example, that family disputes are increasing; or that family disputes are more likely to result in homelessness; or that both conditions apply?

On a political level, a focus on the immediate reasons for homelessness has been associated with suggestions that homelessness has increased because of changes in social behaviour. Thus:

> Nicholas Ridley suggested to the Commons that 'the cause of the rise of homelessness is the change in the way people are behaving'. He was referring to young people leaving home, people unable to stay with friends and relatives, the break-up of marriages and an increase in illegitimate births(48).

An almost inevitable corollary to explaining homelessness in terms of people's behaviour is to see such people as somehow different from the mainstream of society. This assumption has its manifestations in the housing management context in that homeless people are sometimes seen as 'jumping the queue' whilst others, who have been waiting patiently on the council's list, are being excluded or are having to wait longer than they ought to. It may also result in homeless households being offered poorer-quality property and/or being allowed a limited number of offers of housing. Alan Murie has emphasised that the history of local authority response to homelessness illustrates a widely held assumption that homeless households are disreputable and irresponsible, and to rehouse them into permanent stock penalises others who wait their turn or who are more responsible(49).

Housing campaigners have put some effort into claiming that homeless households are 'ordinary' people and part of the community in the area where they present as homeless. The problem with this is that it then undermines the legitimacy of the housing need of those who cannot be so described, for example, people moving from one part of the country to another in search of work, immigrants, refugees, people who have other problems such as drug users, people discharged from psychiatric hospitals. What all these people have in common, including the 'ordinary' families, is a lack of resources to meet their housing need through the existing housing market.

In the context of his research on homelessness amongst young people, Kevin Doogan argues that:

> Homelessness is as much a housing problem as famine is a 'food problem'. Just as with the latter we have to seek out the structural reasons which explain the continual vulnerability of certain countries to famine, so too with homelessness must we locate the same economic, political and social determinants that explain the continual vulnerability of social groups that places them at risk in the housing market(50).

Doogan then goes on to analyse the way in which it is not young people's desire to leave home which has resulted in an increase in homelessness amongst young single people, nor indeed a collapse of housing provision for young people, because their housing needs were never addressed by local authorities. Rather the causes of such an increase in homelessness are to be sought in the social and economic context of being young in Britain of the 1980s. He documents the way in which 'the rise in youth homelessness is but one symptom of the deteriorating economic position of young people that has its roots in the dramatic restructuring of the world of work'(51).

Young people have experienced dramatic rises in unemployment, particularly long-term unemployment, a downward pressure on wages for young workers and reductions in entitlement to benefit. While average housing costs have increased, the average income of young people has fallen back during the 1980s, thus making access to housing more difficult. At the same time, the decline of rented housing means that the housing market cannot meet the needs of young unemployed people who may wish to move to areas where work is available.

189

It remains to be seen whether the demographic trends which have now produced a shortage of young workers will result in a decline in the experience of youth homelessness during the 1990s. If such a decline does occur, it will certainly not be because of a change in the social behaviour of young people, rather it will result from a change in the socio-economic consequences of being a new entrant to the labour market.

Alan Murie also argues that it is socio-economic factors which explain the increase in homelessness, although he places greater stress than Doogan does on the role of the housing market. With specific reference to London, he identifies four important factors: the decline of the private rented sector; increasing social inequality; increasing costs of home-ownership; the decline of council renting. He goes on:

> The four key factors outlined above combine to create real housing problems. The low income and marginalised population have grown at the same time as the costs of house purchase have risen dramatically. Dependency on the rented sector has grown and deepened in a period when the decline of the rented sector is unabated(52).

The increasing gap between rich and poor during the 1980s is well documented by pressure groups such as the Low Pay Unit and the Child Poverty Action Group(53). In the context of London's housing market, this has meant that the better-off sections of the population – for example, those benefiting from the expansion of London's finance sector – have been able to pay more for housing. The associated house price boom, coinciding with the decline of both the private rented sector and the public sector, has reduced the housing opportunities of the increasing number of households experiencing poverty as a result of either low wages or unemployment. This also means that those coming into the capital seeking work, or those leaving institutional care of any kind, experience greater difficulty in finding housing. The consequences are clear in the doubling of the number of households accepted as homeless by London local authorities between 1978 and 1988 and a 1186 per cent increase in the use of temporary accommodation over the same period(54).

Research on women's housing opportunities, and also on disabled people's housing situation, further illustrates that socio-economic factors are a more adequate explanation of homelessness rather than social behaviour. Chapter 4 has illustrated the way in which women's position within the labour market means that they experience difficulties in getting access to housing independent of a man, other than through the statutory rights accorded to households with dependent children under the homeless legislation. It is these broader socio-economic factors, together with the fact that the homeless legislation does give such households some rights, which account for the over-representation of single parents amongst those accepted as homeless.

Disabled people have experienced a disproportionate rise in the experience of homelessness, in that the number accepted as homeless by local authorities has risen at about twice the rate of increase for other groups defined as priority groups under the Act(55). Again, such a phenomenon is explicable not in terms of changes of behaviour but in terms of the increasing difficulty of a low-income group in getting access to housing. Disabled people rely in disproportionate numbers on the public rented sector and as access into council housing has been squeezed, so more disabled people have had to come through the homeless route. Their situation is also exacerbated by the widening gap between the supply of housing either adapted or purpose-built to wheelchair standard and the demand for such housing(56).

The changes apparent in the housing market during the 1980s illustrate a clear relationship between social and economic inequalities and housing disadvantage. While the National Housing Forum has calculated that there is an immediate need for 2 million new homes and an additional 3.2–4m by 2001(57), it is clear that the purchasing power of a large number of people in the greatest housing need is insufficient to stimulate supply of dwellings through the private market to meet this need. The average increase in house prices has outstripped the average increase in earnings(58), the result of which can be seen in the Association of District Councils' estimate that between a third and a half of those living in the South East cannot afford to buy even the cheapest of 'starter' homes on the private market(59). At the same time, low-income households are unable to afford market rents in the private rented sector. Research by Price Waterhouse commissioned by the Department of the Environment found that in England a couple with two children just above the qualifying level for housing benefit could afford the average market rent for a two-bedroom house in only two towns – Leicester and Newcastle(60).

We must therefore conclude that it is economic processes – resulting as they have done in a low-waged economy with significant levels of unemployment and economic inactivity amongst particular groups – which have led to high levels of both concealed and expressed homelessness.

Practical measures

The above analysis has established the importance of socio-economic factors influencing the experience of housing disadvantage in the form of homelessness. In the previous section on problem estates, we identified that the interaction of certain housing management practices and policies with these socio-economic factors was often responsible for exacerbating social disadvantage. The same phenomenon can be determined in the context of homeless households. The unequal power relationship between those in desperate need of housing and those who control access to the scarce resource (whether as allocators or as policy-makers) means that homeless households are vulnerable to prejudices and preconceptions about who 'deserves' access to good housing.

One result of this unequal power relationship is the extent to which the actual experience of homelessness has been written out of the picture. Instead, homelessness is perceived to be a problem for local authorities, whose financial, housing and personnel resources are overstretched; a problem for central government as it tries to insist that local authority inefficiency and irresponsible individual behaviour rather than government policies are to blame; a problem for waiting list or transfer applicants as a higher proportion of lettings go to homeless households, reducing their own chances of getting the housing they need. The major group whose perceptions are not represented are homeless people. Their powerlessness means that their voice is not heard.

A crucial part of this powerlessness is the undermining of the legitimacy of homeless households' demand for housing. This has led to a reluctance amongst many local authorities to accord priority to homeless households for permanent housing, or at least to restrict such households' access to permanent housing – for example, by decreeing that no new properties should be allocated to homeless households. It is not only the gap between supply and demand for local authority housing which has led to the increased use of various forms of temporary accommodation over the last ten years, but also the restrictions on access to the permanent housing stock which has been imposed on homeless households as a result of specific policy decisions.

If we look at the problem of homelessness from the point of view of those experiencing it, we find that the local authority response to homelessness – in the form of an increased use of bed and breakfast hotels – has actually created new problems for homeless households. Jean Conway's research on mothers and their children placed in such temporary accommodation concludes that, from their viewpoint, the problem is not so much that they lack secure accommodation but rather that the provision of temporary accommodation was inadequate. Conway argues:

Hotels have now become a new form of housing for many homeless people. Many children know no other home. The interviews with the women show the appalling standards and conditions of this expanding form of housing. The high level of stress and illness found amongst the families interviewed is likely to be a reflection of the inadequacy of the accommodation(61).

She goes on to describe the conditions which are endured by people living in bed and breakfast hotels:

Most of the families had to share the WC and bathroom with several others and a significant number shared with ten or more other people. Many had an unreliable supply of hot water and heating and found the hotel dirty and unhygienic. Very few of the women in the survey had access to reasonable cooking facilities, and many even had no means of preparing basic food or even making a hot drink.

There was considerable concern amongst the women about the safety of the accommodation. These fears for safety are not misplaced. In the last few years there have been a number of fires in hotels in which people have died, and in July 1987 a child died falling from a fourth-floor window in a hotel in London. People living in bed and breakfast hotels have no sense of security and this exacerbates the stresses of living there.

Hotels are often noisy, and many women complained of the lack of privacy: several said it was 'like a prison'. One woman described how restricting it was to have to sit in the dark in the evening when the youngest child was asleep as there was nowhere to go.

The study found extremely high levels of overcrowding. Nearly half the households were estimated as being over the legal standards for crowding. Many of the children had to share their bed, sometimes with an adult, and the bedrooms often had no space for a table or chairs(62).

A second dimension which was of major importance to the experience of life in a bed and breakfast hotel concerns the treatment (or, more accurately, the neglect) by the local authority housing department. The report details the long stays (often over 12 months) that many families had in these conditions. The resulting difficulties were compounded by the fact that the majority of the women did not know how long they would have to tolerate these conditions and there was a general sense that the various councils did not care about them:

> Many of the women interviewed felt that the council was not keeping them adequately informed of their position. Several said the council officer they had originally dealt with had left and they did not have a new contact person; it was often difficult to get through on the telephone; messages left were not responded to; when they did finally talk to someone in the council they felt they were being 'fobbed off'. Their general sense of having been dumped in a hotel and forgotten made it harder to cope with the conditions they were having to live in, and is likely to have exacerbated their stress and anxiety(63).

As in the case of problem estates, we have seen that it is the interaction of the housing market with wider socio-economic processes which is creating the problem of homelessness. However, the responses to the problem are motivated more by prejudices and preconceptions about homelessness than by these more fundamental factors. It is ironic that the development in London of 'private sector leasing' (where homeless households are placed in, often very high standard, accommodation leased on a short-term basis from private landlords) has been motivated not by a wish to provide good accommodation to homeless households but by a desire to cut back on the cost of bed and breakfast hotels.

If, instead of focusing on individual behaviour as the cause of homelessness, we accept that the explanation is to be found in an interaction of broader social and economic processes with the housing market, then homeless households' need for secure, adequate housing must be recognised. Furthermore, those who present themselves as homeless – and who qualify under the meaning of the legislation – can only be part of the total picture of homelessness in Britain today.

The direct implications for housing management of such an analysis lie with the recognition that the type of strategy adopted by Glasgow City Council – where considerable resources have been put into providing an excellent, supportive service to homeless applicants and a speedy allocation of permanent housing – are more appropriate than policies and practices which penalise homeless households. Glasgow started off by providing 35 self-contained flats, furnished to a high standard, as temporary accommodation for homeless households. This enabled them to save about £17 million on the cost of bed and breakfast hotels. £1.8 million of this was spent on a new Homeless Persons Unit, named the Hamish Allan Centre, which aimed to provide an efficient, professional, customer-orientated service for all categories of homeless households. The philosophy of the Centre was summed up by Glasgow's Chief Housing Officer, Bill Hood, when he said:

> It looks attractive and welcoming and that's the message we want to get across. If your house set on fire you would book into a comfortable hotel, so why shouldn't the homeless get the same kind of service? Not having credit cards doesn't mean you have to be limited to very grotty properties(64).

Homelessness may be a result of social and economic marginalisation but it is not inevitable that the behaviour of local housing authorities towards homeless people be part of this process, as it all too commonly is at present. Indeed, it could be argued that the social housing sector has a key role to play in countering such social and economic disadvantage.

RACIAL HARASSMENT

In recent years, the housing profession has recognised racist attacks on tenants as a social problem of direct relevance to the concerns of housing management. The nature of the abuse, and danger, experienced by black people is illustrated by a report received by Tower Hamlets' Housing Committee in 1987 on the attacks sustained by Bangladeshi tenants and quoted by Charlie Forman in *Spitalfields: a battle for land*:

> Verbal abuse, spitting, physical assault by stabbing, kicking, punching, shooting with airguns, throwing stones, eggs, sticks, using iron bars; criminal damage to property e.g. windows being broken, doors damaged, burning material being put through letter boxes, cars damaged; excreta, stink bombs and rubbish being pushed through letter boxes, rubbish dumped on doorsteps, washing vandalised or stolen, graffiti daubed on doors or walls, banging on doors, thumping on ceilings; dogs, cars, motorcycles, knives, petrol bombs, shot guns and threatening letters have also been used to frighten the victims(65).

Policies on racial harassment have been developed in response to conflicting pressures placed on housing managers, and, most importantly, in the context of housing managers' own preconceptions and prejudices. There are, for example, the pressures from local politicians, faced with caseloads of tenants experiencing racial harassment, demanding that housing managers 'do something'; there are the pressures from local community groups, identifying that the police often do not act on reports of racist attack and demanding that housing managers enable their tenants to live securely within their homes; there is criticism from some white tenants and their associations that housing managers are putting too many resources into meeting the housing needs of black and Asian groups. In the midst of this chaos there are the preconceptions held by some housing managers that tenants may falsely claim experience of racial harassment in order to get a transfer; and there is the conflict between the wish to avoid future management problems on 'white' estates and the desire to ensure that black households are not concentrated on the poorer-quality estates.

Faced with all these conflicting pressures it is not surprising that both politicians and managers are unable to stand back from the chaotic reality. Instead, policies and practices are adopted as responses to what are often seen as crisis situations on particular estates – or the problem is seen as overwhelming and not something that housing management can adequately address.

We want to look at some of the problems encountered by local authorities in attempting to deal with racist attacks on housing estates, identifying the social context of the phenomenon and the implications that this has for the role of local authority housing management.

Definitions

In order to develop policies on racial harassment, local housing authorities and housing associations have attempted to be clear about what is meant by the term. However, a striking feature of the existing literature is the absence of a clearly agreed definition. This no doubt stems partly from the fact that it is not a recognised legal concept – there is no crime of racial harassment, although some racist attackers could clearly face charges under the categories of more general violent crimes against the person. The Association of Metropolitan Authorities (AMA) has attempted to articulate a definition in its pamphlet on racial harassment, where it is defined as: 'Conduct against a person of different racial or ethnic origin in accordance with the schedule below and that conduct has interfered with the enjoyment of that person's dwelling house'(66). The accompanying schedule goes on to list 14 different forms of behaviour, ranging from verbal abuse to property damage and grievous bodily harm.

This definition clearly reflects the preoccupations of housing management in its emphasis on observable behaviour – 'conduct' involving people of 'different racial or ethnic origins'. However, what distinguishes racial harassment from neighbour disputes or other forms of

198

criminal or anti-social behaviour is not simply the racial or ethnic origins of the people involved (the observable characteristic) but the motivation for the behaviour. This is recognised by the National Federation of Housing Associations' guidance to housing associations which states:

> A clear distinction can be made between the activities labelled 'neighbour disputes' and those which are encompassed by the label 'racial harassment'. The latter can be distinguished because they are: racially motivated; frequently premeditated; frequently not carried out by immediate neighbours; more likely to recur over a period of time(67).

In other words, the distinguishing criteria ought to be whether or not there is a racist motive. This is important because the identification of the behaviour as racial harassment – rather than any other form of conflict – is a crucial part of determining the urgency of the situation and the priority that housing management will give to reacting to it.

Faced with the inevitable difficulty of determining the motivations for behaviour, housing organisations have commonly responded by taking the victims' assessment of whether or not they have been subject to racial harassment. This is likely to be the most reliable assessment but it is a difficult definition to adopt in a situation where housing managers may view tenants as essentially untrustworthy, leading to the suspicion that they might claim to be victims of racial harassment for the sole reason of obtaining a transfer. The problem here, of course, lies with the attitude of housing managers and any effective policy on racial harassment will need to address this.

Another problem with the AMA definition of racial harassment is that it applies only to behaviour which inter-feres with the enjoyment of the dwelling. This is a conscious, and unsurprising, attempt to restrict the term to a sphere of direct relevance to housing managers, but the fact is that racial harassment does not only occur in residential areas, it does not only occur on local authority housing estates and it does not only involve neighbours. Racial harassment can be perpetrated by strangers in shopping areas, on public transport, at work, or any other sphere of social life. Moreover, it can be institutionalised when it is perpetrated by people acting in an official capacity. Prison officers using racist taunts on black inmates; police officers stopping and searching black youths; immigration officers conducting vaginal examinations on Asian women; housing visitors insisting that Asian applicants produce their passports – all these are examples of the verbal and physical abuse against black people and their property which is a common feature of our society. In this sense, the housing management profession, in developing policies on the racial harassment experienced by their black tenants, is attempting to confront, not just the behaviour of individual tenants, but the racism which permeates British society. Housing managers may be praised for doing this but the task is a daunting one.

We now want to look at the actual policies on racial harassment which some local housing authorities have developed, looking at the assumptions behind these policies and the problems with their implementation.

Policies

Policies on racial harassment have both stimulated and been stimulated by the publication of guides for housing managers by the Institute of Housing, the Association of Metropolitan Authorities and the National Federation of Housing Associations. Elaine Bowes, from the Commission for Racial Equality, has identified the common elements of policies on racial harassment which have, for example, now been adopted by more than half of the London boroughs:

> *a.* A new clause is added to the Tenancy Agreement specifically making the act of racial harrassment a breach of the conditions of tenancy in addition to the already established 'nuisance' clause;

b. The victim's perception of the motive for an attack is always accepted in the first instance by the housing department until subsequent enquiries prove otherwise. The burden of proof does not lie with the victim but with the council;

c. Every case is recorded and investigated immediately;

d. Repairs are done urgently and graffiti removed within 24 hours;

e. Emphasis is on moving the perpetrator and not the victim;

f. Procedures are also laid down for the letting of properties after a black family has had to move because of harrassment;

g. Costs are sought against the perpetrator for any damage or removal expenses of the victim;

h. Staff are given thorough training in the new policy and procedures(68).

There have been practical problems with implementing such policies. Firstly, local housing authorities have found it very difficult to ensure that the 'emphasis is on moving the perpetrator and not the victim'. Often those experiencing racial harassment are frightened for their lives and quite rightly insist that they should be offered alternative housing immediately. Secondly, local authorities have actually found it quite difficult to use the courts to evict racists. In various cases, judges have failed to be persuaded that behaviour is racially motivated, that the incidents in question are not neighbour disputes (i.e. where both parties are engaging in verbal and physical abuse), that parents can be held responsible for their teenage children's behaviour and so on.

The difficulty of relying on local authority powers to evict tenants who break their tenancy agreements, together with the danger involved in leaving a black family on the estate where they are experiencing harassment, has led to a more common practice of establishing a priority transfer system for those households experiencing racial harassment. However, this policy too has its problems.

As Chetan Bhatt argues: 'At best, transfer, as a long-term solution, provides for a circular moving of black families without affecting the level of racist violence'(69). Transferring a black family away from the estate may well be

the most appropriate immediate solution, because of the
danger they are in, but effectively such a transfer is a victory
for the racists and in the long term does nothing to reduce
the overall level of attacks. Black households who wish to
transfer will usually request housing in 'safer' areas where
the black community has a stronger base. However, these
are usually areas of poorer housing. Furthermore, the long-
term effect will be to create no-go areas for black people.
Bhatt argues that transferring black households out of
mainly white areas – which is where racist attacks are
more likely to be experienced anyway – is particularly
problematic in the long term:

> Moving one black family will, apart from increasing the
> confidence of the racists, make every other family in that area
> far more vulnerable. Keeping the family there will keep it under
> risk. Evicting the racists may mean evicting most of the white
> tenants(70).

Bhatt goes on to identify that racial harassment is not a
problem of 'bad neighbours', the words used by one London
borough's advertisement on racial harassment. To fully
understand the issue it is necessary to move away from the
emphasis on individual tenants to the more general problem
of racism. Racism, and racist behaviour, does not emerge at
random in individual psyches. It is not a question of a few
individuals who can be identified as bad, mad or wicked.
Racism is a product of broader social relations. It is not
surprising therefore that a policy on racial harassment which
focuses to the extent that it does on individuals' aberrant
behaviour, seeking to criminalise that behaviour, has not
been very successful in creating safe and secure environ-
ments for black people in predominantly white areas.

Explanations

Before looking at the underlying social factors in creating
specific instances of racial violence, it is useful to examine

the more general context to the racist ideas which are part of the motivating force of such violence.

Negative views on black and Asian people are held by a large minority of white people in Britain and are an important part of the black and Asian communities' experience of living in a white society. It is generally agreed amongst sociologists that, although the actual content of racist views will vary according to specific social and economic circumstances, the racism of late twentieth century Britain has its origins in colonial exploitation. Robert Miles, for example, argues that an ideological representation of the material differences between Britain and the countries she colonised both provided the basis for making sense of Britain's economic and military superiority and justified the exploitation of other countries' resources and peoples(71). Thus, ideologies of racial superiority and racial stereotyping of exploited nations provided Britain with both explanation and justification of colonial domination.

Such ideas continue to dominate white people's attitude to those originating from Britain's ex-colonies who have now made this country their home. As John Rex says:

> Once a racist ideology emerges as a means of justifying opposition, conflict or exploitation, it can take on a life of its own and begin to operate as an additional factor, determining the nature of group boundaries and promoting group conflict(72).

It can be argued that racist ideas remain particularly strong as Britain enters the 1990s. It is clear, for example, that the major institutions of the legal system, the education system and the police all operate in ways which are to the disadvantage of black and Asian people. However, although racism may form the backdrop to the phenomenon of racist attacks, it does not explain their incidence. One of the most striking characteristics of the incidents of racial harassment that have been documented by the existing housing research is that they are a manifestation of working-class racism. More than this, they are manifestations of working-class racism in areas experiencing other forms of social and economic pressure.

In this context, it has been tempting to view racist attacks as a problem of individual criminal behaviour operating within inner city working-class communities. Charlie Forman identifies the way in which racist attacks are seen in terms of individual pathologies, as a 'disease' or 'cancer' and Chetan Bhatt discusses the current tendency towards treating racist violence as an expression of working-class criminality requiring legitimate and hard policing. Such a perspective ignores both the importance of the racist ideology which permeates British society and the material reality underlying the specific phenomenon of racist attacks.

In his account of the settlement of the Bangladeshi community in Spitalfields, East London and their experience of racism, Forman argues that racist attacks are, in fact:

> Part of a war, like all wars, about territory. Although not centrally co-ordinated, the intimidation is designed to terrorise Bengalis and other peoples from ethnic minorities out of areas which racists want to keep for their own(73).

Forman is in fact echoing the findings of a study carried out of another part of inner London ten years ago which identified the struggle for scarce resources, particularly for housing, as the source of hostility felt by white people against black and Asian people. Robert Miles and Annie Phizacklea interviewed white working-class people living in Willesden, concluding that:

> A large proportion of the racist beliefs expressed in the interviews stem from a perceived conflict with black people over the allocation of scarce resources, particularly housing. In this conflict, black people are seen to be a privileged minority which is seen to be 'taking over'. Moreover, those white workers who were born and brought up in north-west London have been caught up directly in the most recent stage of the

socio-economic decline of the Willesden area. These workers have lived the consequences of this decline and its coincidence with the arrival of New Commonwealth immigrants is viewed as cause and effect. What we are arguing therefore is that the white working class in Willesden can immediately identify the cause of their problems in the very presence of black workers in the area: because *black* people live and work in Willesden then they can be *seen* to live in houses in which white workers did and could have done . . . The working- class racist beliefs in the Willesden area are therefore an attempt to understand and explain *immediate daily experience*, while the real reasons for both the socio-economic decline and New Commonwealth immigration are to be found in much more abstract and long-standing social and economic processes which cannot be grasped in terms of daily experience(74).

Willesden, like other areas of inner London, has experienced the run-down of manufacturing industry and a worsening of both job and housing opportunities in the last 20 years. The Spitalfields area of Tower Hamlets, the subject of Forman's study and the location of some of the worst incidents of racist attacks in recent years, has not only experienced these general trends but has also experienced the pressures emanating from the development of London's Docklands. This has resulted in a squeezing out of a community previously reliant on the manual work which is leaving the area and its replacement by those who work in London's finance and service industries and who can afford the new private sector housing.

Communities where racist attacks are common are, by and large, communities which feel threatened by easily identifiable groups who are seen to be in competition for dwindling housing opportunities. Forman puts it bluntly:

As the government and councils tried to close down people's options of better housing, more people used racism as a weapon in holding onto what they had got(75).

It is a generally held belief amongst white working-class communities that black and Asian households get preferential treatment from local authority housing departments. Such communities do not read the mass of research which proves the opposite to be the case; in the context of a racist culture which permeates throughout all social classes, they are instead responding to a sense of fear that they and their children will not be adequately housed. In such a situation, if the response of housing authorities is confined to attempting to evict racists and giving priority transfers to those experiencing racial harrassment, this will do little to challenge the general identification of black people as 'taking away our housing' and may do much to confirm such a world view.

Susan Smith, in her book *The Politics of Race and Residence*, has also identified the ways in which racist attacks can be read as:

> An expression of territoriality – as a popular means of asserting social identity, of defending material resources and of preserving social status. Racial attack is, from this perspective, a segregationist, as well as an exclusionary practice, affected to keep or force black people out of particular urban neighbourhoods(76).

We thus come back to the crucial issue of unequal power relationships and their particular socio-economic context. Not only is the strength of racism an important factor in explaining the incidence of racial harassment, but also the socio-economic context of the provision of council housing (the gap between demand for good housing and its supply in inner city areas) and the socio-economic marginalisation of working-class communities in particular parts of the country. It is not just black communities which experience a powerlessness in their struggle for decent housing, but white communities are also squeezed by the housing crisis. In this situation, local housing authorities would more successfully deal with racial harassment by increasing their investment in high-stress areas, at the same time working with black communities to help them defend themselves, as communities rather than individuals, against racist attack.

Eviction policies directed at racists serve an important purpose of making a clear statement of a housing authority's abhorrence of racist attacks but in practice they go no further towards enabling black people to live securely in good housing.

Conclusion

We have argued elsewhere in this book that housing studies has suffered from the lack of a sociological input. This is also true for housing management. The absence of a sociological perspective has meant that the policies adopted to deal with so-called problem estates, homelessness and racial harassment are usually responses to crisis situations and/or political pressures. This has left housing management vulnerable to perspectives which are deterministic, politically motivated, prejudiced and generally ill-thought out.

Our discussion in this chapter has identified that the starting point for a sociological perspective on housing management problems is the recognition of a sociological definition of what constitutes a problem. We have seen that a sociological perspective differs from the dominant housing management perspective in that, from the sociologist's point of view, the problem is not the estate or its residents, but their socio-economic context; not homeless households, but the housing system; not the victims or perpetrators of racial harassment but racism. This does not mean, however, that the sociologist will sit back and say that housing management can have no impact on these phenomena. A sociological perspective not only provides a more coherent analysis of housing management problems but also points to housing policy initiatives and management practices which are more likely to have a lasting impact on the issues in question.

The three phenomena which we have taken as examples of housing management problems have very different characteristics. However, the common thread which runs through them all is the powerlessness which is experienced by the people concerned. This powerlessness has a number of manifestations. For example, it is apparent in the very way that these three phenomena are defined as problems for housing management and housing policy, in that the perspective of those experiencing the distress of living on an unpopular estate, having no home, suffering racial harassment is largely missing from both the policy analysis and the development of practice.

Powerlessness is also the key feature of the wider social relationships experienced by the groups concerned. This stems from a number of different sources which are each of importance in all three of our examples – the socio-economic context of the provision of council housing; the socio-economic marginalisation of particular groups; the strength of racism in British society and generally the way in which prejudices define certain groups as 'disreputable' and 'undeserving'.

Sociology has an important role in ensuring that housing practice is based on professional standards rather than the operation of prejudices within an unequal power relationship. It is clear that those groups who find it difficult to get access to housing through the private market are also at a disadvantage in terms of their experience within the public rented sector. If this is recognised, it should be possible for investment decisions to be made and policies and procedures to be adopted which, rather than confirming disadvantage within the market place, actually counteract such disadvantage. Such strategies are difficult within a situation of financial and policy constraints imposed by central government but they are not, in fact, impossible.

Notes

1. Jack London (1977), *The People of the Abyss*, Journeyman Press, p.13.
2. P. Taylor (1979), 'Difficult-to-let, difficult-to-live-in and sometimes difficult-to-get-out of: an essay on the provision of council housing with

special reference to Killingworth Towers', *Environment and Planning* A, Vol.II.

3. Lord Gifford (1986), *The Broadwater Farm Enquiry*, HMSO, p.l9.

4. See, for example, Gifford (1986); O. Gill (1977), *Luke Street: housing policy, conflict and the creation of a delinquent area*, Macmillan; S. Damer (1989), *From Moorepark to Wine Alley: The rise and fall of a Glasgow housing scheme*, Edinburgh University Press.

5. F. Reynolds (1986), *The Problem Housing Estate*, Gower, p.17.

6. A. Power (1987): *Property Before People*, Allen and Unwin, p.238.

7. See, for example, the two seminar papers, by A. Coleman and D. Coleman, in *Altered Estates* (1988), Adam Smith Institute.

8. A. Power (1987), p.234.

9. *Ibid*, p.234.

10. *Ibid*, p.239.

11. P. Taylor, (1979), p.1311.

12. Centre for Environment Studies (1984), *Outer Estates in Britain: Interim Report*, p.20.

13. A. Power (1984), *Local Housing Management: a Priority Estates Project survey*, HMSO, p.12.

14. A. Coleman (1985), *Utopia on Trial: vision and reality in planned housing*, Hilary Shipman, p.98.

15. P. Williams (1985), 'Alice in Wonderland', *Housing*, June; P. Dickens (1986), Review of A. Coleman and E. Krupat in *International Journal of Urban and Regional Research*, Vol.10, No.2; A. Coleman (1987): '*Utopia on trial*: a comment on P. Dickens' review', *IJURR*, Vol.11, No.1; P. Dickens (1987), '*Utopia on trial*: a response to Alice Coleman's comment', *IJURR*, Vol.ll, No.l; B.Hillier (1986), 'City of Alice's dreams', *Architects' Journal*, Vol.9.

16. A. Coleman (1985), p.19.

17. *Ibid*, p.20.

18. *Ibid*.

19. *Ibid*, p.l8.

20. *Ibid*, pp.18–19.

21. R. Anderson, M. A. Bulos and S. R. Walker (1985), *Tower Blocks*, Polytechnic of the South Bank/Institute of Housing, p.8.

22. *Ibid*, p.39.

23. P. Spicker (1987), 'Poverty and depressed estates: a critique of *Utopia on Trial*', *Housing Studies*, Vol.2, No.4, p.284.

24. *Ibid*, pp.286–7.

25. M. Brimacombe (1989), 'Beyond design', *Housing*, September.

26. *Ibid*.

27. S. Damer (1989).

28. S. Damer (1974), 'Wine Alley: the sociology of a dreadful enclosure', *Sociological Review*, Vol.22, No.2, May, p.223.

29. *Ibid*, p.223.

30. *Ibid*, p.227.
31. *Ibid*, p.228.
32. G. Armstrong and M. Wilson (1973), 'City politics and deviancy amplification' in L. Taylor and I. Taylor, *Politics and Deviance*, Penguin; O. Gill (1977); Gifford (1986).
33. O. Gill (1977), p.74.
34. S. Damer (1974), p.232.
35. Gifford (1986), p.17.
36. See, for example, P. Gallagher (1981), 'Ideology and housing management' in J. English (ed), *The Future of Council Housing*, Croom Helm; Henderson and Karn (1987), *Race, Class and State Housing*, Gower.
37. L. Thompson (1988), *An Act of Compromise: an appraisal of the effects of the Housing (Homeless) Persons Act 1977*, SHAC/Shelter.
38. *Ibid*, p.2.
39. G. Bramley (1988), 'The definition and measurement of homelessness', in Bramley et al, *Homelessness and the London Housing Market*, School of Advanced Urban Studies, Bristol, p.26.
40. H. Austerberry and S. Watson (1983), *Women on the Margins: a study of single women's housing problems*, City University, p.37.
41. G. Randall (1988), *No Way Home*, Centrepoint Soho, p.25.
42. G. Bramley (1988), p.31.
43. P. Niner (1989), *Homelessness in Nine Local Authorities*, HMSO, p.95.
44. A. Evans and S. Duncan (1988), *Responding to Homelessness: local authority policy and practice*, HMSO.
45. P. Niner (1989), p.32.
46. A. Booth (1989), *Raising the Roof on Housing Myths*, Shelter, p.45.
47. P. Niner (1989), pp.85–6.
48. J. Stearn (1988), 'Homelessness legislation: a disappearing act', *Housing*, July, p.9.
49. A. Murie (1988),'The new homeless in Britain', in Bramley et al.
50. K. Doogan (1988), 'Falling off the treadmill: the causes of youth homelessness', in Bramley et al (1988), p.87.
51. *Ibid*, p.91.
52. A. Murie (1988), p.11.
53. See, for example, Child Poverty Action Group (1987), *The Growing Divide: a social audit, 1979–87*; Low Pay Unit (1989), *Ten Years On: the poor decade*.
54. D. Friedman and H. Pawson (1989), *One in Every Hundred: a study of households accepted as homeless in London*, London Housing Unit/London Research Centre, Appendix 3.
55. J. Morris (1988a), *Freedom to Lose: housing policy and people with disabilities*, Shelter.
56. J. Morris (1990), *Our Homes, Our Rights: housing, independent living and physically disabled people*, Shelter.

57. P. Niner (1989).

58. Joint Charities Group on Homelessness (1989), *Who Says There's No Housing Problem? Facts and figures on housing and homelessness*, Shelter, p.20.

59. *Ibid*, p.21.

60. *Ibid*, p.22.

61. J. Conway(ed) (1988), *Prescription for Poor Health: the crisis for homeless families*, London Food Commission, Maternity Alliance, SHAC, Shelter.

62. *Ibid*, pp.21–3.

63. *Ibid*, p.35.

64. *Inside Housing*, 24th November 1989, p.8.

65. C. Forman (1989), *Spitalfields: a battle for land*, Hilary Shipman, p.208.

66. Association of Metropolitan Authorities Local Authority Housing and Racial Equality Working Party (1987), *A Strategy for Racial Equality in Housing: a policy and good practice guide for local authorities, No.1, Racial Harassment*.

67. National Federation of Housing Associations (1989), *Racial Harassment: policies and procedures for housing associations*.

68. E. Bowes (1987), 'Racial harassment and local government collusion', *Foundation, Race and Housing Journal*, July.

69. C. Bhatt (1987), 'Racist violence and the local state', *Foundation, Race and Housing Journal*, July.

70. *Ibid*, p.10.

71. R. Miles (1989), *Racism*, Routledge and Kegan Paul, p.80.

72. J. Rex (1983), *Race Relations in Sociological Theory*, 2nd edition, Routledge and Kegan Paul, p.198.

73. C. Forman (1989), pp.207–8.

74. A. Phizacklea and R. Miles (1979), 'Working-class racist beliefs in the inner city' in R. Miles and A. Phizacklea (eds), *Racism and Political Action in Britain*, Routledge and Kegan Paul, pp. 117–8.

75. C. Forman (1989), p.209.

76. S. Smith (1989), *The Politics of Race and Residence*, Polity Press, p.162.

6 | Housing studies and sociology

The previous chapter has shown how a sociological approach to housing problems can help with understanding the nature and causes of such problems, and in so doing can inform both housing policy and housing practice. Earlier chapters have argued that the housing studies literature has been over-concerned with housing policy and that more emphasis needs to be placed on the relationship between housing inequality and the major social divisions of class, race and gender.

This book has had two objectives: firstly, to make some of the housing studies literature more accessible to students; secondly, to place this research, and the issues it generates, in a sociological context. In order to develop a sociological analysis, however, it is necessary to be aware of the theoretical contributions which are already available to the field of housing studies. This chapter therefore outlines the contributions that sociologists and others have made to a 'theory of housing', analysing the major elements of each position together with the main criticisms. We will then discuss the issues which are raised by these contributions, identifying the questions with which a sociology of housing will need to concern itself.

The first four contributions have been developed within the field of urban sociology whereas the last two, those of Jim Kemeny and Mike Ball, are situated within the housing studies literature.

I

Rex and Moore: Housing 'classes' or 'status groups'?

One area of sociological theorising about housing concerns the relationship between housing and class formation. The initial contribution came from Rex and Moore's research on Sparkbrook in Birmingham, published in 1967(1). This began as a study of race relations but it soon became apparent that housing was a fundamental dimension of racial inequality and they looked for a theoretical framework within which to explain this. They were attracted to the work of the Chicago School (a development within American urban sociology) because it emphasised the importance of competitive processes in the distribution of scarce urban resources. However, whereas the Chicago School had suggested that the outcome was inevitable and beyond human control, Rex and Moore argued that they themselves were using a model of class based on the theory of Max Weber to explain the social nature of the competitive processes in cities. It was this that led them to develop their concept of housing classes.

In simple terms, the basic stages in their argument(2) are as follows:

- Classes consist of groups of people who share a common position in the market place (this is the Weberian definition of class).
- The labour market is not the only source of class formation.
- The housing market is an important alternative source of class formation.
- Housing classes consist of groups of people who share the same housing situation. This forms the basis for a class struggle over the use of houses which is the central process of the city as a social unit.

Rex and Moore initially identified six housing situations and, therefore, six housing classes:

1. Outright owners of a whole house.
2. Owners of a mortgaged whole house.
3. Council tenants
   a) in a house with a long life
   b) in a house awaiting demolition.
4. Private tenants of a whole house.
5. Owners of a house compelled to let to meet short-term loan repayments.
6. Tenants of rooms in a lodging house.

In the context of Rex and Moore's book, this classification appeared to make sense because it corresponded with the housing situations of the black and Irish households in Sparkbrook that they had analysed in the main part of the research. Also, their analysis of the unequal distribution of scarce urban resources in terms of social conflict was particularly welcomed at a time when urban sociology was seeking new theoretical directions which encompassed issues of power and conflict.

Considerable interest was shown in their work and a number of people published comments on their theoretical model. However, there were major criticisms that emerged from this debate.

1. Rex and Moore implicitly assume that there is a common value system about the desirability of housing which ranked housing situations in the same way as the above classification. Research on other cities shows that this is not so(3). For example, Cowper and Brindley's study found that the Georgian houses in the private rented sector in central Bath were more desirable than owner-occupied property on the outskirts of the town.
2. They simply offered a list of housing classes without adequately explaining the criteria that had been used to identify them. It was not clear why these particular six categories were chosen. This criticism was given additional weight by the fact that Rex subsequently produced different lists, each increasing the number of classes identified(4).

3. Important groups – particularly large landowners and local authorities – were omitted from the classification(5).

4. The model offered by Rex and Moore did not explain which classes were in conflict with each other or why(6).

5. It has been suggested that Rex and Moore confuse Weber's concept of class with his concept of status. In Weber's original formulation, classes were defined as groups who shared a similar market position in terms of their access to resources, whilst status groups were defined as groups who shared a similar life-style in terms of their consumption of goods and services. Therefore, what Rex and Moore have identified are not housing classes but housing status groups(7).

6. In a particularly influential article published in 1970 in *New Atlantis*, Roy Haddon takes this last point further by showing that Rex and Moore confuse the conceptualisation of housing classes with their empirical identification. Regardless of whether they are called classes or status groups, Rex and Moore claim that the basis of the struggles over housing arise from inequalities of access to housing but their classification is based upon current market position. The essential point that Haddon makes is that the position that people currently occupy does not necessarily reflect their position in terms of access. 'For example, some young people may choose to rent even though they can afford to become owner-occupiers, possibly because it enables them to be more geographically mobile'(8). Rather than looking for divisions based upon present consumption of housing, it might have been more useful to have sought for different social groups – e.g. single parents, black households, women, etc – who share a similar position in terms of access(9). Once this is accepted, the analysis in terms of housing class collapses.

At first, these criticisms were presented in the spirit of aiming to refine and develop the theoretical model offered by Rex and Moore. However, their accumulated weight soon led to disenchantment and the concept was largely discarded.

Peter Saunders: Owners vs. non-owners

More recently, Peter Saunders has attempted to salvage elements from Rex and Moore's concept of housing classes to be used in an alternative model of the relationship between housing divisions and wider social divisions. He began by considering the major criticisms that had been levelled against Rex and Moore and concluded that their work was flawed because it attempted to distinguish housing classes in terms of access to and the consumption of housing(10). In 1978, Saunders argued instead that their existence is based upon the material benefits derived from housing. He identified three distinct 'domestic property classes':

1. Suppliers of housing (those who live off domestic property).
2. Tenants (those who live in domestic property).
3. Owner-occupiers (those who do both).

His main concern was to try to establish that owner-occupiers have different material interests from tenants. Thus, he says:

> The three principal sources of real accumulation are . . . the disproportionately high rate of house price inflation, the level of interest in times of inflation, and government subsidies. In addition to these, of course, the owner-occupier may also accumulate through the expenditure of his own labour power on his property (a possibility not available to the non-owner), but these three provide the principal sources of revenue, and for as long as they remain, owner-occupation will continue to provide access to considerable wealth over and above that which is accumulated through enforced saving(11).

Saunders recognises that there are internal differences within property classes in terms of the extent to which individual households enjoy these benefits. However, he argues that these differences are overridden by the fact that owner-occupiers share the potential to accumulate wealth from their housing. He argues that this forms the basis of what he believes to be a major social conflict between owner-occupiers and tenants. This conflict is seen to be independent of conventional class struggle. Indeed, he argues that there is a 'necessary non-correspondence' between political action based upon tenure divisions and economic class – in other words, there is no relationship between the political action which is based on a group's housing tenure position and the political action which is based on a group's position within production(12).

Some people responded critically to this initial article(13). The major sources of criticism are identified by Saunders, in a subsequent article published in 1984, as:

- Is domestic property an enduring source of real accumulation?
- Are home-owners a homogeneous economic and political interest?
- How significant is housing tenure as a basis for social cleavage?

Saunders stated in this article that he now rejects his earlier view that home-ownership is a determinant of class. However, a closer examination shows that the change is an extension of his earlier position rather than a rejection of it. Thus, he rejects the first criticism by asserting that real house prices will continue to rise because subsidies stimulate demand. In response to the second criticism, he restates his view that owner-occupiers share common material interests and adds that home-ownership may also shape people's political values and party alignments. It is in his response to the third criticism that a change in his position can be detected in that he accepts that class is a concept that refers to divisions emanating from the social organisation of production and that it is confusing to try to use it to analyse divisions emanating from consumption(14). This does not mean, however, that he now believes the latter to be unimportant. On the contrary, he wants to suggest that:

217

Social and economic divisions arising out of ownership of key means of consumption such as housing are now coming to represent a new major fault line in British society (and perhaps others too), that privatisation of welfare provisions is intensifying this cleavage to the point where sectoral alignments in regard to consumption may come to outweigh class alignments in respect of production, and that housing tenure remains the most important single aspect of such alignments because of the accumulative potential of house ownership and the significance of private housing as an expression of personal identity and as a source of ontological security(15).

The term 'ontological security' is not very satisfactorily defined in any of Saunders' writings. He has taken it from Anthony Giddens' assertions on the consequences of the erosion of kinship, tradition and community which are said to be lost with the development of capitalist societies(16). The ontological security which such phenomena provided in pre-capitalist societies is now supposedly provided by home-ownership in that the tenure offers a 'physical . . . and permanent location in the world where the individual can feel literally and metaphorically at home'(17).

The major elements in Saunders' revised position are: firstly, the divisions between owner-occupiers and tenants are presented as part of a wider pattern of 'consumption sector cleavages'; secondly, this division is not only analytically separate from class divisions but also more significant in structuring the nature of social inequality in Britain; thirdly, these cleavages are exploitative in the sense that the improved life chances of one group are acquired at the expense of the exclusion of the other from access to social resources; fourthly, the nature of this exploitation is now presented as being twofold – in addition to the advantages of wealth accumulation, Saunders has added the advantage of ontological security, which he seems to use to refer to control over the immediate environment(18).

Some of the broad points that have been made by the commentaries on this contribution are:

1. The extension of the argument to encompass the idea that owner-occupiers benefit from greater ontological security has been scorned by Barlow and Duncan as consisting of 'broad, empirically unsupported and universalistic generalisations'(19). Similarly, Harloe comments on the fact that Saunders offers no evidence for the existence of a desire for ontological security and he certainly does not demonstrate that it is satisfied by home-ownership rather than the security of tenure enjoyed by council tenants(17).

2. Saunders, along with other writers, has been accused of fetishising tenure. In other words, he is criticised for elevating statistical associations between tenure and, for example, type of dwelling, political behaviour and social status so that they are presented as if there were a causal link between them(21).

3. Saunders' conceptualisation of the relationship between class position and tenure has been strongly criticised(22). His earlier critics had already pointed out that, in practice, there is likely to be a strong relationship between class position and the material benefits of owner-occupation(23). The most recent responses have concentrated more upon analytical weaknesses and have pointed out that the fact that class position does not determine consumption location (i.e. whether someone consumes health services, education, housing through the private or the public sector) does not mean that the two are entirely independent(24). It has been suggested that his over-emphasis on tenure and consumption has blinkered his approach so that he has entirely ignored alternative approaches based upon an analysis of production relations(25).

The latter arguments have usually been presented by authors wishing to advocate a position similar to that adopted by Mike Ball's emphasis on production relationships. We will consider this shortly.

Ray Pahl: Urban managers as gatekeepers

Ray Pahl's concept of urban managers was developed in the context of his attempt to provide an alternative theoretical framework for urban sociology. In his initial work published in 1975, he was concerned that the existing approaches offered a very inadequate understanding of social processes and he attempted to set out 'some preliminary thinking' about how to include an analysis of power and conflict into urban sociology(26.) He suggested that power to control access to these scarce urban resources resides with a range of key occupational and professional groups 'such as housing managers, estate agents, local government officers, property developers, representatives of building societies and insurance companies, youth employment officers, social workers, magistrates, councillors and so on'(27).

These are the groups that he is referring to when he talks about urban managers and the fact that the list starts with housing managers reflects the importance of housing as a resource. Pahl argued that, in order to understand why urban resources are distributed in the particular ways that they are, we need to study the urban managers to discover the reasons why they exercise their power as they do:

> We need to know not only the rates of access to scarce resources and facilities for given populations but also the determinants of the moral and political values of those who control these rates(28).

Despite their brevity and the obviously tentative nature of Pahl's comments, they attracted enormous interest and a number of responses were made. Some of the major criticisms levelled against him were:

1. There was a lack of conceptual clarity in that he offered no criteria by which to identify urban managers(29).
2. The range of groups identified was considered to be too wide and it was suggested that the concept should be restricted to public sector groups only(30).
3. The most damaging criticisms concerned his implicit concept of power and the fact that he attributed too much power to low-level officials. Pahl's critics pointed to a wide range of constraints which restrict the autonomy of urban

managers and confine the exercise of their discretionary powers, such as government policy, organisational policies and practice, the operation of the market and wider cultural influence(31).

Pahl accepted the spirit of these criticisms and subsequently, in 1977, revised his position to restrict the application of the concept to the public sector and to acknowledge that urban managers are not the independent variable that he had originally suggested. In his revised position he put forward the view that Britain has a 'corporate state'. His argument was that the nature of state intervention in British society lies midway between a classical laissez faire model of the capitalist state and the totalitarian model of the state associated with Eastern Europe. In particular, he pointed to the fact that, although there is extensive state involvement in Britain, this tends to occur indirectly through a series of incentives and discouragements rather than as direct instructions. Pahl suggests that the indirect nature of state involvement builds in discretionary powers for the urban managers at lower levels in the power structure as well as defining the parameters for the exercise of such discretion(32). The responses to Pahl's reformulated position have directed themselves largely to a critique of his theory of the state. To a large extent these critiques emanate from the neo-Marxist theory of the state espoused by Castells.

Manuel Castells: the role of the modern state

Manuel Castells has recently revised his position(33) but, in the mid-1970s his earlier work had a profound impact on urban studies(34). It not only provided a new theoretical framework which was adopted unquestioningly by many, it also rewrote the agenda even for those people who were less willing to accept it.

Castells was heavily influenced by the version of Marxism espoused by Louis Althusser and the derivative theory of the state developed by Nicos Poulantzas. To fully understand the nuances of Castells' position would necessitate a long explanation of his mentors' work and his application of it to urban sociology, which would not be appropriate in this context. Instead, we offer a simplified version which summarises the key elements of his position.

In articles published in the years 1976–78, Castells argued that the role of the state in modern capitalist society is to resolve the inherent contradiction he believed to exist between the spheres of production and consumption. Castells stated that the function of consumption is to reproduce labour power – i.e., to feed, clothe, nurse, shelter existing workers and to reproduce and nurture future generations of workers. He argued that, whilst it is vitally important for the capitalist system to perform this function as cheaply as possible, it is likely to conflict with the interests of any particular capitalist whose immediate priority will be to maximise profits from production. In other words, it simply does not pay to invest in cheap housing, schools, hospitals and other socially necessary facilities.

Castells suggested that the contradiction is resolved by the state stepping in to provide these essential services for capital. In this way, consumption becomes collectivised in the form of state provision. Castells went on to argue that state intervention of this kind creates a further set of problems leading to a 'fiscal crisis of the state'(35). The costs of collective consumption are borne by the state but the benefits accrue to capitalists in the form of a cheaper, fitter, better-educated workforce. The gap between state expenditure and state revenue continues to grow until a crisis is reached and the state is no longer able to finance social provisions. At this point the state reduces its expenditure by cutting social provision in an attempt to repair the imbalance.

It may appear as if Castells was postulating a circular process with a movement from minimal state provision to maximum state provision and back again. However, it was central to his position that this movement, in itself, brings about a fundamental social change. He argued that once the state takes over and collectivises consumption, so consumption becomes politicised and any attempt to withdraw will meet with resistance. In fact, Castells went further than this and argued that the 'urban struggles' around collective consumption are a form of class conflict, although he suggested that they can only be assimilated into broader class struggles through coordinated political organisation (of the Communist Party).

Castells used the term 'urban social movements' to describe these new forms of class conflict. He further suggested that they create the potential for a revolutionary change, leading to the overthrow of capitalism and its replacement with socialism.

Some of the major criticisms(36) that have been levelled against Castells are:

His use of the term 'collective consumption' is inconsistent. Sometimes he uses it in the sense of communal consumption in the sense that street lighting or roads are consumed communally. At other times he uses it to refer to socialised consumption in the form of state provision of facilities.

2. Collective consumption (in either of the above senses) is not restricted to the reproduction of labour power. It also involves the provision of a range of non-profitable facilities, particularly communication networks, which constitute the infrastructure necessary for capitalist production(37).

3. Following Althusser and Poulantzas, Castells adopts a crude functionalist view of the state. He asserts that the state acts in the long-term interests of capital. No attempt is made to explain how this happens. It is unquestioningly accepted that this is the case. It is a tautological position. Thus, if you were to ask 'Why does the state act in the interests of capital?' the answer would come back 'Because the state acts in the interests of capital'. Although superficially this position offers an explanation for everything the state does (i.e. it serves the interests of capital), the fact that it offers no possibility of refutation makes it meaningless and it, in fact, explains nothing.

4. There is a contradiction in Castells' position between his model of an all-powerful state which is resistant to fundamental changes and his view of urban social movements which, it is suggested, have a revolutionary potential. Suppose that such a movement emerged in Britain in response to the disposal of public sector housing. Further suppose that the ensuing national rent strike led to radical changes in government policy. Two logical, but directly contradictory, explanations flow from Castells' position. On the one hand, this would be a gain won by the working class from the class struggle over housing. On the other hand, it would be a state ploy designed to further the interests of capital. It cannot be both but Castells' work suggests that it would be. Note that the two explanations are mutually exclusive. It is possible that concessions that have been fought for may subsequently prove useful for capital but this is not the same as saying – as Castells does – that the state manipulated the situation knowing that this would be the case.

Jim Kemeny: the social construction of tenure

Unlike the contributions considered so far in this chapter, Jim Kemeny's book *The Myth of Home Ownership* has emerged from within housing studies rather than urban sociology. Consequently, it has not provoked the same sort of sociological response and his ideas have not been explored in the same way as those of Rex and Moore, Pahl, Castells or even Saunders. This has meant that the potentially fruitful areas of study that he identifies have not been fully considered. It also means that there is not a coherent literature from which to distil a set of standard criticisms and we will, therefore, present his position in a slightly different format by offering some comments of our own, at appropriate points, as we progress through the exposition.

Kemeny's stated aim is to examine the relationship between housing tenure and social structure(38). This might sound like Saunders' project but Kemeny's concerns are rather different. His interest lies in the processes through which housing tenure is socially constructed and the reasons why it takes particular forms. Thus, he begins by identifying a number of largely unquestioned assumptions about home-ownership which reflect the implicit view that it is somehow 'natural'. He goes on to suggest that housing research in English-speaking countries has generally reflected and reinforced the misconceptions about tenure widely held by the general public(39). He concludes that:

> The narrow empiricism and general inability to conceptualise problems outside of traditional and politically conservative frameworks is reflected in the sociological weakness of the housing literature. Although . . . occasional appeals are made for more sociological analysis in housing studies, it is notable that to date there has failed to emerge a body of literature which relates housing to the wider social structure(40).

This is a useful identification of the problems with the housing studies literature. However, as we identified in Chapters 1 and 2, it is doubtful whether the relationship between housing and social structure can be adequately explored solely through a focus on tenure. There are also criticisms to be made about the manner in which Kemeny postulates the relationship between tenure and social structure. For a large part of the book, he appears to reduce 'social structure' to a continuum based solely upon the degree of 'privatism' at one end or 'collectivism' at the other. His basic argument, which he illustrates with reference to Sweden, Australia and Britain, is that there is a relationship between the nature of the dominant form of tenure and the balance between privatism and collectivism in the wider society(41). For example, he suggests that the tendency to live in houses in English-speaking countries has led to greater reliance upon private cars because lower urban densities make public transport less efficient and/or accessible. Similarly, where individual households possess

225

their own gardens there is less space for and less need for the provision of public parks in easy walking distance. He goes on to argue that 'the tendency to the privatisation of urban facilities in house suburbs acts as a stimulus to further privatisation in a process of mutual reinforcement'(42).

A little later he suggests that there may be a relationship between the extent of home-ownership and the level of government involvement through the welfare state. For example, he suggests that there is a direct relationship between home-ownership and the preference for the private payment of medical expenses. He points out that private health schemes in Australia and the USA enable individuals to control their level of medical cover and he says:

> The importance of this is that it allows households which are under heavy financial pressure from housing cost – especially those saving up to buy a dwelling and those who have just bought one for the first time and so have heavy mortgage commitments – to budget their medical expenditure accordingly(43).

A similar link is suggested in the case of pensions. He points to the fact that home-ownership shifts housing costs to the early stages of the life cycle, thus producing an indirect subsidy from the young to the old or, more precisely, a subsidisation by individuals for their own old age. He goes on to suggest that aged home-owners can manage with lower retirement pensions which means that:

> In a home-owning society there is less pressure on politicians to increase real pension levels, or, indeed to increase other forms of care for the aged (such as cheap or free public transport passes, free telephone rentals or high standard public retirement homes)(44).

Kemeny has been attacked for suggesting that there is a simple causal relationship between owner-occupation and these other social patterns(45). This criticism is perhaps unjustified since it ignores the fact that Kemeny is at pains to stress that this was not his intention(46). However, it is not difficult to understand why the criticism was made. Kemeny does sometimes drop his guard and make statements which sound deterministic. Also, he leads us to expect more than a few superficial, tentative links between tenure and lifestyles and it is tempting to assume that more is on offer than meets the eye.

In the latter part of the book, Kemeny discusses the role of power and ideology in producing specific tenure patterns. He suggests that powerful constellations of business and professional interests combine to produce tenure patterns which suit their own interests. He draws back from a conspiracy model by adding that this has been counter-balanced to different degrees by the efforts of labour movements and social democratic parties in promoting and defending cost-rental housing(47). Kemeny appears to be pointing to the importance of examining the dynamic nature of housing struggles and analysing the way in which power relationships mediate housing tenure policies. However, he does little more than identify three groups which on a prima facie basis would seem to be likely candidates to include in such an analysis – i.e. finance institutions, professional groups (solicitors, valuers, surveyors), and organised labour. He says nothing, for example, to indicate how finance institutions and the professional groups have used their influence to try to produce the outcomes that they desired. He fails to consider the possibility that they might have become influential because of the particular form that owner-occupation has taken, rather than the other way around. Neither does he have anything to say about the dynamics of the process of conflict resolution between the groups.

The closest that Kemeny comes to an analysis of the relationship between power and tenure patterns is when, in the final chapter, he discusses the importance of ideology. Here, Kemeny says:

It is testimony to the power of vested interests in home-ownership that monotenurial owner-occupier housing policies can be justified in terms of a set of common and taken for granted economic assumptions which are based upon a complete falsification and mystification of the ways in which housing tenures operate.

It is clearly not coincidental that the ideological bias happens to support the vested interests of powerful groups who stand to benefit from owner-occupation. At the same time, care must be taken not to take a conspiratorial view of housing tenure ideologies. Rather there is a symbiotic relationship between ideology and the power to determine policy(48).

Although he suggests a relationship between power, ideology and the social construction of tenure, Kemeny does not offer much more than an assertion that there is a symbiotic relationship between them. However, his work provides a useful starting point for an analysis of the details of such relationships in the context of the development of particular housing tenure systems.

Mike Ball: the production of housing

Although he has not been consciously engaged in an attempt to develop a sociology of housing, Ball's recent work has much to offer such a project(50). He starts from a critique of what he describes as 'the consumption-orientated approach to housing'(51). He argues that this has led to a narrow focus on immediate political issues whilst ignoring more deep-seated processes(52). For example, although it is possible from within this approach to point to the fact that housing policy benefits the better off, it is not possible to explain why this should be the case(53). The limitations of existing work in housing studies, including Marxist contributions, are blamed upon the failure to consider issues involved in the production of housing.

Ball has been accused of advocating an analysis of production at the expense of consumption(54). However, whilst there may be room to argue about the balance that he strikes between the two, he was clearly attempting to develop a conceptual framework which enables them to be seen as a whole and he suggests that his concept of 'structures of housing provision' provides such a framework(55).

Ball has offered various definitions of this concept none of which is exactly the same but the following passage appears to encapsulate the essentials:

> Breaking with the limitations of consumption orientated approaches necessitates seeing housing provision at any point in time as involving particular social relations. Housing provision via a specific tenure form is the product of particular, historically determined social relations associated with the physical process of land development, building production, the transfer of the completed dwelling to its final user and its subsequent use. They can be defined as 'structures of housing provision'(56).

Ball suggests that the key social relations in the particular structure of provision associated with owner-occupation in Britain are those between landowners, speculative builders, building workers, mortgage merchants and housing consumers, and the planning profession(57). He posits a central role for speculative house builders and argues that the ways in which they have pursued the drive for profit have created what he perceives as the crisis in the provision of owner-occupied housing in Britain. Some of the major components in his many-faceted analysis are:

1. A consideration of the ways in which the organisation of the development process results in the subordination of design to profit considerations leading to a limited number of house types in which individuality is achieved through minor variations in finish and external detailing(58).
2. An analysis of the conflict between speculative house-builders and landowners over the balance between the profit to be made from the development of land (which accrues to the builder) and the profit to be made from the sale of land (which accrues to the landowner). Ball uses the term development gain to mean the difference between house

price and the cost of constructing the dwelling, and such gain is divided between the landowner and the builder, the former getting a price for their land and the latter a profit from housing development on that land(59). Ball then argues that the modern large builders are uniquely placed to ensure that development profit (as opposed to profit from the sale of land) represents a high proportion of development gain(60). He goes on to argue that the very success of speculative builders in maximising development profit has led to a crisis in building production. The central argument here is that builders have not had to rely on minimising unit production costs in order to maximise profits; instead such factors as the increase in the value of land following planning permission for change of use, and the general increase in house prices have provided a more important source of profit. Large speculative builders in particular have been shielded from the rigours of competition, thus weakening the pressures for technical change and more efficient methods of work organisation in the industry. In the absence of such pressures, other considerations become paramount. For example, although the sort of large-scale production methods used in the public sector might reduce unit production costs, they could also lead to stocks of unsold houses and large amounts of working capital being tied up. Speculative housebuilders have therefore adopted the common practice of small batch production. They also adopt different site practices from public sector builders. In the private sector, for example, the pressure to get sales and the accompanying need to show a completed front results in houses being built at the site entrance first which 'militates against efficient building practice'(61).

3. An examination of the nature of the 'struggle' between speculative housebuilders and building workers. Ball suggests that the particular form of employment relationship – labour-only subcontracting – which predominates in the housebuilding industry creates short-term gains for management but also leads to long-term problems(62).

Because of its handicraft nature, building work requires a pool of skilled labour but the poor conditions of employment operate against this. Skilled workers laid off during slumps do not always return to the industry in booms. So:

> When labour-power becomes short during upturns firms start to use gangs of workers of poorer quality in order to achieve their target output levels. The timing of production to hit peaks in demand is especially pronounced in speculative housebuilding, so this sector tends to lead the way in the trend towards lower-quality work. The quality of work, moreover, is not the only problem: less-skilled workers also are less-productive workers. Novice bricklayers, for example, cannot lay bricks at the same speed as a skilled operative; costs therefore start to creep up as well. So one consequence of the loss of more skilled operatives is likely to be a fall in average labour productivity over time(63).

Thus, Ball attempts to dig beneath the surface to reveal the importance of the underlying social conflicts associated with the form in which owner-occupied housing is produced. In doing this, he presents a strong case to suggest that the problems associated with private sector house building – e.g. inefficient work methods, the lack of a skilled labour force and monotonous architecture – can only be addressed by altering the nature of the social relations contained within the structure of provision – i.e. the relationships between the agencies involved in the production and exchange of housing. Ball argues that we are currently witnessing a major crisis in both of the major tenures and that the current climate is, therefore, ripe for radical housing reform. He argues that housing policy has generally taken the existing structures of provision for granted and operated within the constraints that they impose(64). Ball advocates a reform of housing policy which would go beyond tinkering with housing finance by restructuring the social relations upon which it is based. Instead of proposals centred around rent pooling and mortgage tax reform, he advocates nationalising land and the building industry, provided that this is accompanied by changes in the organisation of production, the operating criteria of the building industry (need rather than cost), the nature of planning, the system of housing exchange, and other changes to offset the dangers involved in nationalisation programmes(65).

Ball's concept of structures of provision has been greeted enthusiastically by many writers(66). However, the following criticisms have been made in an attempt to advance the debate further:

1. There is to some extent a lack of clarity about what he is offering. His definitions change and he has created further confusion by talking about both structures of housing provision and structures of building provision without attempting to distinguish between them(67).

2. Ball could be accused of making contradictory claims for his contribution. Thus, on the one hand, he has suggested that he is offering a 'theoretical refocus' for housing analysis(68) and, on the other, that he is not making a theoretical contribution but simply offering a new concept as 'a means of ordering and evaluating sets of empirical material rather than an explanation in itself'(69).

3. His theoretical framework is not made explicit and this creates ambiguity. Whilst it is clear that he draws heavily from the methodology that Marx adopts in *Capital*, it is equally clear that his studious avoidance of any reference to Marx and his use of the term 'structures of provision' (rather than 'relations of production') are calculated to differentiate his approach from a Marxist analysis. However, this is not made explicit and Ball offers no analysis of the material basis for the social relations between the various agents within the 'structure of provision'. This failure results in a tendency for the implied materialist analysis to evaporate, leaving an account of a series of conflicts between competing interest groups.

4. It could also be argued that his departure or 'refocus' is not as radical as it is sometimes assumed. His call to focus on production rather than consumption may turn housing

studies on its head but it does not alter the object of study. It is still concerned with tenure and housing policy. Although it looks at the social relations underlying the former and attempts to break the mould of the latter, Ball's focus is still essentially the same and it remains to be seen whether his approach can be adapted to provide insights into, for example, housing management and inequalities of access to housing.

II

As we have seen, the above contributions are motivated by a variety of different concerns and adopt a wide range of different, and sometimes conflicting, approaches. Nevertheless, all six positions share a common denominator in that they attempt to grapple with the relationship between housing and the wider social structure. They do this in very different ways and they offer widely disparate accounts of the relationship. We now want to look a little more closely at the ways in which housing inequality has been approached in order to identify some of the issues with which a sociology of housing might be concerned.

There is obviously a lot of work to do in conceptualising the nature of housing inequality. As we have seen in Chapters 2–4, this can be measured in numerous ways. The issue is further clouded by the element of subjectivity involved in what is considered to be desirable or undesirable housing. Both academics and practitioners are prone to rely on assertions and assumptions about, to take just two examples, the experience of living in high-rise flats or the residential preferences of Asian households.

A development of the concept of housing inequality should be integrated with attempts to establish the ways in which housing inequality is patterned in accordance with the major social divisions. At present there is an imbalance in existing research with more studies on race than either class or gender. Even in the case of race and housing, the

233

present situation is inadequate. The research consists largely of disconnected case studies of particular housing organisations. There is a clear need for more work to be conducted on the interrelationship between housing inequality and wider racial inequality – both research and theorising.

There is a further need to develop a better understanding of how the major social divisions of class, race and gender interlink with each other in the context of housing. There is already a sociological literature that attempts to address these issues in other contexts. Although this has generally asserted the supremacy of class divisions and devalued the significance of race and gender divisions, nevertheless it may provide a starting point for housing debates about how social divisions combine and/or conflict with each other to produce particular patterns of housing inequality.

All six of the theoretical contributions which we have discussed are also concerned (in one way or another) with conflict over housing and, between them, they have high-lighted some potentially useful areas for housing sociology to explore. One avenue which has probably been too hastily dismissed is Pahl's concept of 'urban managers'. Although Pahl has overstated the power of lower-level officials, this does not mean that this power does not exist nor that it is not important. It is quite clear from the research discussed in our earlier chapters that housing officials do pattern access to housing on the basis of their prejudices and preconceptions. It is equally clear from this research that Pahl's critics are correct to point to the fact that the exercise of this power is influenced by both national housing policies and organisational practices and procedures. However, not only is there a limited amount of research on housing workers and their organisations, but also it has not been informed by a coherent theoretical framework. Consequently, there has been a tendency to produce descriptive reports.

There have been few attempts to integrate direct studies of housing workers into research on housing organisations. Instead, the research has tended to take the form of presenting statistical patterns, from which inferences are then drawn about the behaviour of officials and the effects of organisational policy. This is particularly common in the case of studies of racial discrimination and housing allocation practices. Henderson and Karn's *Race, Class and State Housing* is one example of the very few attempts within the housing studies literature to explore the interrelationship between the actions of officials, the organisational setting and the wider social environment(70). However, this type of analysis has a much greater chance of success if it is able to draw on the wider sociological literature and apply a sociological analysis to housing. There are a number of types of sociological analysis which may have a contribution to make.

For example, labelling theory offers a better understanding of Pahl's basic point about the need to understand the role of front-line officials in imposing stigmatising labels onto less-powerful groups. The labelling theory tradition also spawned a number of studies of magistrates, police officers, psychiatrists, social workers, etc which could easily be extended to housing workers.

Labelling theory had a far greater impact on criminology than Pahl's version has had upon housing studies. Nevertheless, it too has been criticised in much the same way as Pahl's work. However, whereas housing studies has discarded the concept of urban managers (even if it has retained some interest in the effects of officials' attitudes), the sociology of deviance has been concerned not to throw the baby out with the bathwater and has attempted to build upon the lessons of labelling theory by, for example, exploring ways in which the interactive processes of labelling link with the broader structural factors(71).

Another field which may provide a useful starting point is the sociology of organisations. There is a vast literature here which offers many potentially useful insights for housing studies(72) and this could be used to develop a better understanding of the complexity of the ways in which the actions of front-line housing officers are constrained and/or reinforced by the structural processes within their organisations. Initially, this could focus upon the issue of access to housing but it may lead on to other issues about the organisation of housing work which are more commonly considered under the heading of 'management' – e.g. the design of jobs, the forms of internal control mechanisms, the bases of power and conflict within the organisation, and the ways in which workers resist the attempts to control them.

The work of the six contributors that we examined in the first part of the chapter highlight a number of possibly fruitful areas for further investigation. Both Castells and Saunders have pointed to areas of concern about the nature of political mobilisation over housing which are of interest to housing sociology, although, as we have discussed, there are fundamental problems with the particular theoretical frameworks which Castells and Saunders are using.

Saunders has already engaged in sociological research on urban politics in Croydon(73). This is part of a wider body of research which has been concerned with such things as the allocation of resources and the defence of housing space against motorways, encroachments on the 'green belt', high-density housing developments, council house tenants, etc. As we have already seen, there are major problems with attempts to explain this in terms of divisions based purely on tenure. However, even Saunders does not do this in his empirical work and the research is interesting in that it demonstrates some of the mechanisms through which middle-class pressure groups are able to defend their interests more effectively than working-class groups and often, at least indirectly, at the expense of other groups of working-class households who have been deprived of potential resources.

Castells' work also offers some interesting possible avenues of investigation in that he places the spotlight on the relationship between political action and housing policy. Lowe has shown how this focus, coupled with a modified concept of urban social movements, provides a useful starting point for an analysis of the tenants' movement in

Britain. This perspective could usefully be extended and housing sociology could make a valuable contribution through an analysis of recent forms of tenant action, for example, against Housing Action Trusts and the 'tenants' choice' provisions of the 1988 Housing Act and the 'voluntary transfers' of the 1986 Act.

This leads on to a further area which has been identified by both Castells and Pahl – i.e. the role of the state. While there are significant problems with both of their models it is undoubtedly important to develop an understanding of the position of housing workers and organisations within the state. This may, in fact, be far more complex than either Pahl or Castells acknowledge. Debates about the nature of the state in relation to housing need to grapple with the different types of relationship that might exist for local authorities, housing associations, the Housing Corporation – which are all part of the British state – and the variations within sectors or perhaps amongst different departments within the same organisation.

An analysis of the role of the state could be linked to a broader consideration of power and conflict. Despite Kemeny and Ball's subsequent theoretical disagreements about the balance between consumption and production or the role of the individual as opposed to structural and material factors(74), there is a consensus in their earlier work about the importance of the role of power and conflict in shaping the particular content of the owner-occupied tenure. As we have suggested in the previous section, Ball has had more success but this does not necessarily diminish the importance of the questions which Kemeny has raised. What both of these authors highlight is the importance of looking at the social processes involved in the construction of tenure. Between them, they have identified the major interest groups in the British context (as well as suggesting some possible ways in which this is exceptional in an international context). Ball's work has the advantage of locating this firmly within the specific historical context of post-war Britain. Kemeny's work is interesting in that it points to the importance of ideology.

237

Between them they have provided a good basis for the development of a sociological analysis of owner-occupation. This could be usefully built upon by incorporating a clearer analysis of the role of the state. There may also be benefits from future attempts to develop similar analyses of other tenures, particularly local authority housing but also housing associations.

The final area that we would identify from the above contributions concerns what Kemeny calls the relationship between housing and 'social structure'. We must begin by clarifying Kemeny's terms. Firstly, what he has to say concerns tenure – not housing. Secondly, the links that he makes are with patterns of behaviour rather than social structure – i.e. he does not make links with underlying social divisions. What he does is to explore some of the ways in which high rates of owner-occupation may relate to other social patterns such as the use of public transport, private medical schemes, etc. It will be clear from our previous discussions in this book that we believe a sociology of housing could more profitably focus on housing rather than tenure, and social divisions rather than patterns of behaviour.

However, Kemeny's work is valuable, particularly because, despite what some of his critics say, he tries to avoid a deterministic position and he tries to restrict his discussion to concrete effects. This differentiates his position from that of Saunders who appears to have arrived at a crude deterministic position based upon an asssertion that human beings desire ontological security and that home-ownership is the only form of tenure that can provide it. This is not very far from saying that there is a natural desire for home-ownership or that people have an inbuilt need for defensible space. Neither of these positions are compatible with a sociological perspective on housing inequality because of their reliance, in the last analysis, on biological determinism. But the underlying questions raised within the debate initiated by Peter Saunders may be of interest to a sociology of housing, in that they appear to concern the 'meaning of the home'(75). Despite their rather simplistic approach, the article by Saunders and Williams published in *Housing Studies* in 1988 does offer some ideas about how existing sociological work, particularly on gender and the family, can be developed to explore the nature of social relationships in the home.

In this chapter we have offered short summaries of six of the major sociological contributions to a 'theory of housing'. We would hope that this has helped to make these ideas more accessible and that we have provided a framework which will make further reading easier. We have also used these contributions as a way into a discussion about the relationship between housing and sociology.

Although the main aim of this book has been to make the available housing literature more accessible to students, we have also sought to argue that there is a need for more sociological analysis in the field of housing studies. The importance of such an analysis lies not simply in the light that it can shed on housing policy and practice but also in the potential that it offers for a reorientation of the field by locating housing as a central concern in debates about the nature of the social divisions of class, race and gender, and associated forms of social conflict.

Notes

1. J. Rex and R. Moore (1967), *Race, Community and Conflict*, Oxford University Press.
2. *Ibid*, pp.273–4.
3. M. Cowper and T. Brindley (1985), 'Housing classes and housing values', *Sociological Review*, Vol.23.
4. See, for example, J. Rex (1968), 'The sociology of a zone in transition' in R. Pahl (ed), *Readings in Urban Sociology*, Pergamon; J. Rex and S. Tomlinson (1979), *Colonial Immigrants in a British City*, Routledge and Kegan Paul.
5. See, for example, R. Pahl (1975), *Whose City?*, Penguin.

6. *Ibid*.
7. See, for example, R. Haddon (1970), 'A minority in a welfare state', *New Atlantis*, Vol.2, pp.129–133.
8. *Ibid*. p.128.
9. P. Saunders (1981), *Social Theory and the Urban Question*, Hutchinson.
10. P. Saunders (1978), 'Domestic property and social class', *International Journal of Urban and Regional Research* Vol.2.
11. *Ibid*, p.246.
12. *Ibid*, p.249.
13. See, for example, D. Thorns (1981), 'The implications of differential rates of capital gain from owner-occupation for the formation and development of housing classes', *International Journal of Urban and Regional Research* Vol.5, No.2; M. Edel (1982): 'Home-ownership and working-class unity', *IJURR*, Vol.6, No.2.
14. P. Saunders (1984), 'Beyond housing classes', *IJURR*, Vol.8, No.2, p.206.
15. *Ibid*, p.203
16. A. Giddens (1981), *A Contemporary Critique of Historical Materialism. Vol.I: Power, Property and the State*, Macmillan.
17. Saunders (1984), p.223.
18. *Ibid*, p.220
19. J. Barlow and S. Duncan (1988), 'The use and abuse of tenure', *Housing Studies*, Vol.3, No.4, p.221.
20. M. Harloe (1984), 'Sector and class: a critical comment', *International Journal of Urban and Regional Research*, Vol.8, No.2, pp.235–6.
21. See, for example, Barlow and Duncan (1988),
22. M. Harloe (1984), p.228.
23. See, for example, M. Edel (1982); D. Thorns (1981).
24. M. Harloe (1984).
25. See, for example, M. Harloe (1984); Barlow and Duncan (1988); M. Ball (1983), *Housing Policy and Economic Power*, Methuen.
26. R. Pahl (1975).
27. *Ibid*, p.206.
28. *Ibid*, pp.207–8
29. See, for example, P. Norman (1975), 'Managerialism: a review of recent work', in M. Harloe(ed), *Proceedings of the Conference on Urban Change and Conflict*, Centre for Environmental Studies.
30. See, for example, P. Norman (1975); J. Lambert et al (1978), *Housing Policy and the State*, Macmillan.
31. See, for example, J. Lambert (1978); P. Saunders (1981).
32. See R. Pahl (1977), 'Collective consumption and the state in capitalist and state socialist societies', in R. Scase(ed), *Industrial Society: Class, Cleavage and Control*, Tavistock; R. Pahl (1977), 'Managers, technical experts and the state', in M. Harloe (ed), *Captive Cities*, John Wiley.

33. M. Castells (1983), *The City and the Grassroots*, Edward Arnold.
34. For useful discussions of this see, for example, J. Lowe (1986), *Urban Social Movements*, Macmillan; P. Saunders (1981).
35. This concept is borrowed from J. O'Connor (1973), *The Fiscal Crisis of the State*, St Martin's Press, New York.
36. These criticisms have been summarised and clarified by P. Saunders (1981).
37. See, for example, M. Harloe (1979), 'Marxism, the state and the urban question: critical notes on two recent French theories', in C. Crouch (ed), *State and Economy in Contemporary Capitalism*, Croom Helm.
38. J. Kemeny (1981), *The Myth of Home Ownership*, Routledge and Kegan Paul, p.xi.
39. *Ibid*, p.11.
40. *Ibid*, p.17
41. *Ibid*, p.41.
42. *Ibid*, p.50.
43. *Ibid*, p.59
44. *Ibid*, p.60.
45. D. Hayward (1986), 'The great Australian dream reconsidered: a review of Kemeny', *Housing Studies*, Vol.1, No.4, pp.213–4.
46. See, for example, J. Kemeny (1981), p.41 passim.
47. *Ibid*, pp.69–70.
48. *Ibid*, pp.156–7.
49. M. Ball (1983), *Housing Policy and Economic Power*, Methuen. See J. Kemeny (1987), 'Toward a theorised housing studies: a counter critique of the provision thesis', *Housing Studies*, Vol.2, No.4.
50. See particularly M. Ball (1983); M. Ball (1986a), 'Housing analysis: time for a theoretical refocus', *Housing Studies*, Vol.1, No.3; M. Ball (1986b), 'The built environment and the urban question', *Environment and Planning* D. Vol.4.
51. M. Ball (1983), p.13.
52. M. Ball (1986a), p.148.
53. M. Ball (1983), p.13.
54. See J. Kemeny (1987).
55. M. Ball (1986a), p.158.
56. M.Ball (1983), p.17.
57. *Ibid*, Chapters 2, 7 and 8.
58. *Ibid*, pp.142–3.
59. *Ibid*, p.143.
60. *Ibid*, p.155.
61. *Ibid*, p.164.
62. *Ibid*, p.171.
63. *Ibid*, p.180.
64. *Ibid*, pp.344–6.

65. *Ibid*, Chapter 13. See also M. Ball (1982), 'Housing provision and the economic crisis', *Capital and Class*, 17.
66. See, for example, M. Harloe and M. Hartjens (1984), 'Comparative housing research', *Journal of Social Policy*; P. Dickens et al (1985), *Housing, States and Localities*, Methuen; D. Hayward (1986); M. Harloe (1984); Barlow and Duncan (1988).
67. See M. Ball (1986b).
68. M. Ball (1986a).
69. M. Ball (1986b), p.457.
70. See, for example, D. Phillips (1987), 'The institutionalisation of racism in housing: towards an explanation' in S. Smith and J. Mercer (eds), *New Perspectives on Race and Housing in Britain*; H. Flett (1984), 'Bureaucracy and ethnicity: notions of eligibility to public housing', in R. Ward (ed), *Race and Residence in Britain*, Economic and Social Research Council; P. Gallagher (1981), 'Ideology and housing management', in J. English (ed), *The Future of Council Housing*, Croom Helm.
71. See, for example, I. Taylor, P. Walton and J. Young (1973), *The New Criminology*, Routledge and Kegan Paul.
72. See P. Williams (1982), 'Restructuring urban managerialism: towards a political economy of urban allocation', *Environment and Planning* A, Vol.14.
73. P. Saunders (1979), *Urban Politics*, Penguin.
74. M. Ball (1986a) and J. Kemeny (1987).
75. P. Saunders and P. Williams (1988), 'The constitution of the home: towards a research agenda', *Housing Studies*, Vol.3, No.2.

Conclusion

Throughout this book we have argued that housing studies has suffered from the lack of a sociological input. By this we mean that housing provision and housing management has not generally been set within the wider social structure and that housing research (with a few exceptions) has tended to be empirical, failing to concern itself with seeking the underlying causes for the data which is gathered.

The title of this book makes it clear that we believe that an understanding of social inequality is crucial to an understanding of housing provision and housing practice. The emphasis within the housing studies literature has tended to be on housing policy and, while our first chapter does illustrate the importance of housing policy in exacerbating housing inequality, we have also argued that the experience of housing inequality must be analysed in the context of the wider social structure and in particular the major social divisions of class, race and gender.

Chapters 2, 3 and 4 have established the clear relationship between housing experience and these major sources of inequality in modern British society. Chapter 2 argued that the 'tyranny of tenure' which has characterised housing research has inhibited an understanding of the relationship between class and housing experiences. We have argued that class divisions are much more important than tenure in determining the experience of housing advantage and disadvantage. We have also examined some of the key empirical research which undermines the notion that tenure affects class consciousness.

Chapters 3 and 4 have assembled the available research on

the relationship between the two social divisions of race and gender and the experience of housing inequality. There is a considerable amount of empirical research on racial inequality in housing and a growing body of research on women's housing experiences, although both research areas tend to focus on the gathering of empirical data with limited attempts to explain the relationship between race and housing or gender and housing. Our discussions illustrated the ways in which race and gender are key determinants of housing advantage and disadvantage although, of course, more research is required on the ways in which the three key social divisions of class, race and gender interrelate in patterning housing experiences.

Chapter 5 provided examples of how a sociological perspective can be applied to some of the day-to-day experiences of housing managers, illustrating how a sociological body of knowledge can aid professional practice. The issue of inequality is the thread running through the first four chapters and this fifth chapter has shown quite clearly how it is the experience of powerlessness which determines the nature of the three phenomena discussed.

Our last chapter has aimed to 'package' some of the theoretical contributions which are available in the development of a sociology of housing in a form which is more accessible to students. We have also identified the key questions with which a sociology of housing needs to concern itself.

Our concern throughout the book has been to bring together the diverse research material in the field of housing studies and to present it in a form which is more accessible to students. We feel that this has been necessary in order to both clearly establish the body of knowledge about housing inequality which we believe is crucial to the development of a professional housing practice, and also to set the context for the further development of a sociology of housing. We hope therefore that the book will point the way both to better housing practice and to useful housing research.

Select bibliography

This Bibliography contains references which may be useful to anyone wishing to further explore the issues raised in this book. We have not listed all the material which is referred to in the text but have included sociological and housing research publications which are of general relevance to a sociology of housing.

ANDERSON, R., BULOS, M.A. and WALKER S.R. (1985) Tower Blocks, Polytechnic of the South Bank/Institute of Housing.

ARMSTRONG, G. and WILSON, M. (1973) 'City politics and deviancy amplification' in L. Taylor and I. Taylor (eds) Politics and Deviance, Penguin.

AUSTERBERRY, H and WATSON, S (1983) Women on the Margins, City University.

BALCHIN, P.N. (1979) Housing Improvement and Social Inequality, Gower.

BALL, M. (1981) 'The development of capitalism in housing provision', International Journal of Urban and Regional Research, 5 (2).

BALL, M. (1982) 'Housing provision and the economic crisis', Capital and Class, 17.

BALL, M. (1983) Housing Policy and Economic Power, Methuen.

BALL, M. (1985) 'Coming to terms with owner-occupation', Capital and Class, Winter, 24.

BALL, M. (1986a) 'The built environment and the urban question', Environment and Planning D, 4.

BALL, M. (1986b) 'Housing analysis: time for a theoretical refocus', Housing Studies, 1 (3).

BALL, M. (1986c) Home Ownership: a suitable case for reform, Shelter.

BARLOW, J. (1987) 'The housing crisis and its local dimensions', Housing Studies, 2 (1).

BARLOW, J. and DUNCAN, S. (1988) 'The Use and Abuse of Tenure', Housing Studies, 3 (4).

BERRY, M. (1986) 'Housing provision and class relations under capitalism: some implications of recent Marxist class analysis', Housing Studies, 1 (2).

BINNEY, V., HARKELL, G. and NIXON, J. (1985) 'Refuges and housing for battered women', in J. Pahl (ed), Private Violence and Public Policy, Routledge and Kegan Paul.

BHATT, C. (1987) 'Racist violence and the local state', Foundation, Race and Housing Journal, July.

BHAT, A., CARR-HILL, R and SUSHEL, O. (1988) Britain's Black Population, Gower.

BOLEAT, M. and COLES, A. (1987) The Mortgage Market, Theory and Practice of Housing Finance, Allen and Unwin.

BOTTOMS, A. (1982) 'Housing allocation and related issues' in M. Hough and P. Mayhew (eds) Crime and Public Housing, Home Office Research and Planning Unit, HMSO.

BOWES, E. (1987) 'Racial harassment and local government collusion', in Foundation, Race and Housing Journal, July.

BOYS, J. (1984) 'Is there a feminist analysis of architecture?', Built Environment, 10 (1).

BRAILEY, M. (1985) Women's Access to Council Housing, Planning Exchange Occasional Paper N. 25, The Planning Exchange.

BRAMLEY, G. et al (1988) Homelessness and the London Housing Market, School of Advanced Urban Studies, Bristol.

BRAMLEY, G. (1988) 'The definition and measurement of homelessness' in G. Bramley et al.

BRINDLEY, T. and STOKER, G. (1988) 'Housing renewal policy in the 1980s', Local Government Studies, Sept/Oct.

BROWN, C. (1984) Black and White Britain: The Third PSI Survey, Gower.

BULL, J. and POOLE, L. (1989) Not Rich, Not Poor, SHAC and Anchor Housing Trust.

BULOS, M. and WALKER, S. (1987) 'High rise housing in context' in M. Bulos and S. Walker (eds) The Legacy and Opportunity for High Rise Housing in Europe, Housing Studies Group.

BURNETT, J. (1986) A Social History of Housing (second edition), Methuen.

BYRNE, D. et al (1985) 'Housing, class and health: an example of an attempt at doing socialist research', Critical Social Policy, 13.

BYRNE, D. (1986) 'Housing and class in the inner city' in P. Malpass (ed), The Housing Crisis, Croom Helm.

BYRNE, D. et al (1986) Housing and Health, Gower.

CENTRE FOR ENVIRONMENT STUDIES (1984) Outer Estates in Britain – Interim Report, CES.

CLAPHAM, D. and KINTREA, K. (1984) 'Allocation systems and housing choice', Urban Studies, 21.

COHEN, S. (1973) 'Property destruction: motives and meanings, in C. Ward (ed) Vandalism, Architectural Press.

COLEMAN, A. (1985) Utopia on Trial: vision and reality in planned housing, Hilary Shipman.

COMMISSION FOR RACIAL EQUALITY (1984) Race and Housing In Hackney, CRE.

COMMISSION FOR RACIAL EQUALITY (1985a) Walsall Metropolitan Borough Council: practices and policies of housing allocation, CRE.

COMMISSION FOR RACIAL EQUALITY (1985b) Ethnic Minorities in Britain: statistical information on the pattern of settlement, CRE.

COMMISSION FOR RACIAL EQUALITY (1985c) Race and Mortgage Lending, CRE.

COMMISSION FOR RACIAL EQUALITY (1986) Race and Housing In Liverpool, CRE.

COMMISSION FOR RACIAL EQUALITY (1988), Homelessness and Discrimination: report of a formal investigation into the London Borough of Tower Hamlets, CRE.

CONWAY, J. (1988) Prescription for Poor Health: the crisis for homeless families, London Food Commission, The Maternity Alliance, SHAC and Shelter.

COWPER, M. and BRINDLEY, T. (1985) 'Housing class and housing values', Sociological Review, Vol. 23.

DAHYA, B. (1974) 'The nature of Pakistani ethnicity in industrial cities in Britain' in A. Cohen (ed) Urban Ethnicity, Tavistock.

DAMER, S. (1974) 'Wine Alley: the sociology of a dreadful enclosure' Sociological Review, Vol. 22.

DAMER, S. (1976) 'A note on housing allocation' in Political Economy of Housing Workshop, Housing and Class in Britain.

DAMER, S. (1989) From Moorepark to Wine Alley: the rise and fall of a Glasgow housing scheme, Edinburgh University Press.

DAMER, S. and MADIGAN, R. (1974) 'The housing investigator', New Society, 25th July.

DICKENS, P. et al (1985) Housing, States and Localities, Metheun.

DOLING, J. and DAVIES, M. (1984) Public Control of Privately Rented Housing, Gower.

DOOGAN, K. (1988) 'Falling off the treadmill – the causes of youth homelessness' in G. Bramley et al.

DUNCAN, S.S. (1986) 'House building, profits and social efficiency in Sweden and Britain', Housing Studies 1 (1)

EDEL. M. (1982) 'Home ownership and working class unity', International Journal and Regional Research, 6 (2)

EDWARDS, M., GRAY, S., MERRETT, S. and SWANN, J. (eds) (1976) Housing and Class in Britain, Conference of Socialist Economists.

EVANS, A and DUNCAN, S. (1988) Responding to Homelessness: local authority policy and practice, HMSO.

FENTON, M. (1984) 'Costs of discrimination in the owner occupied sector' in R. Ward (ed) Race and Residence in Britain, Economic and Social Research Council.

FENTON, M. and COLLARD, T. (1984) 'Do coloured tenants pay more? Some evidence' in R. Ward.

FLETT, H. (1984a) 'Dispersal policies in council housing: arguments and evidence' in R. Ward.

FLETT, H. (1984b) 'Asians in council housing: an analysis' in R. Ward.

FLETT, H. (1984c) 'Bureaucracy and ethnicity: notions of eligibility to public housing' in R. Ward.

FLETT, H. (1984d) 'Dimensions of inequality: Birmingham council house allocations' in R. Ward.

FORMAN, C. (1989) Spitalfields: a battle for land, Hilary Shipman.

FORREST, R. and MURIE, A. (1980) 'Wealth, inheritance and housing policy', Policy and Politics, 8 (1).

FORREST, R. and MURIE, A. (1983) 'Residualization and council housing', Journal of Social Policy, 12 (4).

FORREST, R. and MURIE, A. (1986) 'Marginalisation and subsidised individualism', International Journal of Urban and Regional Research, 10 (1).

FORREST, R. and MURIE, A. (1987) 'The affluent home-owner: labour market position and the shaping of housing histories', in N. Thrift and P. Williams (eds), Class and Space: the making of urban society, Routledge and Kegan Paul.

FORREST, R. and MURIE, A. (1989), 'Differential accumulation: wealth, inheritance and housing policy reconsidered', Policy and Politics, 17 (1).

FENNELL, G., PHILLIPSON, C. and EVERS, H. (1986) The Sociology of Old Age, Open University Press.

FRIEDMAN, D. and PAWSON, H. (1989) One in Every Hundred – a study of households accepted as homeless in London, London Housing Unit/London Research Centre.

FRYER, P. (1984) Staying Power: Black People in Britain Since 1504, Humanities Press, New Jersey, USA.

GALLAGHER, P. (1982) 'Ideology and housing management' in J. English (ed) The Future of Council Housing, Croom Helm.

GIFFORD, Lord (1986) The Broadwater Farm Inquiry: report of the independent inquiry into disturbances of October 1985 at the Broadwater Farm Estate, Tottenham, HMSO.

GILL, O. (1977) Luke Street: housing policy, conflict and the creation of the delinquent area, Macmillan.

GORDON, P. and NEWNHAM, A. (1986) Different Worlds: racism and discrimination in Britain (second edition), Runnymede Trust.

GRAY, F. (1976a) 'Selection and allocation in council housing', Transactions of the Institute of British Geographers, 1.

GRAY, F. (1976b) 'The management of local authority housing' in Political Economy of Housing Workshop, Housing and Class in Britain.

GRAY, F. (1982) 'Owner-occupation and social relations' in S. Merrett, Owner-Occupation in Britain, Routledge and Kegan Paul.

GREATER LONDON COUNCIL (1984) Council House Sales, GLC.

GREATER LONDON COUNCIL (1986) Women and Housing, GLC.

GREATER LONDON COUNCIL (1986) Private Tenants in London, GLC.

HADDON, R. (1970) 'A minority in a welfare state: the location of West Indians in the London housing market', New Atlantis, 2 (21).

HAMNETT, C. (1984) 'Housing the two nations: socio-tenurial polarization in England and Wales, 1961–81', Urban Studies, 4.

HAMNETT, C., McDOWELL, L. and SARRE, P. (eds) (1989) The Changing Social Structure, Sage Publications.

HARLOE, M. (1984) 'Sector and class: a critical comment' International Journal of Urban and Regional Research, 8 (2).

HARLOE, M. and HARTJENS, M. (1984) 'Comparative housing research', Journal of Social Policy.

HEATH, A., JOWELL, R., CURTICE, J. and EVANS, G. (1989) The Extension of Popular Capitalism, Strathclyde Papers on Government and Politics, No. 60, Department of Politics, Strathclyde University.

HEATH, A., JOWELL, R., CURTICE, J. and EVANS, G. (1990) The British Voter, Pergamon Press.

HENDERSON, J. and KARN, V. (1984) 'Race, class and the allocation of public housing in Britain', Urban Studies, 21.

HENDERSON, J. and KARN, V. (1987) Race, Class and State Housing, Gower.

HOLMANS, A.E., NANDY, S., and BROWN, A.C. (1987) 'Household formation and dissolution and housing tenure: a longitudinal perspective', Social Trends, 17, HMSO.

HOLMES, C. (1986) 'The worsening crisis of single homelessness' in P. Malpass (ed) The Housing Crisis, Croom Helm.

HOUGH, M. and MAYHEW, P. (eds) (1982) Crime and Public Housing, Home Office Research and Planning Unit, HMSO.

HOUSING SERVICES ADVISORY GROUP (1978) The Housing of One-Parent Families, HMSO.

INSTITUTE OF HOUSING AND SCOTTISH HOMELESS GROUP (1985) Housing and Marital Breakdown – the local authority response, University of Strathclyde.

JACOBS, B. (1988) Racism in Britain, Christopher Helm.

JOHNSON, M. (1987) 'Housing as a process of racial discrimination' in S. Smith and J. Mercer (eds) New Perspectives on Race and Housing, Centre for Housing Research, University of Glasgow.

KARN, V., DOWLING, J. and STAFFORD, B. (1986) 'Growing crisis and contradiction in home ownership' in P. Malpass (ed) The Housing Crisis, Croom Helm.

KARN, V., KEMENY, J. and WILLIAMS, P. (1985) Home Ownership in the Inner City, Gower.

KEMENY, J. (1981) The Myth of Home Ownership: private versus public choices in housing tenure, Routledge and Kegan Paul.

KEMENY, J. (1984) 'The social construction of housing facts', Scandinavian Housing and Planning Research, 1.

KEMENY, J. (1987) 'Toward a theorised Housing Studies: a counter-critique of the provision thesis', Housing Studies, 2 (4).

KEMENY, J. (1988) 'Defining housing reality: ideological hegemony and power in housing research', Housing Studies 3 (4).

KEMP, P. (1987) 'Some aspects of housing consumption in late nineteenth century England and Wales', Housing Studies 2 (1).

KERR, M. (1988), The Right to Buy, HMSO.

KETTLE, M. and HODGES, L. (1982) Uprising: the police, the people and the riots in Britain's cities, Pan.

KLEINMANN, M.P. and WHITEHEAD, C. (1988), 'British housing since 1979', Housing Studies 3 (1).

LAMBERT, J. et al (1978) Housing Policy and the State, Macmillan.

LEVISON, D. and ATKINS, J. (1987) The Key to Equality: the 1986 women and housing survey, Institute of Housing.

LOGAN, F. (1988) Homelessness and Relationship Breakdown, National Council for One Parent Families.

LONDON RESEARCH CENTRE (1986) The Docklands Housing Needs Survey, London Research Centre.

LONDON RESEARCH CENTRE (1988) Access to Housing in London, London Research Centre.

McDOWELL, L. (1983) 'Towards an understanding of the gender divison of urban space', Environment and Planning D, 1.

MacEWAN, M. (1988) 'Racial incidents, council housing and the law', Housing Studies, 3 (1).

MALPASS, P. (ed) (1986) The Housing Crisis, Croom Helm.

MALPASS, P. (1988) 'Utopia in context: state, class and the restructuring of the housing market in the twentieth century' in N. Teymur, et al (eds) Rehumanizing Housing, Butterworth.

MALPASS, P. (1990) Reshaping Housing Policy: subsidies, rents and residualisation, Routledge.

MAYHEW, P. and CLARKE, R. (1982) 'Crime prevention and public housing in England' in M. Hough and P. Mayhew (eds) Crime and Public Housing.

MATRIX (1984) Women and the Man-made Environment, Pluto Press.

McDOWELL, L. (1983) 'City and home: urban housing and the sexual division of space' in M. Evans and C. Ungerson (eds), Sexual Divisions, Patterns and Processes, Tavistock.

MEANS, R. (1987) 'Older people in British housing studies: rediscovery and emerging issues for research', Housing Studies, 2 (2);.

MERRETT, S. (1979) State Housing in Britain, Routledge and Kegan Paul.

MERRETT, S. (1982) Owner-Occupation, Routledge and Kegan Paul.

MILES, R. (1989) Racism, Routledge.

MONRO, M. and SMITH, S. (1989) 'Gender and housing: broadening the debate', Housing Studies, 4 (1).

MORRIS, J. (1988), Freedom to Lose: housing policy and people with disabilities, Shelter.

MORRIS, J. (1990), Our Homes, Our Rights: housing, independent living and disabled people, Shelter.

MURIE, A. (1983) Housing Inequality and Deprivation, Heinemann.

MURIE, A. (1988) 'The new homeless in Britain' in G. Bramley et al, Homelessness and the London Housing Market.

MURIE, A. and FORREST, R. (1980) 'Wealth inheritance and housing policy', Policy and Politics, 8 (1).

MURPHY, M. and SULLIVAN, O. (1986) 'Unemployment, housing and household structure among young adults', Journal of Social Policy, 15 (2).

NATIONAL CHILD DEVELOPMENT STUDY (1988) A Longitudinal Study of Housing and Social Circumstances in Childhood and Early Adulthood, NCDS.

NATIONAL FEDERATION OF HOUSING ASSOCIATIONS (1985) Women In Housing, NFHA.

NINER, P. (1985) Housing Association Allocations: achieving racial equality – a West Midlands case study, Runnymede Trust.

NINER, P. (1987) 'Housing associations and ethnic minorities', in S. Smith and J. Mercer (eds) New Perspectives on Race and Housing.

NINER, P. (1989) Homelessness In Nine Local Authorities: Case studies of policy and practice, HMSO.

PARKER, J. and DUGMORE, K. (1976), Colour and the Allocation of GLC Housing, GLC.

PASCALL, G. (1986) Social Policy: a feminist analysis, Tavistock.

PAYNE, J. and PAYNE, G. (1977) 'Housing pathways and stratification: a study of life chances in the housing market', Journal of Social Policy, 1977, 6 (2).

PEACH, C. and SHAH, S. (1980) 'The contribution of council house allocation to West Indian desegregation in London, 1961–71', Urban Studies, 17.

PHILLIPS, D. (1981) 'The social and spatial segregation of Asians in Leicester' in P. Jackson and S. Smith (eds) Social Interaction and Ethnic Segregation, Academic Press.

PHILLIPS, D. (1986) What Price Equality? GLC Housing Research and Policy Report, No. 9.

PHILLIPS, D. (1987) 'The institutionalisation of racism in housing: towards an explanation', in S. Smith and J. Mercer (eds) New Perspectives on Race and Housing in Britain.

POWER, A. (1982) Priority Estates Project, HMSO.

POWER, A. (1984) Local Housing Management: a Priority Estates Project survey, HMSO.

POWER, A. (1987) Property Before People: the management of twentieth century council housing, Allen and Unwin.

PRATT, G. (1982) 'Class analysis and urban domestic property: a critical examination', International Journal of Urban and Regional Research, 6 (4).

RANDALL, G. (1988) No Way Home: homeless young people in Central London, Centrepoint Soho.

RAVETZ, A. (1984) 'The home of woman: a view from the interior', Built Environment, 10 (1).

RAVETZ, A. (1988) 'Malaise, design and history: scholarship and experience on trial' in N. Teymur et al (eds) Rehumanizing Housing, Butterworth.

READE, E. (1982) 'Residential decay, household movement and class structure', Policy and Politics, 10 (1).

REX, J. and MOORE, R. (1967) Race, Community and Conflict: a study of Sparkbrook, Oxford University Press.

REYNOLDS, F. (1986) The Problem Housing Estate, Gower.

RICHARDSON, J. and LAMBERT, J. (1985) The Sociology of Race, Causeway Books.

ROBINSON, R. and O'SULLIVAN (1983) 'Housing tenure polarisation: some empirical evidence', Housing Review, July/August.

ROBINSON, V. (1980) 'Asians and council housing', Urban Studies, 17.

SARRE, P. (1986) 'Choice and constraint in ethnic minority housing – a structurationist view', Housing Studies, 1 (2).

SAUNDERS, P. (1978) 'Domestic property and social class', International Journal of Urban and Regional Research, 2 (2).

SAUNDERS, P. (1979) Urban Politics: a sociological interpretation, Penguin.

SAUNDERS, P. (1981) Social Theory and the Urban Question, Hutchinson.

SAUNDERS, P. (1984) 'Beyond housing classes: the sociological significance of private property rights in the means of consumption', International Journal of Urban and Regional Research, 8 (2).

SAUNDERS, P. (1989) 'The meaning of "Home" in contemporary English culture', Housing Studies, 4 (3).

SAUNDERS, P. and WILLIAMS, P. (1988) 'The constitution of the home: towards a research agenda', Housing Studies 3 (2).

SMITH, D. and WHALLEY, A. (1975) Racial Minorities and Public Housing, Political and Economic Planning.

SMITH, S. (1989), Housing and Health: a review and research agenda, Glasgow Centre for Housing Research.

SMITH, S. and MERCER, J. (eds) (1987) New Perspectives on Race and Housing in Britain, Glasgow Centre for Housing Research.

SMITH, S. (1989) The Politics of Race and Residence, Polity Press.

SOMERVILLE, P. (1989) 'Home sweet home: a critical comment on Saunders and Williams', Housing Studies, 4 (2).

SPICKER, P. (1987) 'Poverty and depressed estates: a critique of Utopia on Trial', Housing Studies, 2 (4).

STUBBS, C. (1988) 'Property rights and relations: the purchase of council housing', Housing Studies, 3 (3).

STUBBS, P. (1987) 'Crime, community and the multi-agency approach: a critical reading of the Broadwater Farm Inquiry

Report', Critical Social Policy, Autumn, No. 20.

SULLIVAN, O. (1986) 'Housing movements of the divorced and separated', Housing Studies, 1 (1).

SULLIVAN, O. and MURPHY, M. (1984) 'Housing pathways and stratification: some evidence from a British national survey', Journal of Social Policy, 13, (2).

TAYLOR, I., WALTON, P. and YOUNG, J. (1973) The New Criminology, Routledge and Kegan Paul.

TAYLOR, P. (1979) 'Difficult-to-let, difficult-to-live-in and sometimes difficult-to-get-out-of: an essay on the provision of council housing with special reference to Killingworth', Environment and Planning A, 11.

THOMAS, A. (1986) The 1985 Physical and Social Survey of Houses in Multiple Occupation in England and Wales, HMSO.

THORNS, D. (1981) 'The implications of differential rates of capital gain from owner-occupation for the formation and development of housing classes', International Journal of Urban and Regional Research, 5 (2).

THORNS, D. (1982) 'Industrial restructuring and change in the labour and property markets in Britain', Environment and Planning A, 14.

TWINE, F. and WILLIAMS, N.J. (1983) 'Social segregation in public sector housing', Transactions of the Institute of British Geographers, NS. 8.

WARD, R. (1984) Race and Residence in Britain, Economic and Social Research Council.

WARD, R. (1987) 'Housing as a process of racial discrimination' in S. Smith and J. Mercer (eds).

WATSON, S. (1986) 'Women and housing or feminist housing analysis?', Housing Studies, 1 (1).

WATSON, S. and AUSTERBERRY, A. (1986), Housing and Homelessness: a feminist perspective, Routledge and Kegan Paul.

WILLIAMS, P. (1976) 'The role of institutions in the London housing market: the case of Islington', Transactions of The Institute of British Geographers, 1, (1).

WILLIAMS, P. (1978) 'Building societies and the inner city', Transactions of the Institute of British Geographers, 3 (4).

WILLMOTT, P. and MURIE, A. (1988), Polarisation and Social Housing, Policy Studies Institute.

Name index

Armstrong, G. and Wilson, M. 75
Association of Metropolitan
    Authorities 12, 78, 85–86,
    101, 198

Balchin, P. 48, 57
Ball, M. 212, 219, 228–233,
    237
Barlow, J. and Duncan, S. 4, 219
Barrett, M. 152
Bhatt, C. 201–202, 204
Binney, V., Harkell, G. and
    Nixon, J. 132, 133, 134
Birmingham Standing
    Conference on Single
    Homelessness 137
Boleat, M. and Coles, A. 6–7
Booth, A. 187
Bowes, E. 200–201
Brailey, M. 126–128, 130, 133,
    148
Bramley, G. 184, 185, 186
Brindley, T. and Stoker, G. 15,
    17, 18, 19
Brown, C. 78, 80, 81, 83, 84–85,
    86, 92, 94
Bull, J. and Poole, L. 140

Castells, M. 221–224, 236,
    237
Coleman, A. 163, 168–174
Commission for Racial Equality
    78, 81, 82, 86, 93, 107, 160
Conway, J. 3, 193–195

Cowper, M. and Brindley, T. 214

Dahya, B. 88
Damer, S. 175–177, 178–179
Daunton, M. 36
Dickens, P. 169
Doogan, K. 189

Edholm, F., Harris, O. and
    Young, K. 151
Edwards, S. 131
Evans, A. and Duncan, S.
    128–129, 130, 134, 186–187

Fennell, G., Phillipson, C. and
    Evers, H. 143
Forman, C. 89, 197, 204, 205
Forrest, R. and Murie, A. 2, 31,
    47, 48, 58, 59, 74

Gibson, M. and Langstaff, M. 20
Gifford Report 177–178
Gill, O. 176, 179–180
Gray, F. 102

Haddon, R. 215
Hamnett, C. 37, 38, 41, 55
Harloe, M. 219
Heath, A., Jowell, R., Curtice,
    J., and Evans, G. 65–72
Henderson, J. and Karn, V. 50,
    80, 81, 83, 87, 89–90, 95, 98,
    102, 104, 166, 235
Hillier, B. 169

Holmans, A. and Nandy, S. 11
Holmans, A., Nandy, S. and
    Brown, A. 125
Hough, M. and Mayhew, P. 132
House Condition Survey, 5, 12,
    16, 53, 141

Institute of Housing 78

Johnston, M. 72–74, 84

Karn, V., Kemeny, J. and
    Williams, P. 60–62, 87, 97
Kemeny, J. 212, 224–228, 237,
    238
Kemp, P. 4, 36
Kettle, M. and Hodges, L. 91–92
Kleinmann, M. and Whitehead,
    C. 30, 43

Local Authority Housing and
    Racial Equality Working
    Party 101, 103
Logan, F. 149
London, J. 160–161
London Docklands Housing
    Needs Survey 129
London Housing Survey 1986–7
    135
Lowe, S. 236

McDowell, L. 144, 146
Malpass, P. 9, 11, 13
Malpass, P. and Murie, A.
    8, 41
Merrett, S. 15, 37
Miles, R. 203
Miles, R. and Phizacklea, A.
    204–205
Munro, M. and Smith, S. 135,
    152–153
Murie, A. 188, 190
Murie, A. and Forrest, R. 55

National Child Development
    Study 52, 122, 135
National Federation of Housing
    Associations 78, 199
Niner, P. 81–82, 105–111, 128,
    134, 186, 187

Pahl, R. 219–221, 234, 235, 237
Parsons, T. 150
Pascall, G. 125
Phillips, D. 95
Power, A. 162, 163, 164

Randall, G. 185
Rex, J. 203
Rex, J. and Moore, R. 89, 213–
    215
Reynolds, F. 162
Robinson, V. 89

Sarre, P. 90
Saunders, P. 6, 216–219, 236,
    238
Saunders, P. and Williams, P. 52,
    64, 239
Smith, S. 206
Spicker, P. 173, 180
Stanko, E. 131
Sullivan, O. 123, 131

Taylor, P. 161, 166, 181
Thompson, L. 183
Thorns, D. 56
Twine, F. and Williams, N. 49,
    173
Walentowicz, P. 12
Ward, R. 81
Watson, S. 147–148
Watson, S. and Austerberry, H.
    136–138, 184
Williams, P. 169
Willmott, P. and Murie, A. 41,
    43, 50

Subject index

Access to housing 1, 2, 3, 8, 24, 44, 47–48, 85–87, 100–105, 108, 130, 136, 154, 180, 184, 190, 193, 208, 215, 233, 234, 236
allocations 49–50, 129, 166, 174, 177, 179, 180, 181, 196
  and class 49, 173
  and gender 117–122, 130, 136, 146, 148
  and race 49, 82–83, 98–105, 107, 109–111
  and stereotyping 49, 89, 98–100, 112, 164, 183, 234

Building societies 17, 18–19, 28, 62
  and racial inequality 96–97
  and 'red-lining' 18, 96

Council house sales 20–25, 36, 44, 73
council housing 5, 8, 13, 37–51, 161, 164, 166, 180, 181, 190
  and class 37–51, 173
  and gender 122, 123–125, 136, 141
  and household type 43–44, 130
  and poverty 41–2, 43, 162
  and powerlessness 41, 47–51
  and race 69, 97–105

Demographic change 9, 10–11, 43, 147

disabled people 3, 191
divorce (*see* relationship breakdown)
domestic labour 146–147, 150–153, 154
domestic property classes 216–219
domestic violence 122, 131–135

Employment patterns 56, 59–60
  and gender 125, 136, 144, 151
  and race 91–94

Feminist sociology 143–153
functionalist sociology 150–152

Gentrification 57–58
government policy 7–9, 12, 14–31, 148–149, 153, 181

Health 2, 52, 127, 136, 194
homelessness 3, 28, 31, 129, 142, 159, 173, 180, 182–195, 207, 208
  attitudes towards 130, 182, 183
  causes of 9, 26, 28, 182, 187–192
    definition of 137, 182–187
  and gender 126–127, 128, 134, 136–137, 148–149
  and increase in 9
  measurement of 182–187
  and race 85–86, 100, 103, 153

Subject index

homelessness, *contd.*
  and single offer policies 100,
    130, 181, 188
  and young people 3, 26, 185,
    188, 189
household formation 10–11,
    123–124, 135
household structure 58–59, 118,
    148, 153, 164, 173
  and gender 117–119, 145, 147
  and race 94–95, 104
Housing Act (1980) 8, 20, 26, 40,
    44
Housing Act (1985) 8, 20, 148,
    182
Housing Act (1988) 8, 23, 24, 25,
    26, 27, 28, 30, 237
Housing (Homeless Persons) Act
    (1977) 8, 42, 142, 182–185,
    191
Housing and Building Control
    Act (1984) 21–22
Housing and Planning Act (1986)
    8, 19, 20, 223, 237
housing associations 23, 24, 30,
    81–82, 96, 105–111, 141,
    142, 238
housing classes 213–219
housing conditions 3, 5, 7, 9,
    11–12, 26, 40, 61, 63, 93,
    129, 176, 194
housing management 49–50, 78,
    130, 159–160, 161, 162,
    163–168, 171–172, 173,
    180–182, 183, 188, 192–196,
    198–199, 200–202, 207, 220,
    233, 236
housing mobility 1, 87–88, 215
housing quality 2, 5–6, 22, 26,
    40, 49, 53, 54, 57, 61, 79,
    80–85, 86, 95, 98, 104, 110,
    120, 130–131, 139, 141, 188,
    197
housing renewal 7, 15–20, 28
housing subsidies 3, 17, 29–31

housing visitors 49, 98, 200

Immigration Acts 92

Labelling theory 163, 175–180,
    180–181, 234
lesbian women/gay men 139
Local Government and Housing
    Act (1989) 8, 17, 28
lone parents 3, 10, 22, 49, 53, 104,
    110, 121, 122, 128–131,
    139–140, 164, 173, 215

Marxist sociology 150–153,
    221–224, 232

Nomination agreements 107–108

Older people 3, 26, 43–44,
    53–54, 59
  and gender 119–120, 123, 138,
    139–143, 145
ontological security 218, 238
owner-occupation 4, 5–7, 13, 29,
    36, 190, 229, 237, 238
  and class 6, 37, 51–74, 219
  and gender 118–122, 124, 125,
    135, 145
  and household formation
    123–124
  and life chances 51, 52–64, 218
  and race 61, 78–79, 87–88,
    96–97, 101
  and sources of finance 29–31,
    54, 61
  and wealth accumulation 6–7,
    54–64, 97, 216–217

Poverty 41–42, 43, 53–54, 141,
    145, 160, 164, 165, 173, 176,
    180, 190
Priority Estates Project 162–168
private housebuilders 18, 24, 229
private renting 5, 23, 25–29, 36,
    40, 42, 138, 141, 161, 180, 190

'problem' estates 49, 159, 160–182, 207, 208
powerlessness 207–208
  and class 26, 47–51, 61
  and gender 26, 126–127, 146–147
  and homelessness 103, 193, 196
  and 'problem' estates 166, 180–182
  and race 100, 206
  and racial harassment 202–208

Racial discrimination 13, 62, 92, 100–111, 112, 153
racial harassment 90, 98, 159, 160, 196–207, 208
  definitions of 198–200
  explanations of 202–208
relationship breakdown 11, 44, 122–128, 128–129, 130, 134, 143, 168, 183, 187
rents 23–24, 28, 30, 49, 162, 168, 231
reserve army of labour 150
residualisation of council housing 8, 41–51, 154, 173

Settlement patterns 60, 80, 87, 106
  and class 48, 49
  and race 60, 88–92, 202, 206
single parents (*see* lone parents)
single people 10
  and gender 26, 134, 135–139, 143
  and homelessness 134, 183, 184
sociology of housing 212, 233–239

spatial divisions
  and gender 146–147
state, the 147, 149, 151, 221, 221–224, 237, 238
structures of provision 228–233

Tenure 3–7, 20–31, 224–228, 233, 238
  changing patterns of 9, 12–13, 25–26, 36–40, 136, 161
  and class 35–64, 217
  and class consciousness 51, 64–74
  definitions of 4
  and gender 117–122
  and household income 53
  and housing conditions 26, 61
  and power 41, 61, 227–228
  and race 78–79
  and voting patterns 65–74

Unemployment 3, 22, 43, 44, 48, 49, 51, 52, 54, 60, 61, 63, 91, 122, 145, 164, 167–168, 189, 190, 192
urban managers 219–221, 234
urban social movements 223–224, 236

Vandalism 159, 162, 168, 173, 175, 177, 178
void rates 49–50, 99–100, 130, 162, 166, 178, 180, 181

Wealth 2, 54, 140

NEWS OUT OF AFRICA
Biafra to Band Aid
Paul Harrison and *Robin Palmer*

'Will shock those who are ignorant of the machinations
of our mass media . . . the information, ideas and
revelations with which this book is packed are depres-
sing as well as fascinating.'

Times Educational Supplement

IN SEARCH OF CHINA
David Kellogg

'There is no better travel book about China today.'

The Observer

*Hilary Shipman is at 19 Framfield Road,
Highbury, London N5 1UU   Telephone 071-226 0246*